SOCIAL RESEARCH AND ROYAL COMMISSIONS

ALSO EDITED BY MARTIN BULMER

Working Class Images of Society (1975)
Mining and Social Change: Durham County in the Twentieth Century (1977)
Sociological Research Methods (1977)
Social Policy Research (1978)
Censuses, Surveys and Privacy (1979)

Social Research and Royal Commissions

Edited by

MARTIN BULMER

Lecturer in Social Administration, London School of Economics and Political Science

London
GEORGE ALLEN & UNWIN
Boston Sydney

First published in 1980

GEORGE ALLEN & UNWIN LTD
40 Museum Street, London WC1A 1LU

British Library Cataloguing in Publication Data

Social research and royal commissions.
1. Governmental investigations – Great Britain – Case studies
2. Social science research – Great Britain – Case studies 3. Policy sciences – Case studies
I. Bulmer, Martin
300'.7'241 JN329.G/ 79-41713

ISBN 0-04-351055-8

Typeset in 10 on 11 point Times by Red Lion Setters, London and printed in Great Britain by Biddles Ltd, Guildford, Surrey

Contents

Contents

Preface

The origins of this book lie in a general interest which I developed while working on an earlier collection of papers, published as *Social Policy Research* (Macmillan, 1978). What impact does social research have on public policy, and how is any impact which it does have exerted? What is meant by 'research' in this context, and what part does theoretical social science play in such research activity? Different models of the relationship between social research and social policy have been proposed, to my mind the most illuminating by Morris Janowitz and Carol H. Weiss. Much might be gained in assessing their usefulness, it seemed, from a more detailed examination of the part which research had played in Royal Commissions and Departmental Committees of Inquiry, particularly since the role of research, and the experience of those charged with conducting such research, seemed to have been so variable between commissions.

The work of commissions had been analysed in general terms in R. A. Chapman (ed.), *The Role of Commissions in Policy-Making* (Allen & Unwin, 1973), G. Rhodes, *Committees of Inquiry* (Allen & Unwin, 1975) and T. J. Cartwright, *Royal Commissions and Departmental Committees in Britain* (Hodder & Stoughton, 1975). None of the three had, however, devoted significant attention to the role of social research in the work of commissions, except for one chapter by Cartwright which oddly includes as 'research' visits of inspection. The broader American perspective provided by M. Komarovsky (ed.), *Sociology and Public Policy: The Case of the Presidential Commissions* (New York: Elsevier, 1975) was a reminder that many issues in relation to Britain remained untreated, and that there was scope to explore them through analysing one particular kind of application.

The selection of British commissions in this volume was partly indicated by the importance of particular inquiries, partly by the role which social research played in particular commissions, and partly by the availability of authors. Apart from direct approaches which I made myself, I am also grateful to my colleague Howard Glennerster and to L. J. Sharpe for suggestions about whom to invite. In addition to those appearing here, I am indebted to Lord MacCarthy, who talked to me about his experiences as Research Director for the Donovan Royal Commission on Trade Unions and Employers' Associations (1965–8), and to Lord Diamond, the Chairman and Mr N. S. Forward, the Secretary, of the Standing Royal Commission on the Distribution of Income and Wealth (set up in 1974), an interview with whom forms the basis of Chapter 11.

It is a matter for regret that some commissions are not represented. The notable part played by social research in the work of the Robbins Committee on Higher Education (1961–3) and in the Fulton Committee on the Civil Service (1966–8) merited their inclusion, but they could not in the end be represented. Other commissions where contributions were sought proved unproductive. In one case, a social scientist who had done a good deal of work for a commission did not reply to my letter. I later learnt that he had since left academic life and was reportedly running an antique shop. The case is atypical. A much greater problem is that academic social scientists with experience of commissions as members or research directors tend to be relatively eminent, busy and extremely active people who can only with difficulty find the time to set down their experiences, apart from the difficulties which there may be in recalling events a decade or more before. There is scope for others to follow where this volume leaves off. Be that as it may, I hope that the commissions which are, selectively, represented in this book provide scope for understanding and generalisation about the social role of applied social research.

MARTIN BULMER

Acknowledgements

To the Publisher of *New Society*, London, the weekly review of the social sciences, for permission to reproduce Chapter 2 by David Donnison and Chapter 5 by Sir Andrew Shonfield, which first appeared in that publication in 1968 and 1969 respectively.

To the Royal Institute of Public Administration and Mr Gerald Rhodes for permission to reproduce Chapter 8, which first appeared in *Public Administration*, 51 (1973), pp. 449–60.

To the National and Commercial Banking Group Ltd and Professor A. R. Prest for permission to reproduce Chapter 12, which first appeared as part of an article discussing the Royal Commission on Civil Liability 1973–8, in *Three Banks Review*, no. 119 (September 1978), pp. 3–30.

Contributors

Dr HENRY ACLAND currently teaches the Sociology of Education in the School of Education at the University of Southern California in Los Angeles. The re-analysis of the Plowden national survey data reported here was carried out for his D.Phil. at Oxford University. The greater part of this work was done at the Center for Educational Policy Research, a group headed by Christopher Jencks and David Cohen at the Harvard Graduate School of Education. The re-analysis was related to their shared interest in the effects of family background and schooling on educational and occupational success. The results of the group's work were published in C. Jencks *et al., Inequality* (1972), of which Dr Acland is co-author. Since then, he has worked at the Huron Institute and the Rand Corporation studying the effects of teachers on academic achievement and the impact of certain federal educational programmes. His current research, supported by the Carnegie Corporation, is into the way schools use information to reach decisions about the instructional programme. His publications also include 'Stability of teacher effectiveness: a replication', *Journal of Educational Research* (1976), and 'Are randomised experiments the Cadillacs of design?', *Policy Analysis* (1979).

MARTIN BULMER is Lecturer in Social Administration at the London School of Economics and Political Science. Previously he worked as a statistician in the Office of Population Censuses and Surveys, London, and taught at the University of Durham. His main teaching and research interests are in methods of social research and in the applications of social research in policy-making. He is currently a member of the executive committee of the Social Research Association. He has also edited *Censuses, Surveys and Privacy* (1979), *Social Policy Research* (1978), *Sociological Research Methods* (1977), *Mining and Social Change* (1977) and *Working Class Images of Society* (1975).

DAVID DONNISON is Professor of Town and Regional Planning at Glasgow University. Previously he was Chairman of the Supplementary Benefits Commission, 1975–80, Director of the Centre for Environmental Studies, 1969–75, and on the staff of the London School of Economics and Political Science, 1956–69, where he was Reader and then Professor of Social Administration. He has been Chairman of the Public Schools Commission, 1968–70, a member of the Plowden Committee on Primary Education (discussed in Chapter 4), 1964–7, and a member of the Milner-Holland Committee on Housing in Greater London, 1963–5. His publications include *Housing since the Rent Act* (1961), *The Government of Housing* (1967), *London – Urban Patterns, Problems and Policies* (with D. Eversley, 1973) and *Social Policy and Administration Revisited* (jointly, 1973).

A. D. J. FLOWERDEW is Professor of Management Science at the University of Kent at Canterbury. Previously he was Senior Lecturer in Economics at the London School of Economics. From 1968 to 1970 he was Deputy

Director of Research for the Commission on the Third London Airport (Roskill). He has also worked in the coal and steel industries and in the Planning Department of the Greater London Council. His main current teaching and research interests are in operational research in the public sector, especially urban, regional and transport planning, and in the economics of information.

PHOEBE HALL is a Research Liaison Officer at the Department of Health and Social Security. Previously she held research posts at Bristol University, the Centre for Studies in Social Policy (now part of the Policy Studies Institute) and the London School of Economics. Her publications include *Caring for Quality in the Caring Services* (with R. Klein, 1974), *Change, Choice and Conflict in Social Policy* (with H. Land, R. A. Parker and A. L. Webb, 1975), and *Reforming the Welfare* (1976).

O. R. McGREGOR (Lord McGregor of Durris) is Professor of Social Institutions in the University of London at Bedford College, where he has taught since 1947. From 1972 to 1975 he was also Director of the Centre for Socio-Legal Studies, University of Oxford, and a Fellow of Wolfson College. He was a member of the Finer Committee on One-Parent Families, 1969–74, and Chairman of the Royal Commission on the Press, 1974–7. He is also a member of the Countryside Commission, and President of the National Council for One-Parent Families. His publications include *Divorce in England* (1957) and *Separated Spouses* (with others, 1970).

Dr A. R. PREST is Professor of Economics with special reference to the public sector at the London School of Economics and Political Science. Previously he was Stanley Jevons Professor of Political Economy at the University of Manchester, and Lecturer in Economics at Cambridge University. He was a member of the Royal Commission on Civil Liability (Chairman: Lord Pearson), 1973–8. His publications include *War Economics of Primary Producing Countries* (1948), *Consumers' Expenditure in the UK 1900–1919* (1954), *Public Finance in Theory and Practice* (1960), *Public Finance in Underdeveloped Countries* (1962), *The UK Economy* (editor, 1966), *Public Sector Economics* (editor, 1968), and *Self-Assessment for Income Tax* (with N. A. Barr and S. R. James, 1977).

GERALD RHODES is currently doing research on inspectorates in British administration at the Royal Institute of Public Administration. He has previously carried out research for the RIPA, the EEC, government Committees of Inquiry, and the Greater London Group at the London School of Economics. He was an SSRC observer on the Younger Committee on Privacy, 1970–2. His publications include *Committees of Inquiry* (1975), *The Government of London* (1970) and *Public Sector Pensions* (1965).

L. J. SHARPE is University Lecturer in Public Administration with reference to local government and Fellow of Nuffield College, Oxford. He is also currently Editor of *Political Studies* (the journal of the Political Studies Association of the United Kingdom). From 1962 to 1965 he was Lecturer in Government at the London School of Economics. From 1966 to 1969 he was Director of Intelligence and Assistant Commissioner on the Royal Commission on Local Government in England (the Redcliffe-Maud Commission). His publications include *A Metropolis Votes* (1963), *Why Local Democracy?* (1965), *Voting in Cities* (editor, 1967) and *Decentralist Trends in Western Democracies* (editor, 1979).

Sir ANDREW SHONFIELD is Professor of Economics at the European University Institute, Florence. Previously he was Director of the Royal Institute of International Affairs, 1972–7, Director of Studies there, 1961–8, and Chairman of the Social Science Research Council, 1969–71. He was a member of the Royal Commission on Trade Unions, 1965–8, and of the Duncan Committee on Overseas Representation, 1968–9. His publications include *British Economic Policy since the War* (1958), *The Attack on World Poverty* (1960), *Modern Capitalism* (1965) and *Social Indicators and Social Policy* (editor, 1972).

JEREMY TUNSTALL is Professor of Sociology at City University, London, where he also played some part in establishing the post-graduate course in Journalism. He previously held posts at the Open University, University of Essex and LSE. In 1978–9 he taught at the University of California, San Diego. He was an academic consultant to the Royal Commission on the Press, 1974–7. His books include *The Media are American* (1977), *Journalists at Work* (1971), *The Westminster Lobby Correspondents* (1970), *Old and Alone* (1966) and *The Fishermen* (1962). He is editor of the Communications and Society series of books published in London by Constable and in the USA by Sage. He is currently writing a book about the mass media in California.

Chapter 1

Introduction

MARTIN BULMER

What part do social science and empirical social research play in public policy-making in Britain? This book seeks to answer that question by looking at the role which social research has played in the work of those venerable British institutions, the Royal Commission and the Departmental Committee of Inquiry. It does so by means of case studies of the work of particular commissions during the last fifteen years. Each contributor examines in detail the part played by social research in the commission he or she was associated with.

The generic term 'commission' will be used throughout to refer to public bodies set up by central government to consider specific policy problems, to gather evidence about them, and to report and make recommendations for action. The Royal Commission, at least since the Poor Law Commission of 1834, is the archetype of this form of inquiry. It is appointed by the Crown, acting on behalf of the government of the day, it enjoys the authority and prestige which such appointment confers, and it reports to the monarch through Parliament.[1] Departmental Committees of Inquiry appointed by ministers rather than the Crown are not, in practice, distinguishable from Royal Commissions in terms of importance and function, though they lack some of the prestige which Royal Commissions enjoy.[2] The conventional view that Royal Commissions are appointed to consider matters of greater importance and weight does not nowadays carry conviction. Many of the most important commissions of the last twenty years – the Robbins Committee on Higher Education (1963), the Fulton Committee on the Civil Service (1968), the Seebohm Committee on the Personal Social Services (1969) and the Roskill Commission on the Third London Airport (1970) – have not been Royal Commissions. Som Royal Commissions have been appointed on highly specialised an even abstruse topics (such as Dundee University, and Doctors' an Dentists' Pay) which are of much less significance than gener policy issues considered by certain departmental committees.[3]

A detailed description, classification and taxonomy of differe types of commission will not be offered here, since thorough studi

have already been made by G. Rhodes[4] and T. J. Cartwright.[5] It is clear that while some commissions are of major national importance, many others have much more restricted or specialised scope producing reports likely to have only limited circulation. The commissions whose work is described in this volume have been selected because the subject of their work was important for one or another aspect of national social policy, their reports received wide public attention, and their deliberations have had major implications for subsequent action. They share in common the characteristics that the government sought advice from an independent body on a major issue of current social policy; and that the asking of such advice involved the recognition by government that it would (or might) take action upon the recommendations of the commission when it had reported.[6]

The primary aim of this collection, however, is not to generalise about the place of commissions in the British political system. To do so on the basis of ten case studies would be of doubtful validity, particularly when more extensive surveys exist. Rather, the purpose is to understand and generalise about the part which social science can play in the formulation of public policy. In all of the commissions examined here, social research has played some part although they range from the Royal Commission on the Distribution of Income and Wealth, which is exclusively devoted to research, to the Seebohm Committee on the Personal Social Services, which lacked an explicit research programme altogether.

In terms of subject-matter, the coverage of commissions here is broad and diverse, including local government, primary education, overseas representation, personal social services, air transport and planning, privacy, the press, and income and wealth. The experience on which these accounts are based is varied. Six chapters are contributed by members of commissions, four by research staff working for commissions on a programme of research which their commission initiated, and two by academic researchers who had made either a special study of a particular commission (Phoebe Hall of Seebohm) or a re-analysis of a commission's research data (Henry Acland of the Plowden Committee on Primary Education).

What does 'research' mean in the context of a Royal Commission or Departmental Committee of Inquiry? Since such committees are intended, in Wheare's words, 'to advise and inquire',[7] is not research an integral part of their work? Are not commissions by definition bodies which carry out research? This presumption is reinforced by the history of the nineteenth-century 'golden age' of Royal Commissions, where they were a principal means of social inquiry and played a major part in what has come to be called 'blue book sociology'. The procedure of commissions: to issue invitations

to submit evidence; to receive written evidence; to hold public hearings at which oral evidence is presented; to make visits of inspection relevant to their subject – all reinforce the impression that such bodies are seeking to inform themselves and inquire.[8]

The very considerable limits to the openness of this process should be borne in mind. Governments tend to set up commissions with a view to a certain sort of outcome:

> The statesman who nominates the commission can almost always determine the course that it is going to take, since he will have a pretty good knowledge beforehand of the minds of the experts whom he puts on it, while, of course, avoiding any appearance of 'packing' his team.[9]

This is exaggerated, but it makes an important point. Potential members of commissions are usually public figures. Their views are not unknown, and even if judges, academics, lawyers, businessmen and civil servants (serving or retired) are commonly appointed,[10] people in such occupations often have definite views, if not of a party political kind.

The same point can be made in a different way if one classifies commissions by type, for example, as representative, expert and impartial.[11] 'Representative' commissions, where membership is intended to reflect the different interest groups involved, are almost by definition not open-minded, since particular members have particular axes to grind. 'Expert' commissions, too, since they are composed of specialists on a particular subject, are likely to a certain extent to have predetermined views often quite strongly held. 'Impartial' commissions hold out the greatest promise for free inquiry, though the definition of impartiality is crucial. For as the Webbs observed, 'when we are told that a particular person has been appointed to a Royal Commission . . . on the ground that he is or claims to be an "impartial party", we may rest assured that this means merely that the selector and the selected agree in their bias'.[12]

The ideal of impartiality in the ability to carry out a 'thorough and disinterested investigation of the facts pertinent to the subject' and the 'unprejudiced weighing of causes and effects'[13] nevertheless remains an appealing one, that is reflected in the preference for judges as chairmen of commissions. In the postwar period, judges and other lawyers have chaired more than one-third of all commissions.[14] But the most common mode of gathering 'impartial' evidence is not by means of systematic social research. It is rather by written deposition and by oral statement, kinds of evidence which are particularly likely to lack objectivity. Many of those who submit written evidence to commissions are those who have particular views to put forward – that is why, indeed, they responded to the commission's invitation – while the taking of oral evidence is a procedure which lends itself particularly to the vagaries of those who appear. Either there is too little evidence – a state described by Rhodes below in Chapter 8 – or there is too much and it is too undifferentiated. 'Witnesses troop before the committee one after another, each to say much the same as the previous witness. Yet there is normally little a committee can do to select its evidence – especially if it wants to canvass public opinion – without distorting the overall effect or arousing howls of protest.'[15]

These are obviously broad generalisations, but point to an important reason why recent commissions have come increasingly to rely on social research in addition to taking written and oral evidence and making visits. There are, of course, distinguished historical precedents but these should not be exaggerated. The history of the 'golden age', as Pinker has pointed out, embraces much more than Royal Commissions. The work of government inspectors, medical men with research interests, local statistical societies and the census all provided alternative sources of data to the written and oral evidence presented to Royal Commissions.[16] Even where commissions sat and used Assistant Commissioners to make visits and gather evidence at first hand, to dignify this as 'research' is perhaps a misnomer. The Poor Law Commission of 1834, indeed, the father of all such inquiries, undertook extensive investigations of this kind and claimed to have assembled 'the most extensive, and at the same time the most consistent, body of evidence that was ever brought to bear on a single subject'.[17] Critics have poured scorn on this claim, pointing to the lack of rigour in research design, collection of evidence and its analysis. The preconceptions of the commissioners, moreover, were dominant. McGregor describes it as 'of all the empirical investigations before the 1850s . . . the least open-minded, the most concerned to validate the dogmatic presuppositions of political economy'.[18]

The contrary approach, the view that the 'facts speak for themselves', or what Shonfield in Chapter 5 calls 'the pragmatic fallacy', also holds powerful sway. 'Just plunge into your subject; collect as many facts as you can; think about them hard as you go along; and at the end, use your common sense, and above all your *feel* for the practicable to select a few proposals . . .'[19] Certainly, factual material is important in helping a committee form a view of a subject. The Fulton Committee on the Civil Service, for example, had available to it a vast amount of such material, much of it in very detailed Treasury memoranda, 'probably the largest amount of factual information about the British civil service that has ever been published'.[20] But such material is the raw material of research; to yield understanding it has to be organised and analysed.

Can one trace any trends in the use of social research in commissions? Academic social science in Britain is a twentieth-century phenomenon, and on a significant scale, a later twentieth-century one. Though academics sat on commissions, for instance, Mrs Webb on the Poor Law Commission of 1909 and Tawney on the Sankey Coal Commission of 1920, it is principally since the Second World War that large research projects have been mounted as aids to the work of commissions. An early notable example was the Royal Commission on Population (1944–7), which spent more than £100,000 on research into the growth and distribution of population, organised under three scientific sub-committees dealing with statistics, economics, and biological and medical aspects.[21] In the 1960s one of the more striking early examples was the Committee on Higher Education chaired by the economist Lord Robbins, for which Claus Moser (later Sir Claus and head of the Government Statistical Service 1967–78) mounted an impressive programme of educational research. Since the mid-1960s, it has become much more common for commissions to have their own research staffs, and to publish a greater amount of research which they have commissioned. Is such 'research', however, all of a kind? It is probably helpful to distinguish different types of social research which are employed by commissions.

(1) *Research as statistics and intelligence*. The gathering of existing quantitative data of a descriptive, factual nature is a significant kind of research in the work of commissions. The Fulton example quoted is one instance; some of the work of the Royal Commission on the Distribution of Income and Wealth, described in Chapter 11, is another.

(2) *Research as analytic description*. The gathering of primary data as part of the Commission's own research programme frequently plays an important role in mapping out the terrain which the commission seeks to cover. Such mapping is often descriptive, though it may involve more difficult features – such as attitudes – than under (1). Examples would be some of the studies on the press described by Tunstall in Chapter 9; the attitude survey carried out for the Younger Committee, described in Chapter 8; and the attitude surveys carried out for the Kilbrandon Royal Commission on the Constitution.[22] This is probably the most common type of original research instigated by commissions.

(3) *Research as causal analysis*. Once such data is gathered, it is also possible to use it to explore relationships between two or more explanatory factors. There was a modest attempt to do so in the Younger survey on privacy described by Rhodes.

More full-blown analyses were those carried out for the Redcliffe-Maud Commission, described by Sharpe, into the relationship between size of local authority and efficiency; and the Plowden national survey which is dissected by Acland in Chapter 4.

(4) *Research as the testing of a theoretical model.* A mature conception of social science involves the recognition of the value of incorporating explicit theoretical models or hypotheses into one's empirical research. Shonfield argues for such an approach in Chapter 5. Tunstall implicitly seems to advocate such a course in Chapter 9. Prest discusses the resistance to economic concepts which he encountered in Chapter 12. The cost-benefit analyses for Roskill which Flowerdew discusses in Chapter 7 are, however, the only really worked-out examples of such an approach in the contributions to this volume. No doubt this reflects the economic orientation of the Roskill research, the greater facility there is in measuring economic variables, and the tighter fit between theory and evidence which economists manage to achieve. Whether such testing of models, and the tight fit between theory and data can be achieved in other social sciences, remains to be seen. There is little evidence of it in the applied research reported here, though that is less a reflection on British social scientists than of the hold which Shonfield's 'pragmatic fallacy' tends to have over the average member of a commission.

(5) *Research as generalised understanding or enlightenment.* One persuasive view of applied social science argues that it exists less to provide policy-makers with facts or analytic descriptions or narrow technical solutions than to provide the general intellectual conditions for social problem-solving. Its role is to put specific problems into a broader context in relation to general theoretical notions.[23] Weiss's identification of policy research as conceptualisation is analogous, seeing it as a means of influencing the ways in which society defines phenomena as 'problems' or revising the ways in which issues are thought about.[24]

In the present collection, the Roskill research perhaps represents one attempt to do this, and Tunstall's work for the Royal Commission on the Press an instance which failed. The most successful example is perhaps the interpretive role which Dr (now Professor) Roy Parker played on the Seebohm Committee, described in Chapter 6. Paradoxically, although formal research played no part in that commission's work, social science nevertheless played a part.

The use made of social research by commissions differs, as the following chapters make clear. Moreover, as Acland suggests in Chapter 4 the latent function of research may differ from its manifest function. Its underlying purpose may not be quite the open, impartial and objective inquiry that the canons of science embody.

Nevertheless, systematic social inquiry based on the research procedures and theories of social science has an important and necessary role to play in the work of modern commissions, and an increasingly important one, as several of the following chapters demonstrate. Before turning to these examples, David Donnison will introduce some of the *dramatis personae* in the next chapter.

NOTES: CHAPTER 1

1 The classic survey is H. M. Clokie and J. W. Robinson, *Royal Commissions of Inquiry: The Significance of Investigations in British Politics* (Stanford, Calif.: Stanford University Press, 1937).

2 'The distinction between a Royal Commission and a committee is of some theoretical importance, but does not today amount in practice to very much more than a question of prestige.' R. V. Vernon and N. Mansergh (eds), *Advisory Bodies* (London: Allen & Unwin, 1940), p. 24. See G. Rhodes, *Committees of Inquiry* (London: Allen & Unwin, 1975), ch. 2, and T. J. Cartwright, *Royal Commissions and Departmental Committees in Britain* (London: Hodder & Stoughton, 1975), ch. 2.

3 Cartwright, p. 29.

4 G. Rhodes, *Committees of Inquiry.*

5 T. J. Cartwright, *Royal Commissions and Departmental Committees.*

6 Rhodes, p. 14.

7 K. C. Wheare, *Government by Committee* (London: Oxford University Press, 1955), chs. 3 and 4.

8 cf. Clokie and Robinson, ch. 5; Cartwright, chs 7 and 9. Rhodes (p. 26) suggests that three elements are involved in the work of Committees of Inquiry – investigation, appraisal and advice. Their task is not just to find out the facts, but to analyse the situation and to suggest possible remedies.

9 W. Dibelius, *England* (London: Cape, 1930), p. 254, quoted in Cartwright, p. 62.

10 cf. Cartwright, ch. 5.

11 cf. Clokie and Robinson, esp. ch. 4; Cartwright, pp. 62–6.

12 S. and B. Webb, *Methods of Social Study* (London: Longman, 1932), p. 24.

13 Clokie and Robinson, p. 164.

14 Cartwright, pp. 71 ff.

15 Cartwright, p. 145.

16 R. Pinker, *Social Theory and Social Policy* (London: Heinemann, 1971), pp. 61–7.

17 The 1834 Commissioners, quoted in S. and G. Checkland (eds), *The Poor Law Report of 1834* (Harmondsworth: Penguin, 1974), p. 32.

18 O. R. McGregor, 'Social Research and Social Policy in the Nineteenth Century', *British Journal of Sociology*, 8 (1957), p. 148.

19 Shonfield, p. 59.

20 R. Chapman, 'The Fulton Committee', in R. Chapman (ed.), *The Role of Commissions in Policy Making* (London: Allen & Unwin, 1973), p. 17; see Vol. IV of the Fulton Committee Report, *Factual, Statistical, Explanatory Papers* (London: HMSO, 1968).

21 See its *Report*, Cmd 7695 (1947).

22 cf. Royal Commission on the Constitution, *Devolution and Other Aspects of Government: An Attitudes Survey*, Research Paper 7 (London: HMSO, 1973). For a more general discussion see E. Craven 'Issues in representation', in R. Davies and P. Hall (eds), *Issues in Urban Society* (Harmondsworth: Penguin, 1978), pp. 242–67.

23 M. Janowitz, 'Sociological Models and Social Policy', in *Political Conflict: Essays in Political Sociology* (Chicago: Quadrangle, 1970), pp. 243–59.

24 C. H. Weiss, 'Research for policy's sake: the enlightenment function of social research', *Policy Analysis*, 3 (1977), pp. 531–45. C. H. Weiss (ed.), *Using Social Research in Public Policy Making* (Farnborough: D. C. Heath/Teakfield, 1977), ch. 1.

Chapter 2

Committees and Committeemen

DAVID DONNISON

Committees of Inquiry are now an established part of British government. Scarcely a year passes without the appearance of one important report or another, though seldom has the economy given so little scope for acting on their advice. A lot of people are going to be disillusioned about this instrument of policy-making. But governments grappling with increasingly complex fields of administration need some procedure of this kind, and a roll-call from the 1960s of committees and commissions – Younghusband, Robbins, Heyworth, Milner-Holland – shows a decade or more later that they can be a force to reckon with. What followed from their inquiries was not exactly what these committees intended, but their work generated and focused reforming impetus which would have been difficult to mobilise in other ways.

Most of the people on a Committee of Inquiry are usually appointed on the recommendations of officials. Interests will be carefully balanced: the right professional and administrative groups; Scotland and Wales; the north and the south; women and men; the left and right – all will be carefully matched, though the representatives of each generally come from the middle of the political road.

But the selection of personal talent is less skilled. Whitehall is politically sophisticated but alarmingly ignorant about people, particularly if they live more than an hour's journey from London. It is too easy to pick the willing horses, already known and trusted. To the official selection there will generally be added a sprinkling of more eccentric names chosen by the minister and his friends. Among them will be found some of the best members of the committee, and some of the worst.

What happens next? This account is drawn from my own experience of five committees inquiring into education, housing and town planning. The committees on which I served were the Milner-Holland Committee which reported on London housing in 1965; the Denington sub-committee of the Central Housing Advisory Committee whose report, *Our Older Homes*, appeared in 1966; the Research Advisory Group which made an unpublished report to the Minister of Housing and Local Government in 1965; the Plowden

Committee which reported on *Children and their Primary Schools* in 1967; and the Public Schools Commission (of which I was Chairman, 1968–70). All these committees were attached to spending departments and concerned with the growth of public services. A study of other committees, set up to reorganise administrative structures and reduce public expenditure (Lord Plowden's, as it were – not Lady Plowden's) might have produced different conclusions. But I doubt it. Both types of inquiry call for the analysis of problems, the synthesis and arbitration of conflicting views, and the mobilisation of opinion inside and outside the committee. And so does any attempt to formulate new policies. Hence patterns of the kind I describe can be seen in all sorts of working groups which deal with problems that are at once administrative, professional and political. In a Committee of Inquiry these patterns are only more sharply and dramatically focused.

The government tells Committees of Inquiry what they are to do. They may not be asked for recommendations: some, like the Milner-Holland Committee, are only asked to find the facts. But in practice they will imply recommendations whether they are asked for them or not. Terms of reference give all concerned a sense of purpose and urgency, and ensure that other people know the kind of help the committee needs. The Central Advisory Council for Education and the Central Housing Advisory Committee are entitled by law to advise their ministers about any aspect of education or housing. But the education council abides by the terms of reference given it by the Secretary of State for Education and obediently disbands as soon as it has reported upon them. The housing council, likewise, only becomes fully effective when asked to make a specific inquiry such as those the Parker Morris and Denington Committees carried out. Committees need terms of reference. They always complain about those they are given but without them their job could be neither defined nor completed.

The committee does not work in a vacuum. It depends on other groups and organisations which together make up the environment in which it sinks or swims. The main ones are: the committee's secretariat; the research workers, if any, helping the committee; the witnesses, pressure groups and others giving advice and information; the government department responsible for the committee's sphere of inquiry; the Treasury; other departments of government; and the press and other means of mass communication. The committee cannot work well unless it establishes the right relations with each of these at the appropriate phases of its work.

The *secretariat* serves the committee; its staff draft some, possibly all, of the final report. It prepares agendas, briefs the chairman before each meeting, writes the minutes, and organises, summarises (and often filters) the evidence seen by the committee. The secretary is helped by a small team of executive and clerical officers, and probably by professional advisers and assessors who devote only a small part of their time to the committee's work. The secretary must lead this team (though he may be junior to some of his assessors), maintaining both their loyalty to the committee and their capacity to give independent and critical advice.

Research staff may be employed directly by the committee. More often they work part-time for the committee in the department, the Government Social Survey or the universities. They are generally interested in particular aspects of the committee's work, in teasing out particular problems and discovering the truth about them. Often they are less concerned than the committee – sometimes scarcely concerned at all – about the final recommendations to be made. They are most unlikely to have a grasp of all features of the situation which the committee must consider before framing its recommendations.

If they had it might distract them from their main task – which is to discover objective and sometimes embarrassing truth: to show, for example, that there appears to be no clear correlation between the attainment of schoolchildren and the size or streaming of the classes in which they are taught; or between housing conditions and the physical or mental health of the household.

The committee can quickly mount straightforward survey work and make fresh analyses of existing data. But the scope for more fundamental studies depends on the quality of current research in the committee's field of work that was probably begun for purposes quite different from the committee's. If little research is being done, or if the people doing it are not good enough, fresh research mounted specially for the committee is unlikely to penetrate very deep. For a major inquiry it takes at least nine months to hire good staff, plan, pilot and launch a study, and another year to gather data and write up the findings. If the committee is not well on the way to making up its mind in less than two years, its report will be long delayed. Drafting, redrafting, printing, proof correction, binding and publication will probably take yet another year. Committees with narrow terms of reference and brisk methods can work faster. But for them there will be even less opportunity to mount entirely fresh research.

This means that research workers, if they are good enough to make a major contribution in the time available, will generally have views of their own, well-established working methods and public reputations. They will have friends and enemies, collaborators and allies. They will not be a neutral element providing a merely technical service. From time to time they will find the committee's outlook and methods irritating, and some committee members will be equally irritated by the researchers. Their contribution and the way it is used will depend heavily on members of the committee – often academics – who are familiar with research in relevant fields. These members can make, or break, the link between research workers and the main body of the committee.

Then there are the *witnesses*. In a well-developed sphere of professional knowledge, many organisations will be equipped to prepare evidence. The stronger they are, the less original their ideas are likely to be. Their evidence will usually be prepared by a group, representing various branches of the profession, whose draft must then be submitted to a larger body. By the time it is approved there will seldom be anything new left in it. But what powerful groups such as the BMA or the Association of Education Committees have to say about developments in their own field must always command attention.

Other groups represent more specialised or general interests – the Comprehensive Schools Committee, for instance. Consumer groups, such as those representing parents of schoolchildren or tenants of rented housing, play an increasingly important part; university research groups (still contributing too rarely to such inquiries), political parties at a local or national level, and individuals of all kinds from the most expert to the arrant cranks also contribute information and views.

The first evidence submitted will be studied carefully. But after a year or so, the committee becomes so submerged in paper and so familiar with its witnesses' views that only the most cogent statements will make much impact. Besides reading their evidence, the committee will meet the more prestigious or interesting witnesses. Such hearings are often a waste of time, but if the committee is well briefed and led, opportunities can be made to set fresh thinking going that will prepare the ground for action on the committee's recommendations.

The dramatic developments in thought about social work which have taken place while the Seebohm Committee was at work were partly provoked by the discussions which preceded and followed the presentation of evidence to that committee. Some of the best evidence given to the Public Schools Commission was prepared by people who were encouraged to present second thoughts after discussing their first thoughts with the commission.

A committee often makes visits to 'see for itself'. This can be fruitful, often in unforeseen ways (in public relations or by enabling members to explore each others' views and reactions in the field), but it is expensive in time and money – particularly if the committee travels to foreign countries. Foreign visits will not help much unless the committee understands its field thoroughly, meets the right people and is well briefed. The Plowden Committee's proposals for educational priority areas were sharpened by lessons, positive and negative, learnt during a carefully prepared visit to the United States.

The *department responsible* for the committee's work will be watching all that happens with interest. Committee members, once a report is signed, go back to their jobs – or to other public service – but the department has to cope with the outcome of their inquiry. Its officials will be asking whether the committee is likely to reach sound conclusions and back them with effective arguments. Will the report disrupt their work – or even redistribute precious bits of it among other departments? Will it hang an albatross around the department's neck for years to come? The assessors attached to the committee by the department can steer the committee off dangerous ground and rephrase its proposals more acceptably.

All the committee's papers circulate among senior officials of the ministry concerned. When the press says no action can be taken because the minister is 'waiting for *Milner-Holland*' or '*Plowden*', this either means the committee has not yet made up its own mind or it is nonsense. If a decision has been reached the minister's advisers know it. There is no constitutional reason why he *should* wait: Anthony Crosland did not wait to hear Plowden on 'the transition to secondary education' before announcing his own decisions on this issue in Circular 10/65.

Other departments may be equally interested in some of the work. But it can be almost as difficult for committees as for members of the public to get information from them. Bureaucracies are not unitary, smoothly articulated, closely co-operating machines. Official secrets do not belong to government: they are the property of particular departments, or even of one division within a department, and they will not be divulged automatically to committees set up by other departments or divisions. The more departments an inquiry involves, the greater the difficulties.

The *Treasury*'s views will seldom be publicly expressed. But its vote on the committee's proposals is the first to be cast and, in the short run at least, the most important. If a report is to be taken seriously, every argument in it must be framed with the Treasury reader in mind (but not only the Treasury reader). He will be more impressed by the claims of a department which knows its job, appreciates the arguments ranged against it and refutes them, than by favourable comments in Parliament or the press.

The *press*, the mass media and the professional journals must not be forgotten. A committee wants to launch its proposals upon a flood tide of popular and expert support, and it can help to achieve this. It may at least ensure that its work is not forgotten or seriously misunderstood. Although its proceedings are technically secret, information can be leaked. Leaks may be destructive: more often they waste a great deal of the chairman's and the secretariat's time by provoking further inquiries or parliamentary questions. But they can also focus attention on the right issues, disperse suspicion and anxiety, and keep alive public interest in a forthcoming report. Before the Milner-Holland Report was published a leak to the *Sun* (not from the committee) provoked widespread speculation in the Sunday newspapers and helped to achieve the excellent coverage the report was given when it appeared.

If the committee keeps the press at arm's length others will not be so scrupulous. The statements published by the NUT a few days before the Plowden Report appeared may not have been deliberately timed, but they certainly helped to focus the immediate response to the report on particular issues such as the employment of teachers' aides in schools. The Maud Commission on English Local Government and the Public Schools Commission were exposed to a continuing barrage of comment and speculation by interested parties.

The key people in the committee's work are its chairman and its secretary. They operate on the boundaries of the committee, being responsible for communication with government departments, researchers, the press, witnesses and others with whom the committee must do business.

The chairman sets the pace and tone of the proceedings, and the general level of the members' aspirations. He must refrain from taking sides on contentious issues until other members' views are known. Otherwise he may destroy consensus instead of creating it. A really good chairman can create an effective committee against heavy odds, but even a good committee is unlikely to be effective if it has a poor chairman.

The secretary is almost as important. He is probably a civil service principal, more rarely an assistant secretary. Thus he still has a career to make. After the initial honeymoon phase of shedding his usual responsibilities, getting to know the (generally very nice) people on his committee and setting up the secretariat team, he gets down to the hard grind. Within a year more inquiries will have been set on foot than he can easily handle; the committee will ask for yet more information and research, but he knows it is increasingly unlikely that there will be time or opportunity to use the findings of further studies.

As drafting begins in earnest, members of the committee become muddled, contradictory and sometimes ill-tempered. They complain about drafts, and then about revisions made to satisfy them. They always grumble about points of style. The secretary's superiors in the ministry breathe down his neck, taking an increasingly anxious interest in the proceedings. Later the committee's promised deadlines disintegrate – and there have to be deadlines to get a report into the queue at HMSO for printing and publication. There may be disagreement in the committee and in the secretariat, illness among crucial members of the team, unforeseen delays in the collection of data . . . and the computer breaks down.

As signing day approaches, the committee develops an end-of-term euphoria, but the secretary knows he must live with the report amongst his colleagues for years to come. If things go badly wrong, he may find himself side-tracked to some administrative graveyard for the next ten years. He may look as if he is getting ulcers, and he probably is. His central problem arises from the fact that the committee needs a good administrator to discipline and organise its ideas to make them viable; but it is most unlikely that any one man can fully understand and completely convey every idea and nuance thrown up in the course of the committee's work – and put it all into clear and vivid prose.

Look now at the committee itself and the parts played by its members. It may be large (say, twenty-five) or small (say, six); distinguished (full of Lords, Dames, and FRSs) or more humdrum; entirely male or largely female; paid for its work (rarely) or attending on an expenses-only basis. (There are rules, difficult to interpret, about payment. If a committee consists largely of lawyers, engineers, surveyors and others who work for fees and lose money by attending its meetings, it is likely to be paid. If it consists largely of teachers and other salaried workers who lose no money by taking time off, it will not be.) Whatever the committee's composition and character, certain roles must be filled if it is to do its job effectively. These roles reappear, in one form or another, in working groups of many different kinds. The main ones are as follows.

Some members are treated as *experts*; they know far more than anyone else on the committee about certain parts of the field to be studied, and they know where to find even more expert advice. They speak with a formidable but limited authority. If they confine their contributions to their own territory, this enables them to avoid contentious discussion and helps to assure their expert status. No one ever disagrees with them.

Occasionally the expertise of a member of the committee is so central to the committee's terms of reference that he becomes a 'general expert' – a sort of guru – unwillingly it may be. Every major issue awaits his comment before a decision can be reached; the decisions taken may not accord with his views, but progress is slow on days when he is absent. He will not be away much, however, and he will be trusted and respected by his colleagues – otherwise he would not be accorded this role.

A role closely allied to that of the expert, but one that can seldom be combined with it, is that of the *representative of an interest*. He, or she, knows exactly how the average nursery schoolteacher, or the average architect, or the average medical officer of health would feel about particular arguments, proposals and phrases – or he is believed to know. He worries more than most, for he – like the secretary – will have to live with the report among his colleagues for years to come. If the people for whom he speaks are to play an important part in carrying out the committee's proposals, the committee must be aware of their potential reactions. Their spokesman may later play a crucial part in 'selling' the committee's proposals to them. A committee 'educates' such a man out of his automatic understanding of such groups' feelings at its peril.

Another role may be regarded as an extreme version of the preceding one: it is that of the man who retains deeply rooted and passionate prejudices widely held among relevant groups outside the committee. He can be relied on to 'blow up' if the committee's views or phraseology part company too seriously with the assumptions and attitudes of those 'at the coal face'. He is a *fuse box*.

Tiresome though he may sometimes be, he is also one of the committee's assets. If it is well briefed and works hard, the committee will in time become collectively expert and very sophisticated about its subject. During its second or third year it can too easily part company with the world outside the committee room; its views (about corporal punishment, for example) may be sound, but they are no longer expressed in language that ordinary people would understand or accept. One or two sensitive fuse boxes can help to avoid this error.

An altogether different animal is the *advocate of a particular philosophy*. He is someone with more than a partisan viewpoint or specialist expertise: he thinks in terms of general principles derived from a frame of reference that extends well beyond the task in hand. If he has a political philosophy it will be more profound than a party programme. He applies a system of thought derived from general assumptions about people, their rights and the character of the future society the committee is helping to create.

His capacity to generalise the committee's concerns and to show how they relate to a broader social context may be highly articulate, or intuitive and implicit. He can help a committee to reason about its proposals and convey a sense that it is making history as well as getting through the agenda. He can give the report a social context and direction that will mobilise support beyond the groups immediately concerned with its recommendations. His strength lies partly in his irresponsibility: he represents no one and worries less about the reception that may be given to the report by colleagues outside the committee.

The committee must have one or more (preferably more) *consensus builders*. They take an altogether different role. These people do not make the running in the early stages of a discussion; they are good listeners, capable of sensing and synthesising potentially conflicting opinions. When sufficient tension has built up, they propose a formulation or clarification which maximises consensus and builds on it. Such people must be trusted and respected by the rest of the committee. They trust and respect others, and do not mind who gets the credit provided progress is made. A committee with too few consensus builders is liable to disintegrate altogether; a committee with too many will relapse into cosy unanimity which fails to penetrate beyond the superficial.

Very important, too, are the *genial hosts* – those who are sensitive about the committee's expressive functions (the things that are done purely for their own sake). These are the people who remember that it is time the committee had a party and arrange this with the minimum of fuss and the maximum of innocent enjoyment; they remember who has just become a grandfather, or been awarded a CBE, or been promoted, and ensure that proper note is taken of these events. They also ensure that the less articulate or prestigious members of the group do not become isolated. Unless the committee enjoys its work, it will not do its job well. These are the people who create that essential condition of success. Their role is one of the few that the secretary can also play.

The roles I have listed are not all distinctive or mutually exclusive: some can be combined – 'consensus builder' and 'host', for example; or 'representative of an interest' and 'fuse box'. But 'fuse boxes' do not build consensuses, and the advocates of particular philosophies seldom represent interest groups effectively. In one form or another all these roles must be played if a Committee of Inquiry is to work effectively. They are called into being by the situation in which such a group finds itself and by the work it has to do.

Some people may be better fitted for one role rather than another. But the most diverse and unexpected personalities seem capable of ensuring that all the parts in the drama are filled. And the same people may find themselves cast in altogether different roles in the next committee on which they serve.

Chapter 3

Research and the Redcliffe-Maud Commission

L. J. SHARPE

I INTRODUCTION

In September 1965 Richard Crossman, then Minister of Housing and Local Government, startled the Association of Municipal Corporations at their Annual Conference by announcing that he had decided to reverse his earlier decision to allow the existing seriatim procedures for local government reorganisation under the aegis of the Local Government Commission for England[1] to continue. Instead he suggested the creation of a small and powerful committee to establish some first principles of reorganisation in England on which a new and a more thorough round of reorganisation could be based.[2]

In the event, Mr Crossman changed his mind, evidently under some pressure from the local authority associations and civil servants, and the small powerful committee became a conventional Royal Commission. Strangely enough Mr Crossman's threat to what he called 'the dinosaurs' of local government, by which I think he meant the counties and county boroughs, was received with a standing ovation from the representatives of one branch of the species, the county boroughs.[3] Whether the cheering delegates on that bright September morning comprehended the full implications of the minister's pronouncement it is impossible to know, but the polite, sometimes enthusiastic and occasionally deferential manner in which the existing local authorities co-operated in the task of drawing up the indictment against themselves and setting up the gallows, so to speak, is still one of my more abiding impressions during the Commission's proceedings and was a source of wonder and bafflement for foreign visitors to the Commission's headquarters at Gwydyr House.

The intention to create a Royal Commission was announced by the Prime Minister in the Commons on 10 February 1966. Owing to difficulties experienced by Mr Crossman in finding a chairman,[4] the Royal Warrant establishing the Commission was not published until 31 May 1966. The Commission consisted of the following eleven members:

Chairman:
Sir John Maud (later Lord Redcliffe-Maud) Master of University College, Oxford, and former Permanent Secretary of the Ministries of Education, and Fuel and Power. He had been Ambassador to South Africa and at the time of his appointment he was already the Chairman of the Committee on Management in Local Government.
Vice-Chairman:
Mr J. E. Bolton Director of a number of private companies and former Chairman of the Council of the British Institute of Management.
Members:
Mr Victor Feather Deputy General Secretary of the TUC. He had spent his whole career in the trade union movement. He was also a member of the Committee on Management in Local Government.
Sir Francis Hill Chairman of the Association of Municipal Corporations, formerly a Conservative Alderman on Lincoln County Borough Council and President of the International Union of Local Authorities. He was also a member of the Committee on Management in Local Government.
Mr Jack Longland Chief Education Officer of Derbyshire County Council and member of the Sports Council. He was also Chairman of the BBC programmes *Round Britain Quiz* and *My Word*.
Dr A. H. Marshall Deputy Director of the Institute of Local Government Studies at the University of Birmingham, formerly Treasurer to the Coventry County Borough Council. He was the author of a comparative study of local government administration that was published as Volume 4 of the *Report of the Committee on Management in Local Government*.
Mr Peter Mursell Fruit farmer and an Independent Chairman of the West Sussex County Council. He was also a member of a number of committees of the County Councils Association, and was a member of the Committee on Management in Local Government.
Mr Derek Senior Freelance planning journalist, gardening editor of the *Guardian* and its former local government correspondent. Member of the Executive of the Town and Country Planning Association.
Dame Evelyn Sharp Formerly Permanent Secretary of the Ministry of Housing and Local Government. Apart from a

period in the Treasury, she had spent her whole career in the central department principally responsible for the oversight of local government.
Mr T. D. Smith Chairman of the Northern Region Economic Planning Council, and public relations consultant. Formerly Leader of Newcastle-upon-Tyne County Borough Council.
Mr Reginald Wallis Retired former Labour Party regional organiser for the North-West. Former parish councillor.

The Commission's terms of reference were:

> to consider the structure of Local Government in England, outside Greater London, in relation to its existing functions; and to make recommendations for authorities and boundaries, and for functions and their division, having regard to the size and character of areas in which these can be most effectively exercised and the need to sustain a viable system of local democracy.

The Commission began work in late May 1966 and its report was published in June 1969.[5] Its main recommendations were accepted by the Labour government on the day the report was published and the government set in motion almost immediately the procedures necessary prior to the introduction of a Bill.[6] In January 1970 a lengthy White Paper appeared setting out the government's policy towards the report.[7] They accepted the Commission's case for change and adopted most of its main proposals with only minor amendments. However, the Conservatives in opposition did not accept the proposals in the White Paper or, in effect, the Redcliffe-Maud Report, and reserved the right to bring in their own proposals should they be elected in what had to be an impending general election. This they did when they were elected in June 1970 and they published their own White Paper in February 1971.[8] A Bill was presented to Parliament on 4 November 1971. This passed through all its stages with relatively little change and received the Royal Assent on 26 October 1972. The new structure came into effect on 1 April 1974.[9]

II THE RESEARCH PROGRAMME

I was appointed by the Commission at its first meeting in June 1966 as Director of Intelligence and Assistant Commissioner. The latter title meant that I was able to attend the meetings of the Commission and contribute to its discussion as well as conducting the Commission's research.

The appointment of the Commission may be seen in retrospect as the culmination of a prolonged process of discussing and proposing local government reorganisation that had begun in 1946; and it was the accumulated knowledge and understanding that had been gathered, especially by the 1958 Local Government Commission for England, which seems to have influenced Crossman's original preference for a small 'principles' committee rather than a full-dress Royal Commission. However, the accumulated knowledge and the vast collection of data that had been gathered by the large staff of the Local Government Commission[10] was not lost to the Redcliffe-Maud Commission since Dr Stanley Vince, a social geographer and planner seconded from the Ministry of Housing, and a team of colleagues, were transferred to the Royal Commission from the Local Government Commission, where they had been responsible for its research. I would like to take this opportunity to pay tribute to the considerable contribution to the work of the Commission made by his incredibly detailed knowledge of the physical, social and economic characteristics of different localities up and down the country, that bore upon the re-designing of local government. Without Dr Vince and his team the task of the Commission would have been wellnigh insuperable since it was unable, given the scope of its task, to make direct visits. Nor was it able to call for detailed information from local authorities, of the kind that its predecessor was required to do. Indeed, the local authorities had relatively little time to concoct even a conventional presentation of their views on reorganisation, since they were given a deadline of 1 October 1966 for making their written submissions to the Commission.

In addition to Dr Vince's team, I was also able to recruit a group of five research staff from universities and other research organisations.[11] They too proved to be an invaluable asset, not only for servicing the short-term research needs of the Commission and appraising the research commissioned from outside, but for undertaking a sizeable number of in-house projects.[12]

At one of the early meetings of the Commission it was agreed that it would complete its work in two years. As it turned out this was too optimistic a timetable, but at the time it did place very severe limits on the kind of new research that we could initiate or undertake ourselves. David Donnison, who has probably had as much experience as anyone of organising and assessing research for inquiries, has quite rightly claimed that it takes a minimum of a year and nine months to complete an entirely new research project of any scale.[13] This time constraint needs perhaps special emphasis and warrants a brief diversion from our main discussion, since the shortage of time that commissions like Redcliffe-Maud face seems to be insufficiently appreciated, particularly perhaps by academics.[14] Baiting committee and commission reports for research inadequacies can be a diverting and relatively costless exercise, if only because there is unlikely to be any riposte, and I have indulged in the practice myself.[15] However, a Royal Commission that is specifically created to examine the case for complex institutional change and recommend action will always fall short of the desirable in terms of its research effort. It is not like, for example, the Royal Commissions that are set up to carry out research and nothing else without any assumption of subsequent legislative action in the manner of the interwar commissions set up by the Ministry of Agriculture.[16] A commission of the Redcliffe-Maud variety can never be in the position of drawing up an exhaustive list of all the possible research possibilities that its terms of reference may suggest, even supposing its members were persuaded that such research would in the end be of any utility, which itself may be a large assumption. To do so would considerably extend its period of cogitation well beyond the normal span of two and a half years.[17]

In the case of the Redcliffe-Maud Commission, as I have already noted, there was a predisposition among its members to keep to a fairly strict timetable in any case. Moreover, whatever may be thought to be the deficiencies of its actual programme, by conventional standards it was remarkably receptive to the notion of research and this receptivity seems to have been part of what has been identified as a new phase in the importance attached to research by Royal Commissions.[18] It may be that for all its virtues, which are undoubtedly considerable, the Royal Commission mode is not appropriate or is inadequate for the determination of complex institutional change. But consideration of different modes raises questions about the role of long-term policy research and its possible place in the internal organisation of central departments. This is unquestionably an important issue that is rarely examined in any depth,[19] but it lies outside the scope of this article. What perhaps does merit brief mention here is the commendable suggestion by Andrew Shonfield, that a Commission or Committee of Inquiry that is examining the case for institutional change ought to have, as a matter of course, a research team which is charged by the committee with the initial task of drawing up a conceptual framework, which places the institution under scrutiny in its setting and explains in theoretical terms its role and rationale within the wider system.[20]

To return to the Commission's research programme, given the time constraints it became imperative that a programme of research priorities be drawn up. However, sorting out what could or ought to be done within the time available was not the most important constraint in drawing up a programme. There was also the problem of trying to guess what the Commission might be wanting to know eighteen months hence. In other words, some careful prior assessment had to be made of the principal structural models that were likely to be engaging the Commission's attention at what would be a crucial stage in the proceedings. But that did not mean that we could narrow down the priorities solely to the most likely 'runners'. It was absolutely essential at that stage to create the maximum degree of trust in the research team and this meant that any list of priorities had to contain items which reassured members that their own particular interests and predilections were not going to be ignored. Perhaps I felt this need for generating trust particularly acutely since I had already publicly aired my views on local government reorganisation, albeit in skeletal form.[21] But I have no strong memory that this did count much when the research programme was drawn up and the reason is, I think, that the Commission was created at a time when institutional change in government was very much in the air. Mr Crossman's standing ovation at Torquay reflected a more widespread public expectation of fundamental change in local government that had already found expression in the increasingly radical proposals of the Royal Commission's predecessor, the Local Government Commission for England.[22] As is often the case with government inquiries, the Redcliffe-Maud Commission began its work in an atmosphere of expectation about change. As Gerald Rhodes has put it in his valuable study of Committees of Inquiry, 'The circumstances of its origin powerfully affect the limits within which a committee can operate'.[23] This public expectation increased in strength as the Commission's work proceeded and, of course, it strongly affected its recommendations. We shall return to the importance of the expectation effect later. Having some sympathy for change, then, was not wholly out of order and this also explains to some extent the appointment of Derek Senior who was to write a very powerfully argued Dissenting Memorandum and whose public commitment to a particular form of change before the Commission was appointed[24] has caused some eyebrow-raising in critical assessments of the Commission's report.[25]

It is impossible to tell whether the research programme fulfilled the requirement, noted earlier, of covering all the most likely options open to the Commission without arousing suspicions among Commission members that some aspects were going to be neglected. This is partly because most members of the Commission were themselves probably inhibited about revealing their own position so early in the life of the Commission. At this stage, given that some members had never even met each other before they joined the Commission, there was clearly a premium on being, or appearing to be, as open-minded as possible. Valuable stores of moral capital could be amassed at relatively little cost for future deployment. Some members had as yet no coherent view to defend or promote in any case so that the possible implications of a research programme were unlikely to matter very much. For one or two of this group the open-minded, uncommitted posture was to remain their chosen role. They were for this reason to become extremely important when it came to building up firm support for specific proposals since the Commission was not only large by local government inquiry standards,[26] some members had strong views which they were capable of expressing with both clarity and force. During the early days of the Commission this crucial counter-balancing role of the strongly uncommitted group was yet to be revealed, but they were possibly the most sympathetic to the idea of a concerted research effort.[27]

Finally, a few members were sceptical about the role and influence of any research. For them the contents of a research programme were likely to be of only marginal importance when the crucial stage of the Commission's proceedings was reached and each member had to reveal his views unequivocally in relation to specific sets of proposals. At that point, so these sceptics may have surmised, skill in advocacy, doggedness and a feel for the practicable would count for most. In the meantime the contents of a research programme did not seem to be of great consequence.

With the aforementioned considerations more or less in mind a research programme was drawn up and agreed in July 1966. Broadly speaking, most of the programme fell into three basic areas that related to the adequacy of the territorial extent of existing top-tier local authorities (counties and county boroughs) in relation to land-use planning and cognate services; that related to whether or not the scale of existing local government units was adequate for the performance of the mainly personal health, welfare and education services; and, finally, public attitudes towards local government, in particular the nature and extent of the sense of local allegiance and identity.[28] I knew from my experience as a member of the Greater London Group at the London School of Economics in preparing evidence for the Herbert Commission on London Local Government a few years earlier, that there was a great deal of work on the first, the socio-geographic aspect. However, the position in relation to the second research area, that on functional capacity, was vastly different. This did not mean there was nothing to be done in relation to the socio-geographic aspect; on the contrary. But given the material already gathered by our predecessors, it could be tackled by the in-house research team and a wide range of in-house projects were carried out on the socio-geographic aspect, some of which appear in Volume III of the Commission's *Report*. In addition, the

South-Eastern region of England had not been covered by the Local Government Commission so the Greater London Group was asked to make a special study of this area. In marked contrast to the socio-geographic research sector there was very little existing research on the relationship between the population scale of local units and their performance of the major services, although there had been a great deal of assertion by the advocates of reorganisation that a relationship did exist.

This disparity between fact and assertion was not entirely fortuitous for there are considerable problems involved in devising satisfactory ways of measuring the relationship between scale and service performance and substituting expenditure figures for the service is the most favoured solution, but there remains the problem of interpreting variations in expenditure in qualitative terms. Equally, there are the difficulties arising from the likelihood that population scale has different implications for service performance according to the way the population is distributed spatially. Contemplating such problems in the light of the time constraints already alluded to and realising, perhaps rather naively,[29] that the outcome of such research could have some influence on the real world, rather than just grace the pages of an academic journal, was a chastening experience not unlike having your bluff called. This formed part of a wider rude awakening that I experienced which merits some mention since it has a bearing on the contribution of social science research to the work of Committees of Inquiry and Royal Commissions generally, especially when it is undertaken by academics. Successive meetings of the Commission brought home to me how wide the gulf was between the academic world and the world of practice. At the risk of sounding unduly portentous, whereas I had imagined that, freed from the distractions of the ephemeral, the social scientist deals with the inner reality of social and political phenomena, I discovered that this was not the view of at least some of the practitioners in the political and administrative process. Knowledge for them was practical experience: 'He who does, knows.' Unless the academic had some esoteric historical knowledge to impart, or some plausible explanatory technique that looked as if it had an immediate application, academics had surprisingly little standing. I do not wish to exaggerate this practitioner scepticism, nor was it directed to the research programme, but it is a characteristic of public policy-making in this country that is not always appreciated by academics, especially perhaps those who proffer memoranda to Committees of Inquiry unasked. P. J. Grigg, who had himself been both a civil servant and a politician, has expressed this type of practitioner view of outside experts with candour:

> Let me say plainly, however, that I do not like 'experts' and technicians who have never occupied, or alternatively have failed in executive positions of responsibility, and yet write books to prove how wise they are and how foolish is everybody else.[30]

As I have said, this sceptical predisposition did not give rise to any questioning of the efficacy of the research programme by Commission members. Indeed, I must record that it always received the warmest support. So, within the time limits already noted, there was no objection to commissioning research on the possible effect of scale, and I was convinced that such research was essential, since it became increasingly clear that the Commission would be unable to avoid the question of the relationship between scale and local government capacity. A number of projects were therefore commissioned from outside research organisations.[31] Literature appraisal exercises were also undertaken by the Commission's research team, together with an analysis of local authority staff quality in relation to scale, using data gathered by the Mallaby Committee on local authority staffing.[32]

The last section of the research programme concerned public attitudes towards the existing system of local government and in particular the nature and scope of its sense of local identity. Here again there was surprisingly little material available but there were some valuable findings on public attitudes to local government and other useful information related to councillor attitudes and behaviour that had been gathered by the Committee on Management in Local Government. This Committee was already sitting when the Commission was set up and it overlapped the Commission not only in its subject-matter, but also in that it shared the same Chairman and three further members. Indeed, one of the members of the Commission, Dr Marshall, was the Committee's research director. This probably unique form of overlap had implications for the Commission's research programme apart from the advantage it gave the Commission in providing a great deal of important research data just noted. In the first place, it meant that four members of the Commission were already aware of the contribution research could make to its deliberations since the Committee on Management had already completed a fairly wide-ranging research programme by the time the Commission was set up.[33] Secondly, it meant that the four members had thought at some length and were familiar with a great deal of information about the internal decision-making processes of local government, central–local relations, the role and attitudes of councillors and public attitudes to local government. This enriched the Commission's discussions immeasurably, and it also undeniably affected both the character of its report and its strong advocacy of the unitary concept for local government reorganisation which was to be so firmly rejected in the new local government system inaugurated in 1972.

All the outside research bodies delivered their reports more or less on time so that most of the research programme was completed well before the Commission had formulated its final proposals. But the programme formed only part of the job of the Commission's research staff. By far the biggest task was the provision of regular background papers to the Commission. This consisted mainly of summaries of existing research, and special fact-gathering exercises on topics that were relevant to the Commission's deliberations. From time to time there was also the need to interpret the more complex and esoteric findings of the research the Commission had itself commissioned from outside bodies for internal consumption. In retrospect, it seems likely that the members had too many papers to cope with. For, as well as the different kinds of research reports just described, there was a constant flow of background papers from the secretariat. In addition, there was the voluminous body of 2,155 items of evidence submitted to the Commission from local authorities (1,269), professional associations (350) and private individuals (536).[34] Not all of the latter flowed directly to each Commission member and the secretariat performed the herculean task of summarising those which seemed to be of more marginal importance. Some idea of the amount of paper that was actually circulated to each member of the Commission can be gauged from the fact that it comprises thirty-five bulging foolscap ring folders which together occupy 6½ feet of shelf space.

The British civil service is especially renowned for its ability to provide support services for higher decision-making.[35] I was certainly struck by the amplitude of such services on the Commission, not just in terms of secretarial provision and the expeditious circulation of paper, but equally by the cornucopian flow of up-to-date information. Until I joined the Commission I had no idea of the handicap I had laboured under as an academic student of British government by being 'outside' rather than 'inside' the government apparatus. However, the sheer amount of material to be read by Commission members, most of whom had to hold down full-time jobs, did strike me as being beyond most people's capacity if they were to do justice to the reading matter placed before them. Of course, the quality of the material that regularly thumped through members' letter boxes varied widely, and some did as much justice to the secretariat's assiduity in ensuring that members were kept fully informed as it did to the requirement of coming to agreed conclusions. Moreover, the ability to absorb material quickly and to sort out the wheat from the chaff are presumably attributes that many members of inquiries will have acquired in the process of reaching the level of eminence in their chosen fields that got them appointed to the inquiry in the first place. Nevertheless, some of the Commission's papers needed very careful digestion and appraisal and I have little doubt that Shonfield's plea for full-time members for at least the earliest phase of the proceedings of an inquiry into complex institutional change is wellfounded.[36] Naturally, some members will be more knowledgeable about the general subject-matter of the inquiry than others and they may also have a firmer grasp of the principles informing the role and functions of the institution under scrutiny, but it is in the very nature of our tradition of lay membership that many, perhaps most, of them will not. At the risk of seeming to endorse an over-exalted role for the research director, Shonfield's case for at least a preliminary period of full-time membership is worth quoting:

> There must, for a start, surely be a period in which members of the committee are engaged full-time in reading themselves into the subject-matter, discovering what up-to-date thinking there is on their problems, and discussing at length with the research director appointed to guide them what are the major issues for investigation and how to set about acquiring the relevant data.[37]

Processing and interpreting the various research projects, both external and in-house, so as to ensure they received due consideration was sometimes difficult, since the completion of a project did not necessarily coincide with that point in the Commission's deliberations where it would be most relevant. Occasionally, too, one was aware that although directly relevant to the topic then engaging the Commission's attention, some research never seemed to make the impact that was expected. This is perhaps an occupational hazard of social scientists involved in the policy-making process: their main concentration is on the trees rather than wood. In a few minor cases the research findings did arrive too late to have any impact on the final conclusions. This was a rare occurrence, but all of these almost certainly inevitable hazards do raise the wider question and the one that seems to fascinate academic Royal Commission watchers: did the research really affect the Commission's proposals? Behind this question there often lurks an assumption that the Redcliffe-Maud Commission's proposals ought to have been mainly 'applied social research'. My own view, which I have stated at greater length elsewhere,[38] is that, by its very nature, the social sciences are unlikely to have the direct impact that such a claim assumes. This is not to say that research had no impact on the Commission's report, but we can, of course, never know what it was with any precision since we do not know what they would have decided without benefit of any research. There can be no doubt, however, that the various kinds of statistical material which demonstrated the degree of population mobility, urbanisation and town and hinterland linkages had a cumulative impact on the Commission's willingness to contemplate the large unitary authorities they did.

Research that almost certainly did have some indirect and negative effects is likely to have been the various studies of the possible impact of scale on service performance already mentioned. Bearing in mind the inherent deficiency that all such studies share because it is impossible to measure the quality of a public service satisfactorily, the overall impression they give is that scale appears to have much less impact than was claimed by those who were pressing the Commission to recommend that the whole local government system be replaced by thirty or forty city regional authorities. Although not numerous, this group did include all the major home front central departments in addition to one of its own members, Derek Senior, who was both highly articulate and dogged in his advocacy. Never before had Whitehall expressed itself in such an emphatic and unambiguous way on the issue of local government reform. And it must also have been a very rare example of virtual unanimity among the major departments. Seldom in the long history of Royal Commissions can Whitehall have provided such a united front on a major policy issue. Had the research shown that these were significant economies of scale, or that more effective provision of major services was provided by the very largest authorities, then the Commission would have found it much more difficult to resist the Whitehall phalanx. With the exception of the two studies conducted by the central departments themselves, the research on scale effects that the Commission undertook or commissioned suggested overall that assumptions about the efficiency advantages of larger authorities were, at the very least, questionable. This placed a large question mark against the Whitehall thesis.

It may be claimed, too, that the community attitudes survey which the Commission instigated also had an important indirect influence on their willingness to contemplate new authorities substantially larger than the existing top-tier local authorities. Now it may be argued with some justification that the survey's conception of local identity is too narrow and as its begetter I accept that criticism. Nevertheless, so far as the Commission was concerned – faced as it was by severe time constraints – the survey's results did suggest that in large urban areas local loyalties were, by one measure, on a surprisingly small scale. This ruled out such loyalties having any bearing on the design of major service-providing authorities.

In the case of the Redcliffe-Maud Commission we must take into account not merely the normal conditions that tend to render social science research of limited direct utility. For the Commission was born in an atmosphere of expectations of a quite formidable kind. As we noted earlier, most inquiries are influenced to some degree by this contextual factor and to understand its strengths in the Redcliffe-Maud case it must be appreciated that the Commission was the third attempt to reorganise local government since 1945[39] and the origins of the case for reorganisation reach back even earlier to the impact of the interwar depression on local government.[40]

What these expectations amounted to is impossible to say precisely, for like all such movements of opinion its very vagueness was its strength. Obviously, the two earlier officially sponsored attempts to correct the inadequacies of the local government system were influential in suggesting that all was not right with it. Throughout the 1960s there had also been a build-up of opinion which argued that the importance of locality had diminished with the rise in population mobility and the growth in communications of all kinds. Society at the sub-national level, it was argued, was now organised on a wider regional basis and the local government system ought to reflect this change. Another strand of the expectations placed in the Redcliffe-Maud, which was perhaps more prevalent in Westminster and the media than elsewhere, was the belief that Britain suffered from too many out-of-date political and administrative institutions. None was more urgently in need of 'reform', so it was argued, than local government with its aura of neo-gothic town halls, geriatric aldermen and parochial bureaucrats. No assessment of the role of research in the Commission's proposals can ignore these expectations, any more than the Commissioners themselves could. Perhaps it was also this vague public desire for some kind of change – almost for its own sake – which made it so easy for Mr Heath's government to ignore the Commission's three years of intensive labour and substitute its own proposals; proposals whose provenance remains something of a mystery, but the evolution of which we can be reasonably certain was unencumbered by research.

NOTES: CHAPTER 3

1 For a discussion of the work of the Local Government Commission for England see H. V. Wiseman (ed.), *Local Government in England, 1958–69* (London: Routledge, 1970), ch. 2.

2 Mr Crossman's speech is reproduced in the *Municipal Review*, November 1965.

3 R. H. S. Crossman, *The Diaries of a Cabinet Minister*, Vol. 1 (London: Hamish Hamilton and Jonathan Cape, 1975), pp. 331 and 622.

4 Crossman, *The Diaries*, Vol. 1. References to the difficulties he experienced in finding a Chairman for the Commission are scattered throughout Vol. 1, but see, for example, pp. 367, 381, 393, 400, 453 and 485.

5 The report is published in three volumes and is entitled *Royal Commission on Local Government in England: Report*, Cmnd 4040 (London: HMSO, 1969). Volume I comprises the actual conclusions and proposals of the Commission and contains two dissenting notes on relatively minor items by three members of the Commission. Volume II is a formal *Dissenting Memorandum* by Derek Senior, the one member of the Commission who did not sign Volume I. Volume III comprises a series of research papers written by various members of the Commission's in-house research team plus two by, respectively, the Department of Education and Science and the Home Office.

In the course of its life the Commission published a series of ten *Research Studies*. These were all published by HMSO under the auspices of the Commission. The titles and authors of the *Research Studies* were as follows:

1: *Local Government in South East England* by the Greater London Group (1968).
2: *The Lessons of the London Government Reform* by the Greater London Group (1968).
3: *Economies of Scale in Local Government Services* by the Institute of Social and Economic Research, University of York (1968).
4: *Performance and Size of Local Education Authorities* by the Local Government Operational Research Unit (1968).
5: *Local Authority Services and the Characteristics of Administrative Areas* by the Government Social Survey (1968).
6: *School Management and Government* by the Institute of Education, University of London (1968).
7: *Aspects of Administration in a Large Local Authority* by the Institute of Local Government Studies (1968).
8: *The Inner London Education Authority: A Study of Divisional Administration* by Anthea Tinker (1968).
9: *Community Attitudes Survey* by Research Services Ltd (1969).
10: *Administration in a Large Local Authority: A Comparison With Other County Boroughs* by the Institute of Local Government Studies (1969).

6 A considerable literature has arisen which discusses the Redcliffe-Maud Report and the 1972 Local Government Act and note ought to be taken of the following:

J. Bowen-Rees, *Government by Community* (London: Charles Knight, 1971).
J. A. Brand, *Local Government Reform in England, 1888-1974* (London: Croom Helm, 1975).
Lord Redcliffe-Maud and Bruce Wood, *English Local Government Reformed* (London: Oxford University Press, 1974).
Jane Morton, *The Best Laid Schemes?* (London: Charles Knight, 1970).
Peter G. Richards *The Local Government Act 1972: Problems of Implementation* (London: Allen & Unwin, 1975).
Geoffrey Smith (ed.), *Redcliffe-Maud's Brave New England* (London: Charles Knight, 1969).
Douglas E. Ashford, 'Reorganizing British local government: a policy problem', *Local Government Studies*, vol. 2, no. 4 (1976).
S. L. Bristow, 'The criteria for local government reorganization and local authority autonomy' *Policy and Politics*, vol. 1, no. 2 (1972).
C. J. Davies, 'The reform of local government with special reference to England', *Studies in Comparative Local Government* 7 (Winter 1973).

W. Hampton, 'Political attitudes to change in city council administration' *Local Government Studies*, 2 (April 1972).
G. W. Jones, 'The Local Government Act 1972 and the Redcliffe-Maud Commission', *Political Quarterly*, vol. 44, no. 2 (1973).
G. W. Jones, 'Intergovernmental relations in Britain', *The Annals of the American Academy of Political and Social Science,* November 1974.
G. W. Jones 'Varieties of local politics', *Local Government Studies*, vol. 1, no. 2 (1975).
R. Newman, 'The relevance of "community" in local government reorganization', *Local Government Studies*, 6 (October 1973).
Roderick Rhodes 'Local government reform: three questions' *Social and Economic Administration*, vol. 8, no. 1 (1974).
Derek Senior, 'Metropolitan planning and local government reform', *Town and Country Planning*, vol. 40, no. 2 (February 1972).
L. J. Sharpe, 'The weak points of the Bill', *Municipal Review*, February 1972.

7 Ministry of Local Government and Regional Planning, *Reform of Local Government in England*, Cmnd 4276 (London: HMSO, 1970).

8 Department of the Environment, *Local Government in England: Government Proposals for Reorganisation*, Cmnd 4584 (London: HMSO, 1971).

9 An informative account of the whole process of reorganisation from the publication of the Redcliffe-Maud Report to the birth of the 1972 Act is given in Bruce Wood, *The Process of Local Government Reform: 1966–74* (London: Allen & Unwin, 1976).

10 Crossman, *The Diaries*, Vol. 1, p. 381, states that the Local Government Commission had a staff of eighty.

11 They were Miss J. Allsop, R. S. Hough, John Shepherd, Dr Paul Spencer and Bruce Wood. The research staff seconded from the Ministry of Housing and Local Government, in addition to Dr Vince, were Miss Dorothy Emmens, Allan Walkden, Miss L. Shepley and J. W. Worth.

12 Some of these were published in volume III of the Commission's *Report*.

13 David Donnison, Chapter 2, above, p. 11.

14 Jeffrey Stanyer, for example, has been particularly critical of the Redcliffe-Maud research effort. However, there is no evidence from his critique that he understands the time constraint and this nullifies much of his case. Nor does he invite serious consideration of his almost wholly critical analysis by accusing the Commission of 'grotesque impertinence' and concluding that the whole report was 'a waste of public money'. See J. Stanyer 'The Redcliffe-Maud Royal Commission on Local Government' in Richard A. Chapman (ed.), *The Role of Commissions in Policy-Making* (London: Allen & Unwin, 1975), pp. 138 and 140.

15 L. J. Sharpe 'Thin gruel from the Local Government Commission', *Town and Country Planning*, August 1963.

16 Angus Mackintosh, 'The use of advisory bodies by the Ministry of Agriculture and Fisheries' in R. V. Vernon and N. Mansergh (eds), *Advisory Bodies* (London: Allen & Unwin, 1940).

17 T. J. Cartwright, *Royal Commissions and Departmental Committees in Britain* (London: Hodder & Stoughton, 1975), p. 222.

18 Cartwright, *Royal Commissions and Departmental Committees*, p. 159. This point is also made by Gerald Rhodes, *Committees of Inquiry* (London: Allen & Unwin, 1975), pp. 110, 111.

19 One exception is of course the *Report of the Committee on the Civil Service*, Cmnd 3638, (London: HMSO, 1968).

20 Andrew Shonfield, Chapter 5, below.

21 L. J. Sharpe, *Why Local Democracy?*, Tract No. 361 (London: Fabian Society, 1965).

22 See Wiseman, *Local Government in England* (Note 1, above).
23 Rhodes, *Committees of Inquiry*, p. 161.
24 Derek Senior, 'The city region as an administrative unit', *Political Quarterly*, vol. 36, no. 1 (1965).
25 Richard A. Chapman, 'Commissions in policy-making' in Chapman (ed.), *The Role of Commissions in Policy-Making*.
26 Bruce Wood, *The Process of Local Government Reform: 1966–74*, ch. 1.
27 Donnison's discussion in the previous chapter remains the best account available of the different and perhaps essential roles that Commission and Committee of Inquiry members tend to play.
28 A more detailed discussion of the Commission's research is given in *Royal Commission on Local Government in England: Report*, Vol. I, ch. V.
29 For a discussion of the tendency for social scientists to exaggerate the contribution of social science to public policy-making see L. J. Sharpe, 'The role of social science in policy-making: some cautionary thoughts and transatlantic reflections', *Policy and Politics*, vol. 4, no. 2 (1975).
30 P. J. Grigg, *Prejudice and Judgement* (London: Cape, 1948), p. 7. Also see R. V. Vernon, 'Introduction' in Vernon (ed.), *Advisory Bodies*, p. 22, for similar sentiments. For a more recent example of practitioner scepticism see A. R. Isserlis, 'The usefulness of political science to the public service', paper given to the Political Studies Association Annual Conference, March 1978.
31 The results of these studies were published under the auspices of the Commission in its *Research Studies* that are all listed in Note 5. A special tribute must be recorded to Allen Wilson, now Professor of Geography at Leeds University, who was then mathematical adviser to the Ministry of Transport. He was of considerable assistance in suggesting ways in which the relationship between population scale and service performance could be analysed, and was particularly helpful in suggesting a way of coping with the spatial distribution of population. In the event there was not the time to pursue this approach, but some idea of its main characteristics is given in Appendix 1 of *Research Study No. 4*.
32 This is published as Appendix 10 in *Royal Commission on Local Government in England: Report*, Vol. III.
33 This is contained in Volumes 2, 3, 4, and 5 of *Management of Local Government – the Report of the Committee on the Management of Local Government* (London: HMSO, 1967).
34 For an analysis of this evidence see I. Gowan and L. Gibson 'The Royal Commission on Local Government in England', *Public Administration*, vol. 46, no. 1 (1968). Not all of this evidence was published but most of it is contained in the nineteen volumes of *Written Evidence*.
35 Anne Stevens, 'Can the efficiency of the French civil service be improved?', paper given to Nuffield College Seminar on Current Trends in the British and French Central Bureaucracies, February 1979 (mimeo.).
36 Shonfield, chapter 5, below, p. 64.
37 Shonfield, chapter 5, below, p. 64.
38 Sharpe, 'The social scientist and policy-making', op. cit.
39 For an account of the postwar reform saga see Bryan Keith-Lucas and Peter G. Richards, *A History of Local Government in the Twentieth Century* (London: Allen & Unwin, 1978), ch. X.
40 Norman Chester, 'The problems of a local authority in an industrially distressed area,' *Public Administration*, vol. XV, no. 3 (1937).

Chapter 4

Research as Stage Management: The Case of the Plowden Committee

HENRY ACLAND

I INTRODUCTION

In this chapter I shall provide an account of the way the Plowden Committee, an advisory group appointed by the Secretary of State for Education and Science, used research in developing policy recommendations for primary schools. Though the policies and researches are specific to the Plowden Committee, they illustrate general problems in understanding the connection between research and policy. My aim is to analyse the way the Committee used, and ignored, research, in a manner that can illuminate attempts of other committees, commissions and councils to employ research in policy-making. In describing one case, I hope to provide insights into the operation of comparable decision-making groups.

I use this case study to advance the idea that research can be viewed as stage management for the development of policy. This theatrical metaphor directs attention away from rigidly rational notions about the connection between research and policy. Seen from the rational point of view, policy research is understood to provide authoritative evidence that justifies one among several policy options. In other words, there is seen to be a close connection between specified policy alternatives, the design of the research, the research findings and the ultimate choice among the policy options. Set against this rational standard most policy research is inadequate. In addition, it is an approach which blinds us to other ways of viewing the interaction of policy and research. I shall show that the Plowden research does not measure up to the rational standard in several ways. The research was not designed to resolve questions about policy alternatives. The research design could not provide substantial evidence for the policies with which it was to be connected. The findings were both misused and ignored. Nevertheless, the research was important in creating the setting in which a potentially sensitive policy could be introduced. The research set the stage for a new policy. The purpose of the stage management metaphor is to expand the number of ways of thinking about the connection between research and policy, and to point to the dangers of mistaking this kind of policy research for authoritative evidence.

The chapter has three sections and a conclusion. In the introduction I describe the origins of the Plowden Committee, its role and ambitions, connecting it to previous committees with similar functions. The second section analyses the Committee's policy for increasing parent involvement in schools, examining the original research and my own re-analysis of the research data. The third section deals with the policy for improvement of schools attended by disadvantaged children.

Central Advisory Councils

The Education Act of 1944 required the Secretary of State for Education and Science to appoint a continuing advisory group known as the Central Advisory Council (CAC). The Act establishes that the CAC will 'advise the Secretary of State upon such matters connected with educational theory and practice as they think fit, and upon any questions referred to them by him'.[1] Although set up by the government, CACs are independent inquiries and in that sense the government is not obliged to adopt any proposals they make. The Councils usually come to be referred to by the name of their chairperson, in this case, Lady Plowden. At no time has a Council met to examine extremely sensitive issues, nor to respond to focused public pressure. Each has been handed a broad mandate, usually to examine a particular segment of the education system, for example, the primary schools. Each has summarised current practices, pointing to weaknesses, but more obviously praising strengths. Each has developed a long list of recommendations on the basis of impression, informed opinion and hard data. However, there is no apparatus to enforce these proposals. Their influence seems to operate through generating interest and thought at the time the committee deliberates and, after publication, in setting new standards and expectations about schools. Clearly identified with the main government agency responsible for education, their effect is considerable in a country respectful of its central government.

It is relevant that previous CACs, though spreading their energies over many issues, have always been concerned with the extension of educational opportunity. *Early Leaving*[2] had recommended several ways to increase the proportion of secondary pupils, especially those from poor homes, who stayed in school beyond the minimum leaving age. The CAC had suggested allowances for needy children to facilitate their staying beyond the age of 15, the payment of family allowances for all children in school and an increase in the proportion of grammar school places. The Crowther Report[3] recommended raising the school-leaving age to 16 followed by compulsory part-time education to 18. The policies were explicitly aimed at decreasing the wastage of talent. Four years later, Newsom's committee[4] repeated the plea for longer schooling and added recommendations for lengthening the school day. Again, the CAC was concerned with improving the development of the country's talent. Newsom also foreshadowed Plowden's priority area policy by pointing to the special needs of slum areas that would require co-ordinated improvement of social services including the provision of schools.

It is also relevant for my purposes that each Council has used research, though Plowden was clearly more research-minded than any of its predecessors. For example, arguments for extending the school-leaving age in earlier reports had been buttressed by studies showing the significant relationship between pupils' home background and their educational performance. Thus, the Crowther Report had shown how educational attainment correlates more closely with social background than with ability.

The Plowden Committee

Plowden was to continue these traditions of concern with the extension of educational opportunity and of the use of research evidence. The Plowden Committee, appointed in 1963, was asked to 'consider primary education in all its aspects'.[5] The Committee's travels, researches and topics of study reflected the width of its mandate. The Committee was composed of a large number of people, twenty-five in all, representing a wide range of interest groups.[6] However, it is fair to say that the professional educational establishment carried the greatest weight. Of the twenty-five, six were headteachers, one an educational psychologist, another the principal of a teacher training institution and three were educational administrators. In this, the Committee looked much like previous CACs. However, Plowden's Committee was distinctive in having four university professors, of logic, economics, social administration and child health. The Chairman of the SSRC, Michael Young, was also included.

Despite these outsiders, it could be anticipated that the Committee would be broadly supportive of schools. In the first place, it had to act through persuasion. Secondly, its size would act as a ballast against wild departures from accepted ideas. Nevertheless, the Plowden group was assertive in advancing its recommendations. Each recommendation was associated with careful costing and proposed time lines for its adoption. Like other CACs, the Plowden Committee did not want its report to gather dust, yet knew that one way to guarantee this was to shriek for unrealistic reforms. Its

Secretary wrote that Plowden and previous CACs were 'slightly in advance of official opinion; the tugboats of gradualist radicalism'.[7]

The Committee probed almost every area of the primary school scene. However, for the purposes of this chapter I shall concern myself with only two of its proposals, both designed to extend educational opportunity. The first called for further involvement of parents in schools, primarily through creating new arrangements by which parents could become familiar with the goals and methods of the school. The second recommendation pointed to the need for improvement of schools attended by 'deprived children', known as the Educational Priority Area (EPA) policy. Both policies sought to improve the quality of education, the parent involvement scheme for all pupils, the EPA policy for those in especially difficult areas. Both were designed to make the school system more efficient, both were expected to improve the life chances of the individual pupils and to contribute to the economic and social development of the country.

At heart, parental involvement meant parental education. Parents were to become informed of school methods and goals so that they could enhance their children's education. For instance, schools were to provide two opportunities each year for parents to meet with the class teacher, who should also be open for unplanned contacts. Open days were suggested in addition to the printed material for parents describing the organisation of the school. Schools were to make written reports on each child at least once a year. The language is revealing: 'Each parent should be invited to an interview with the head, to meet the class teacher and see at work the class into which the child is to go . . . '[8] 'Parents need information not only about their own children's progress but also of a general kind about what goes on in the school'.[9] Yet although the parent involvement scheme was modest because tailored to schools' tolerance for the participation of parents, it should be remembered that the policy was radical if seen in the light of previous practice. Parents had been firmly and explicitly excluded from most schools up until this time. The present climate, which has produced the Taylor Report[10] with suggestions for parent participation in decision-making, is much different from that which prevailed in the early 1960s, and the shift may be partly attributed to the Plowden Report.

The EPA policy was also concerned with upgrading schooling, but focused attention on the most difficult schools. Recognising the multiple forces which create the special problems associated with schools attended by deprived children, the Committee defined ways both of identifying these special areas and of improving the schools in them. Priority areas were to be selected on the basis of social indicators of the schools' catchment area such as the incidence of poverty, the proportion of overcrowded housing, the attendance rate at the school and the number of students whose first language was not English. These schools were to receive special funds for lowering the staff/pupil ratio, providing a salary incentive of £120 per annum for teachers, making more aides available and increasing the provision of nursery education. The schools were to be improved by upgrading the basic ingredients of the basic school: the teachers, buildings and resources.

While the parent involvement scheme seems to have made its mark indirectly and without formal recognition, the EPA idea was adopted in several ways, though half-heartedly. For example, special funds were established for school-building in deprived areas and a salary increment was allowed to teachers in deprived area schools. Further, an action-research project was launched in four districts both to demonstrate the need for positive discrimination and to suggest ways this could be accomplished.[11] However, little is now heard about the idea of priority areas.

My main concern is to describe the way research was used to support those two policies. I have indicated that the Plowden Committee was research-minded. The companion volume to the main report was given to the research studies either directly commissioned by the Committee or used by it. The Committee spent over £67,000 of its budget of £120,000 on research. These studies covered the management of primary schools, the special educational problems of gypsies, the National Foundation for Educational Research study of ability grouping and the National Child Development study of children's growth. A demonstration project was also launched in a school fitting the priority area description, to promote parental involvement. I shall describe this special project later. But at the centre of the stage was a special national survey designed to relate the multiple influences of home and school to pupils' academic performance. It is on this study that I concentrate my attention.

The Plowden Committee was well informed about the evidence that home background was linked to educational achievement. In addition to the studies of previous CACs, the relationship between social background and achievement had been repeatedly documented. Much of this research dealt with the standard measures of home background that are crudely described as socio-economic status.[12] However, attention was being focused on the softer aspects of social class differences; in fact, there was suggestive evidence that attitudes and cultural differences might be even more important than income or status distinctions.[13] The national survey can be seen as a reflection of this growing interest in attitudinal determinants of pupils' school performance. As much as anything else, the currents of academic research shaped the Plowden research.

With even greater certainty it can be said that the survey did not emerge in response to needs to examine the consequences of specific policy alternatives. There was no explicit link between policy and research at the time the survey was commissioned. At this early stage in its work it might be expected that the Committee was finding its feet and so unable to chart a course for the research. This would explain the loose linkage between research and policy, but it does not account for the urgency with which the research was initiated. Ostensibly, it made good sense to make a start because the findings, to be useful, would have to be ready within about two years, since the Committee's life was limited to three. However, this takes for granted the need for a large, time-consuming survey as opposed to quicker studies that could have been planned to relate to the Committee's nascent policies. The fact is, the large survey was waiting in the wings, its outlines largely defined, before the Committee met for the first time.

At the first meeting, on 7 October 1963, the terms of reference for two working parties were already defined, later to be adopted with few alterations. One working party, eventually chaired by Professor Donnison, was charged, among other things to

> prepare a statement for the council on the interaction between primary schools and the communities of which they form part, taking into account (i) the effect on the schools and on individual pupils of consciously held parental attitudes to education, (ii) the extent to which . . . adult attitudes and behaviour and material setting, including socio-economic neighbourhood and regional setting, affect the work of the schools and the performance of pupils, (iii) . . .[14]

The same document points out that the Government Social Survey was 'prepared to conduct surveys' should the working party need them. At the first meeting of this special working party, on 1 November, the idea for the national survey was rapidly advanced. On this and later occasions the working party was assisted by Miss S. M. C. Duncan, a former HMI, who acted as technical expert for the group. Mr G. F. Peaker, another former HMI, had also been consulted on the survey design. He would later take primary responsibility for the analysis of the survey data. At the first meeting, Miss Duncan provided details about important issues such as sample design: important because the size and dispersion of the sample would control the time taken to conduct the survey and shape the kind of information it could yield. The sample design discussed then was very similar to that eventually used. At the same meeting, it was agreed that the questionnaire should be developed by the secretariat in conjunction with the Government Social Survey. In sum, the research was already partially defined and much of the remaining work was handed to technical experts who were not part of the Plowden Committee. Formal approval of the survey was given by the full Committee in its second meeting on 18 December 1963.

The overall goal of the survey was described later by Peaker who noted that:

> The association between the occupation of the parent and the achievement in school of the child must arise, at any rate in part, from the association between occupations and attitudes, and that the variation in attitudes might account for a good deal more of the variation in achievement. It therefore seemed desirable to attempt to estimate the influence of occupation irrespective of attitudes, and of attitudes, irrespective of occupation.[15]

To this end, three broad classes of variables were distinguished: parent attitudes, parent circumstances and school variables. Each class contained many variables. The effect of the three groups on pupil achievement was assessed through application of regression analysis which yielded percentage figures indicating the relative importance of these three classes of explanatory variables.

In the following sections I shall describe in greater detail how the findings were generated and how they were interpreted. In outline, the survey results were used to legitimate the Committee's proposals for increasing parent involvement in schools. However, the research data were not considered in connection with the Educational Priority Area policy. I shall show that important assumptions that underlay the EPA idea could have been examined with these data. In the concluding section, I present an explanation for the use of research to support parent involvement and its lack of application in the case of EPAs.

II THE RESEARCH AND THE PARENT INVOLVEMENT POLICY

I have described the initiation of the main piece of research commissioned by the Committee, and indicated its overall purpose. In the first part of this section I examine the way the research data were collected, analysed and interpreted by the Plowden researchers. I am only concerned with the findings about the relationship between attitudes, circumstances and achievement and with the connection between these findings and the parent involvement policy. The second part of the section is given to my re-examination of the same issue. I shall ask how strongly the data support the parent involvement policy.

The original analysis

As the full title implies, the 1964 National Survey of Parental Attitudes and Circumstances Related to School and Pupil Characteristics was a large-scale cross-sectional survey aimed at estimating the factors which influence educational performance. A complex sample of over 3,000 7-, 8- and 11-year-old children was drawn and extensive data gathered from them, their parents and teachers. This information was supplemented by data on the schools collected by administrators and HMIs. The dependent variables were four measures of reading performance: one given to the 11 year olds, and two each to the 7 and 8 year olds. In addition, the headteacher was asked to supply his estimate of the relative ability of each of the sampled children in his school. These dependent variables feature in different analyses.[16]

The independent variables fall into three broad classes: parent attitudes, parent circumstances and school variables. The parent questionnaire contained eighty questions designed to elicit attitudes and twenty to obtain information on their circumstances, for example, their income and the material possessions in the home. The school survey, completed by the headteacher, covered twenty-five aspects of the school environment, and a further ten variables described characteristics of the child's classroom teacher. The central question of the analysis was which of the three classes of variables, attitudes, circumstances and school, had the greatest influence on academic performance. In the language of regression analysis, the issue was which of the three accounted for the greatest proportion of the variance in achievement.

In all, twenty-four analyses were carried out to provide the answer. The sample was treated as consisting of three separate age groups, and each age group was divided by sex. Within each of the six groups, four kinds of analysis were conducted: between-group and within-group, and long- and short-list analyses. Between-group analysis, in this case, means that schools were treated as the unit of analysis. That is, the average standardised test scores for the sampled schools were related to students' average scores on attitude, circumstance and school variables. For example, the attributes of the school would include the average rating of teacher quality, and the attributes of the home would include the average level of literacy for the children sampled in each school. The within-group analysis uses the student as the analytic unit, and relates each student's performance, relative to the average for his school, to similar deviation scores for the independent variables. In within-school analyses, Peaker used the headteacher ratings of student ability rather than the standardised test score. Long-list analyses refer to analyses in which all of the 104 independent variables were potentially included in the analysis, though only those which made statistically significant contributions to the percentage of variance of the dependent variable emerged in the final tables. This meant that different subsets of independent variables were selected in the twelve long-list analyses. Perhaps because the results are convoluted, they are presented in summary form only in terms of the aggregate effects of the three classes of variables: attitudes, circumstances and school variables. It is this table that features in the body of the report. Peaker notes the long-list summary table is 'probably a better guide than the short-list summary to the total amount of variation accounted for by each of the three.classes of variables'.[17] It is reproduced in Table 4.1.

Table 4.1 *Percentage Contribution of Parental Attitudes, Home Circumstances and State of School to Variation in Educational Performance.*

	Between Schools				*Within Schools*			
	Infants	*Lower Juniors*	*Top Juniors*	*All Pupils*	*Infants*	*Lower Juniors*	*Top Juniors*	*All Pupils*
Parental Attitudes	24	20	39	28	16	15	29	20
Home Circumstances	16	25	17	20	9	9	7	9
State of School	20	22	12	17	14	15	22	17
Unexplained	40	33	32	35	61	61	42	54
Total	100	100	100	100	100	100	100	100

Source: *Plowden Report*, Vol. 2, p. 184.

Short-list analyses seem to have played a smaller role in building the final conclusion. Their purpose is not fully explained, but Peaker describes his goal as that of deriving comparable estimates of effects for variables which consistently appeared in the long-list analyses.

The interpretation gives pride of place to the strong association between attitudes and achievement: 'The most striking feature of [the results] is the large part played by parental attitudes.'[18] The result reinforced common sense: 'it should astonish no one to find that, when these attitudes can be assessed separately from socio-economic class, they emerge as more important than occupation taken by itself'.[19] Separate analyses had been conducted to show how far attitudes were, in turn, determined by circumstances. If attitudes were highly correlated with social class that would suggest attitudes could not be changed independent of changing social class position. However, the results showed the two sets of variables to be weakly related, which implied 'that attitudes could be affected in other ways, and altered by persuasion'.[20]

The two results together underpinned the parent involvement policy. Parents' attitudes could be changed through the agency of the school, and these changes would in turn bring about substantial improvements in pupils' educational performance. It would be an exaggeration to say the findings were the sole prop for the policy, yet they provided the setting for the initiative. Other factors added to the momentum. For instance, the idea of parent involvement was clearly being supported by Michael Young from the start of the Committee's work.

At about the time that the national survey was launched, Young promoted the idea of a small demonstration project carried out by the Institute for Community Studies of which he was the Director.[21] The idea was to make changes in one school to increase parent involvement and at the same time assess the effects of these changes on parent attitudes and children's performance. In the school chosen, a letter was first sent by the headteacher to encourage parents to help their children with schoolwork. This was followed by an invitation to open meetings to discuss the same issue. Private talks between teachers and parents were then arranged at which both could exchange views about the child's education. There were further group meetings on teaching methods and some home visiting. The effects of these changes were difficult to assess for want of a satisfactory control group. The research results indicated 'some improvement over the period in children's performance, particularly in arithmetic'.[22] The main effect had been to enlighten parents about modern teaching methods ('a number of parents stopped worrying about their children's apparent lack of progress').[23]

Despite the tentative conclusions, the demonstration project bolstered the findings of the national survey. The Committee begins the chapter entitled 'Participation by parents' with:

> The National Survey pointed to the influence upon educational performance of parental attitudes. It follows that one of the essentials for educational advance is a closer partnership between the two parties to every child's education.

> A strengthening of parental encouragement may produce better performance in school, and this stimulates the parents to encourage more.[24]

The parent involvement policy was launched with the push of research findings.

Re-analysis of the data on attitudes

I have shown that the research provided a significant prop for the Committee's recommendation that parents be more involved in schools. In this section I report the results of research in which I re-analysed the original raw data of the national survey. This re-analysis shows that the independent effect of attitudes on achievement is weak and uncertain and so gives little support for the view that improved attitudes will lead to improved performance levels. This does not mean that it is undesirable to change attitudes, only that it is inappropriate to expect such changes to result in great alterations of performance. I shall also examine the question of whether alterations in schools recommended by Plowden could reasonably be expected to improve attitudes. Again, I arrive at a pessimistic conclusion. In sum, the research evidence provides no solid support for the Committee's recommendations.

The most important finding of the national survey was that parental attitudes rather than circumstances were the most important influence on children's school performance. However, the published results show there is a range of estimates to support this conclusion. Some sub-groups showed that attitudes were considerably less important than either school or circumstance variables. This variation became even more evident when the original computer printouts for the between-school analysis were examined. This revealed that variables had been incorrectly identified – attitude variables being mistaken for circumstances and vice versa. It also showed that the summary analyses for the bottom junior and infant groups represented averaged results based on the two standardised achievement tests administered to these groups. Recalculations based on correct identification of variables showed the range of results was even larger but the values of R^2 even closer than had originally been reported.[25] The results suggested that attitudes were almost equal in importance to circumstances (see Table 4.2).

Technical problems of analysis can be resolved. But there are other reasons for looking at these statistics with great caution. In the first place, social science does not provide satisfactory reasons for differentiating attitudes and circumstances. In other words, the classification of variables must, to a degree, rest on judgement. For example, one variable the Plowden researchers identified as an

Table 4.2 *Comparison of Published and Re-Estimated Results*

Values are the percentage of the variance in achievement that is associated with one of three sources of influence: parental attitudes, parental circumstances and school variables.

	Published results			*Re-estimated results*		
	Highest	*Average*	*Lowest*	*Highest*	*Average*	*Lowest*
Attitudes	45	28	19	37	25	10
Circumstances	29	20	10	36	20	11
School	23	17	7	28	18	7

attitude was based on a question about whether the parents went on outings with their children. It can be argued that this is mainly a reflection of affluence, or circumstances, in Plowden's terms. Since the classification of variables is suspect, so too must be the estimates of the influence of these two classes of variables on achievement.

Further, judgement must play an even larger role in deciding how many of these variables to include in the analysis. In the collection of data, about four times more attitude variables were measured than circumstances. In the long-list analyses, a statistical procedure was used to select from this potential pool. The procedure pays attention to the statistical relationship between any given variable and all other variables, including the achievement scores. However, it is blind to the theoretical or practical importance of a particular variable. In sum, the selection of independent variables was governed by obscure assumptions and a-theoretical statistical techniques.

The second kind of problem also defies resolution. The mode of analysis and the explicit statements of the researchers imply that achievement is determined by attitudes. For example, 'the variation in parental encouragement and support has much greater effect than either the variation in home circumstances or the variation in schools'.[26] Yet attitudes may well improve when children do better in school, as the authors of the main body of the report are aware: 'Surveys of this kind do not establish causes, only associations. There is certainly an association between parental encouragement and educational performance. This does not tell us which way round the relationship is.'[27] So though there was clearly awareness of this vexing difficulty, the research was nevertheless used to support the view that parent involvement would improve achievement scores. It is relevant to note the way the attitude variables were described. Remember, an assorted bunch of variables was included within the set labelled 'attitudes'. Yet in different parts of the report it is implied that this amalgamation really meant 'parental support' or 'interest' or 'encouragement'. These were the particular characteristics the Committee thought important to change. But I shall show that these specific measures are quite weakly related to achievement.

In re-analysing the data I had the opportunity to try different groupings of the home background variables. My strategy was also

Table 4.3 *Effects of Home Background on Achievement*

Values are the percentages of variance in achievement that are associated with the six sources of home influence. For each set of independent variables these values are presented first with no other variables entered in the equation (first three columns). Separate values were estimated when eight variables measuring social background of the home were first entered in the equation. Items making up the six sets of independent variables are specified at the foot of the table.

	No SES control			*SES controlled*		
Age group (in years)	*11*	*8*	*7*	*11*	*8*	*7*
Contact with school	5	2	3	2	1	2
Sense of exclusion	4	0	2	2	1	2
Level of help at home	5	5	2	1	4	1
Child's response to schooling	9	2	9	5	9	5
Parental aspirations	23	7	6	13	1	2
Parental literacy	14	16	12	6	9	7

Contact with school: Number of times parent had seen teacher. Parent had seen teacher on child's progress. Parent thinks teacher is pleased to see them. Parent thinks teacher is interested in their ideas.

Sense of exclusion: Parent thinks it interfering to go to school. Parent thinks teachers would like to keep parents out. Parent thinks teaching should be left to teachers. Parent thinks teacher is not pleased to see them. Parent thinks teachers not interested in their ideas.

Help given at home: If parent asked for homework for child. Amount and kind of help child receives at home. If mother has time to do things with child. Mother does things with child in evening.

Child's response to schooling: Child talks about school to parent. Child brings school books home. Child reads at home or is read to.

Parents' aspirations: Parent would like child to go to grammar school. Leaving age parent would like for child.

Literacy of home: If child reads at home or is read to. If both parents belong to library. Type and amount of reading parents do at home.

based on vulnerable common-sense assumptions. First, it seemed unrealistic to arrive at generalisations about the relative importance of such broad groups of variables as attitudes and circumstances, in part because the original results appeared so unstable across groups. Secondly, I selected those items which were intuitively most interesting and most clearly relevant to the parent involvement policy. Thus, the first set of items (Table 4.3) measures the level of contact between home and school, while the second set measures the opposite: parents' feelings of exclusion from school. The level of help parents give their children at home and the child's response to schooling form the third and fourth sets. The fifth and sixth are similar to Plowden's variables, measuring literacy and aspiration. The component items of each of the six sets is explained in Table 4.3.

In the first section of the table the figures indicate the total variance that can be associated with each set of independent variables. In the second set, effects of social background are first taken into account. The smaller values of variance associated with the independent variables can be thought of as the conservative estimates of the influence of these variables.

The findings indicate the importance of the set of variables identified as measuring literacy. Parental aspirations are also significant and clearly more strongly associated with achievement for the 11 year olds than for the younger pupils. However, it should be remembered that at this age in England many children were being differentiated into academic and non-academic secondary schools and this decision would determine the length of time they would probably spend in school. The aspiration measure asks parents how long they expect their child to remain in school so it would not be surprising to find a closer association between achievement and aspiration at this age than for the younger age groups. The more important observation is that the variables most closely identified with parent involvement are relatively weakly related to achievement. For example, parents' contact with the school is a very poor predictor of children's achievement levels. Similarly, the level of parental help given in the home is not powerfully associated with achievement scores. The child's response to schooling shows a somewhat stronger relationship, but the variables which make up this composite may well be a consequence, not a cause, of learning. In all, these results provide slim support for the view that changes in parents' attitudes and behaviour envisaged by the Committee would alter achievement levels. In other words, increasing the frequency of visits with the classroom teacher, making parents feel at ease with teachers, or encouraging parents to help their children with homework, while desirable goals in themselves, are not likely to make radical changes in achievement scores. Peaker acknowledges this fact when he observes that variables 'intended to measure aspects of persuasion already in use . . . often failed to reach significance in the regression analyses'.[28] Yet despite the unimportance of these crucial variables the image was created that parents' attitudes were important, and this conglomerate continued to be referred to as meaning parental 'encouragement', 'support', and 'interest'.

The determinants of attitudes

The second finding of importance was that parental attitudes were only loosely related to circumstances. This 'leaves open the possibility that attitudes may be changed by persuasion'.[29] The persuasion was to be exercised by the school in the form of providing new opportunities for parents to learn about the school's goals and practices, and for them to express their concerns to the teachers.

The key assumption is that circumstances are the only likely determinant of attitudes. The weak association is interpreted to mean that attitudes are malleable. However, the evidence in no way excludes the possibility that attitudes are firmly connected to unmeasured variables. Certainly, Peaker is ambivalent. In one place the evidence is interpreted cautiously to mean attitudes 'may' be changed by persuasion, but in another the unexplained variation in attitudes 'must be conditioned to a large extent by communication and persuasion, so that it is reasonable to hope that an attempt to improve the co-operation of parents and teachers by persuasion might attain some success'.[30] A possibility became a probability, and the probability set the stage for the parent involvement policy.

At the same time as these results were over-interpreted, opportunities for testing the likely success of the parent involvement policy were overlooked. The analysis had focused only on the relationship between circumstances and attitudes. But the data could have been used to explore the relationship between school variables and attitudes. In the re-analysis I examined the association between variations in the school environment of the kind described in the parent involvement policy and the measures of supportive behaviour and attitude on the part of parents.[31]

The dependent variables are measures of the average level of parent contact with the school, the parents' feeling of exclusion from the school and the level of help with schoolwork given their child. For this analysis, data were aggregated at the school level; the question being asked is whether variations in the school environments are associated with variations in parent behaviour and attitude. The measured differences in the schools include the number of meetings held for parents, the existence of a PTA and a rating of school–home relations made independently by a visiting HMI. The results (Table 4.4) show two things. First, there is a relatively strong association between the school variables and the amount of contact parents have with schools. It seems the more schools provide opportunities for meeting with teachers, the more they make use of those opportunities. However, here too, the direction of causation is uncertain. The correlation may reflect the fact that the more parents

Table 4.4 *Effects of School Variables on Parent Attitude and Behaviour*

Values are the percentages of variance in the dependent variables (indicated in the left-hand margin) associated with variation in four measures of school provision for parent contact. The dependent variables are composites and the items making up these composites are specified in Table 4.3. The school variables are: if school has PTA; number of meetings in school on education; number of school functions; HMI rating of the school–home contact.

Age group (in years)	*11*	*8*	*7*
Contact with school	43	40	23
Sense of exclusion	4	4	3
Level of help at home	12	11	3

pressure schools to provide those opportunities the more schools will respond to the demand. If this is the case, increasing parent involvement depends on more than changes in the school. Secondly, there is a much weaker association between the measures of school provision and parents' attitudes. Though schools may make more opportunities available, parents may still feel excluded or discouraged by schools. They are not likely to dramatically increase the time they give their children on schoolwork. Perhaps increasing the visibility of schools leads to as much encouragement as discouragement. Perhaps when parents find out what goes on in schools they feel even less certain they can help their children. The results cannot sort out these tentative explanations. The point is, increasing opportunities for parents to be involved with schools leads to insignificant overall improvements in the parents' attitudes to the school or to the level of help they give their children.

To repeat, the original findings were used to create the ground on which the parent involvement policy would be promoted. Despite the weakness of the evidence, the research played an important role in advancing this policy. Later, I shall argue that the innovative and potentially radical nature of this policy could explain the need for the undergirding of the research. Before that, I turn to the EPA policy, where research played an insignificant role.

III THE RESEARCH AND THE EPA POLICY

This section deals with the relationship between the research and the Educational Priority Area policy. I concentrate almost entirely on my re-analysis of the survey data because the Committee did not marshal research to justify the priority area policy in the same way they used research to support the parent involvement scheme. In fact, there is almost no research backing for the EPA policy at all.[32] However, the data collected in the survey provide the opportunity for examination of two key issues in the EPA policy, one concerning the identification of target pupils, the other concerning the effects of improving schools on the lines laid down by the Committee.

Priority areas were to be identified by one or more measures of the social composition of the neighbourhood such as its social class characteristics, the overcrowding of houses and the number of incomplete families. The assumption was that deprived areas contained the majority of deprived children. The Plowden Committee did not define either aggregate or individual deprivation precisely, but it is implied that deprived children are those falling behind in school. Learning is the chief problem for these children: 'homes and neighbourhoods from which many of [the] children come provide little support and stimulus for learning. The schools must supply a compensating environment.'[33] I identified schools that would conform to Plowden's definition of a priority school and estimated the proportion of low achieving pupils in those schools.[34] I defined 'low achievers' as those students scoring below the tenth percentile, because the Plowden Committee aimed its EPA policy at this fraction of the population. The assumption behind the policy is that students with learning problems would be highly concentrated in the schools identified on the criteria Plowden defines. The national survey happened to contain data closely related to five of the eight criteria of priority areas. These were: the social class of parents, the percentage of incomplete families, foreign-born parents, family size and overcrowding. I selected those schools with aggregate scores on any two of these criteria that fell below the tenth percentile of the distribution of scores for all schools. Next, I found the proportion of pupils in these schools that score below an arbitrary level on the standardised tests. I chose a cut-off of the tenth percentile on achievement. Contrary to the expectation that a large number, even a majority, of the pupils would score below this level, only one-fifth of the pupils in my identified schools fell into this category. Certainly this means there is some concentration of poorly performing students, but it is not marked.[35] Pupils who do badly on achievement tests are quite well spread around schools, making it much harder to deliver special programmes or benefits to them. The data collected for the Plowden Committee thus undercut one important assumption of the EPA policy.

The second assumption of the policy is that improvements in the schools would lead to improvements in educational performance. Little attention had been paid to the basis for this belief, and where the issue had been addressed using research evidence, it was to dismiss the findings. For example, Peaker noted that the class size variable was positively related to achievement levels, which might imply the wisdom of raising class size. But: 'It is very hard to believe that, if other things are equal, merely adding more children to the class will improve the average achievement.'[36] The awkward result is explained away because by statistically controlling other variables the relationship between class size and achievement falls below statistical significance. However, this only works for the between-school analyses; within-school analyses show that the relationship persists even when other factors are taken into account. This gets no mention. However, in another part of the body of the report, a possible explanation is found: 'general experience . . . shows that backward pupils are often, as a matter of policy, put into smaller classes'.[37]

This example again underlines the impossibility of deriving conclusions about causal relationships from cross-sectional, non-experimental data.[38] Thus, if teacher experience is found to be related to achievement the optimist might argue that more experienced teachers would raise achievement levels. Another interpretation would be that experienced teachers are assigned to the more able pupils, so the association reflects the way teachers are allocated to classes rather than the superior skills of more mature teachers. If positive associations of this kind cause problems, evidence of the lack of association is more readily interpretable. Re-analysis of the original Plowden data indicated that school variables were weakly and unpredictably associated with achievement. For example, a variable which had a positive relationship for one age group would have a negative association for another. Clumping school variables together, I found that less than 6 per cent of the variation in achievement could be associated with variations in the quality of the school environment as measured by conventional indices of quality such as staff/pupil ratios, expenditures on books, and staff turnover rates.[39] To be sure, the EPA policy involved much more, for example, suggesting ways of making it easier for teachers to buy houses in the school neighbourhood and ways that colleges of education could have extensive links with priority schools.

However, the evidence that changing schools would upgrade the academic performance of the deprived students was missing; in fact, the data were not even considered in the development of the Plowden Committee's policies.

IV CONCLUSION

The re-analysis undercuts Plowden's policies. The research does not support the view that schools, by greater involvement of parents, would improve their attitudes and behaviour, nor that these in turn would significantly influence children's achievement. The re-analysis also suggests two weaknesses of the priority area policy. Low achievers are not highly concentrated in priority schools and the effects of EPA improvements are almost certainly trivial. Better schools do not equate with higher test scores. So closer examination of the original data indicated less, not more, support for the Committee's conclusions.

In part, the differences in findings and interpretation can be attributed to differences in technique and the fact that I did not have to meet pressing deadlines. But more important than the technical aspects of analyses are the political or philosophical predispositions which shape interpretations of findings. For instance, my own attitude was influenced by the experience of working with a group that was evaluating the effects of home and school background on school and adult success.[40] This group was predisposed to thinking that schools were hard to change, that these changes have short-term or capricious effects on achievement and that achievement was more weakly related to adult success than had been supposed. I conjecture that Plowden's use of research was shaped by quite different considerations. I said in the introduction that CACs have always been concerned with the extension of educational opportunity. This usually meant raising the school leaving age. The Plowden Committee, limited to primary schools, could not take this approach, though it did promote the idea of lowering entry age by expanding nursery education. Its parent involvement and EPA policies are its main contributions to extending equality of opportunity. Yet these policies are quite different when examined closely. The EPA recommendation fell within the tradition of CACs. EPA schools would be improved by making them like the best schools, and this meant supplementing the familiar ingredients of schools: materials, buildings and teachers. The parent involvement policy, though cautious, was a departure from this tradition of providing more-of-the-same. First, it implied that the extension of schooling was not, by itself, sufficient to improve the chances of the disadvantaged. Taken too far, this proposal might undermine faith in the power of schooling and this was dangerous for a pro-school committee. Secondly, the new group that was to form a partnership with schools, the parents, had until this point been regarded as a detriment rather than support to children's learning. Schools, after all, were explicitly established to counteract the effects of homes, as the Plowden Committee itself recognised. Now parents and schools were no longer opposed. They were to work together, providing parents could learn their proper function. Thirdly, the plan required careful definition of this function. Once allowed in, parents' influence had to be limited otherwise it might threaten the authority of teachers and administrators. Recall that educational professions were well represented on the Committee and in addition much of the testimony presented to it came from these same interest groups. In sum, parent involvement was a potentially dangerous area; the EPA policy was one that was more familiar and less threatening.

A course had to be found which would be acceptable to schools but which would also hold promise for genuine improvement. The Committee was intent on finding innovative ways of confronting the persistent failure of the educational system to erode the influence of home background on educational achievement. Attitudes held the key. On the one hand they were seen to be strong influences on achievement. On the other, they were not merely reflections of the ancient division of social class, so they might be altered by the agency of the school.

These propositions were not tested stringently but they gained credibility. The research played a role in creating this credibility, a role that can be described as stage management. This theatrical analogy implies a distinction between the stage and the play, where the stage and its contents are the research background to the play which is the policy itself. In any play, the stage and its management make action more efficient, focusing the audience's attention on new boundaries and new possibilities. Thus a stage set will identify a particular historical period, or define a certain interior or provide the set-up for a twist in the plot. Less need be explained to the audience. Yet though the stage provides the outlines and a few details, room is left for the interpretation and movement which constitute the play itself. The play could make sense without the stage, but its meaning is communicated much more effectively and dramatically with the stage set. In the case of Plowden, the research directed attention to a new arena on which the policy of parent involvement would be enacted. The research did not create the policy any more than a set constitutes the play. But the research did make it easier for the audience to share the understanding the Committee had about the need for increasing parent involvement. The research both established the ground on which this policy could be advanced, and left the Committee discretion to shape the policy to fit the many pressures to which it was sensitive. As the Secretary,

Maurice Kogan, later said, the research created a slogan,[41] and slogans are convenient rallying cries that can focus attention and generate enthusiasm.

But the problem with slogans, and the problem of stage management research, is that they simplify. Further, these simplifications will be misinterpreted or overlooked. To extend the metaphor, the set will seem to define the play precisely rather than provide a setting in which several different dramas could be enacted. The same set can accommodate many plays. Yet the temptation is to ignore these alternatives because they require us to attend to an exhausting array of possibilities. It is simpler to take the course of action suggested.

The Committee won acceptance of its play – its policy – for parent involvement. There were minor disagreements, but these were not voiced in conspicuous places.[42] Contrast the reception of the Plowden Report with the avalanche of debate that surrounded the release of the Coleman Report[43] in America at about the same time.[44] The Coleman research, like Plowden's national survey, sought to estimate the relative importance of home and school influences on pupil achievement. Like Plowden, the Coleman survey was flawed by the same problems of measurement and design. Like Plowden, Coleman concluded that school influences are weak relative to the effects of home background on children's educational performance. However, the finding was not used to promote any particular policy. Still, the Coleman finding unleashed powerful forces and a long rumbling academic argument ensued. A sustained effort was made to re-analyse the Coleman data, though the most dramatic finding was not overturned, rather it was reinforced by these re-analyses. The productive outcome of this debate was an increasingly well-informed and even cautious attitude to the use of research in policy-making even though Coleman's was not a policy report in the manner of Plowden.[45] This debate was dormant in England perhaps only because little social research had been used in policy-making while in America the connection between research and policy had been made more often.[46] Experience with policy-related research reveals both its potentials and problems.

A practical implication of this chapter is that research commissioned for policy-makers should be tested against alternative analyses and competing interpretations. This will not guarantee that the truth is magically derived as some compromise between two sets of conclusions. Indeed, the likely effect of exposing social research to several views would be to complicate or even obscure its message. Naturally this flies in the face of our conventional belief that science should simplify, not elaborate, problems. Yet this belief, in the softer sciences, is increasingly shown to be naive and in need of correction.

NOTES: CHAPTER 4

1 Education Act, 1944, Section 4(1).
2 Central Advisory Council for Education, *Early Leaving* (London: HMSO, 1954).
3 Central Advisory Council for Education, *15 to 18* (the Crowther Report) (London: HMSO, 1959).
4 Central Advisory Council for Education, *Half Our Future* (the Newsom Report) (London: HMSO, 1963).
5 Central Advisory Council for Education, *Children and Their Primary Schools* (the Plowden Report), 2 vols (London: HMSO, 1967), Vol. 1, p. iv.
6 The Committee members were: Lady Plowden, JP; Sir John Newsom, Chairman, Public Schools Commission; Mr H. G. Armstrong, educational psychologist; Professor A. J. Ayer, professor of logic; Miss M. F. M. Bailey, headmistress; Mrs M. Bannister, housewife; Miss M. Brearley, college of education principal; Dr I. C. R. Byatt, lecturer in economics; The Hon. Mrs J. Campbell, housewife; Professor D. V. Donnison, professor of social administration; Miss Z. E. Dix, headteacher; Professor C. E. Gittins, professor of education; Miss S. E. Grey, organiser of infant education; Mr E. W. Hawkins, director of language teaching centre; Miss E. N. Parry, inspector of schools; Mr A. Puckey, deputy headteacher; Mr T. H. F. Raison, editor of *New Society*; Alderman Mrs E. V. Smith, JP; Mr R. T. Smith, headmaster; Professor J. M. Tanner, professor in child health and growth; Brigadier L. L. Thwaites, Vice-Chairman, West Sussex County Council; Mr T. H. Tunn, director of education; Mr Martin Wilson, CBE; Mr F. M. White, headmaster; Dr M. Young, Chairman, Social Science Research Council.
7 Maurice Kogan, 'The Plowden Committee on Primary Education', in Richard A. Chapman (ed.), *The Role of Commissions in Policy Making* (London: Allen & Unwin, 1973), p. 87.
8 Central Advisory Council for Education, 1967, Vol. 1, p. 40.
9 ibid., Vol. 1, p. 41.
10 Tom Taylor, *A New Partnership for Our Schools* (London: HMSO, 1977).
11 A. H. Halsey, *Educational Priority: Problems and Policies* (London: HMSO, 1972).
12 The earliest studies of this kind had been done in the 1920s in England, for example, J. E. Duff and G. H. Thompson, 'The social and geographical distribution of intelligence in Northumberland', *British Journal of Psychology*, 14 (1923), pp. 192–8, and Kenneth Lindsay, *Social Progress and Educational Waste* (London: Routledge & Kegan Paul, 1926). More recent work had added little to the basic evidence as demonstrated in the review contained in E. D. Fraser, *Home, Environment and the School* (London: University of London Press, 1959).
13 Particularly influential works at that time were J. E. Floud, A. H. Halsey and F. M. Martin, *Social Class and Educational Opportunity* (London: Heinemann, 1956) and J. W. B. Douglas, *The Home and the School* (London: MacGibbon & Kee, 1964). Douglas made a presentation to Donnison's working party (see below) which described his book as the 'most useful single document the working party had seen'.
14 Central Advisory Council for Education, Agenda 1, 7 October 1963, Appendix C.
15 Central Advisory Council for Education, 1967, Vol. 2, p. 91.

16 The National Survey is described in Volume 2 of the Plowden Report.
17 ibid., Vol. 2, p. 184.
18 ibid., Vol. 1, p. 34.
19 ibid., Vol. 1, p. 36.
20 ibid., Vol. 1, p. 36.
21 Michael Young and Patrick McGheeney, *Learning Begins at Home* (London: Routledge & Kegan Paul, 1968).
22 Central Advisory Council for Education, 1967, Vol. 1, p. 43.
23 ibid., Vol. 1, p. 43.
24 ibid., Vol. 1, p. 37.
25 H. D. Acland, 'Social determinants of educational achievement', unpublished D.Phil. dissertation, Oxford University, 1973.
26 Central Advisory Council for Education, 1967, Vol. 2, p. 180.
27 ibid., Vol. 1, p. 37.
28 ibid., Vol. 2, p. 181.
29 ibid., Vol. 2, p. 181.
30 ibid., Vol. 2, p. 189.
31 Acland, 'Social determinants of educational achievement', pp. 194–9.
32 There is one passage which implies that the research evidence supported the EPA policy. Between-school analyses tended to show stronger associations between the independent and dependent variables than did the within-school analyses. This was because 'pupils, parents and teachers in the same school and neighbourhood resemble one another more than they resemble pupils, parents and teachers in general, just as apples growing on the same tree resemble one another more than they resemble apples in general' (Central Advisory Council for Education, 1967, Vol. 1, p. 34). However the data were not analysed by Peaker to reveal that this was a dangerously inaccurate generalisation. In fact, only 20 per cent of the variance in pupils' achievement scores lies between schools (see Acland, 'Social determinants of educational achievement', p. 81).
33 Central Advisory Council for Education, 1967, Vol. 1, p. 57.
34 Little and Mabey analysed data from ILEA schools from a different point of view to explore the feasibility of defining priority areas. Their main concern is with the possibility of measuring criteria by which these areas might be designated and with the interrelationships among these variables. See Alan Little and Christine Mabey, 'An index for designation of priority areas' in A. Shonfield and S. Shaw, *Social Indicators and Social Policy* (London: Heinemann, 1972).
35 The action-research conducted on the EPA project indicates that concentration of low achievers is greater in particular schools. The demonstration project was limited to schools which were in the lowest 2·5 per cent of all schools in terms of 'exceptional difficulty'. In these schools, up to 49 per cent of the pupils scored below the tenth percentile (A. H. Halsey, *Educational Priority*).
36 Central Advisory Council for Education, 1967, Vol. 2, p. 179.
37 ibid., Vol. 1, p. 291.
38 The ambiguity of non-experimental data points to the desirability of experimental data. The need for this kind of evidence has been expressed more clearly in America, for example, John P. Gilbert and Frederick Mosteller, 'The urgent need for experimentation', in Frederick Mosteller and Daniel P. Moynihan (eds), *On Equality of Educational Opportunity* (New York: Vintage Books, 1972). The problems of experimenting with social programmes have also been more fully explored (see James G. Abert and Murray Kamrass, *Social Experiments and Social Program Evaluation*, Cambridge, Mass.: Ballinger, 1974, as one example).
39 Acland, 'Social determinants of educational achievement', pp. 105–21.

40 See C. S. Jencks, *et al.*, *Inequality: A Reassessment of the Effect of Family and Schooling* (New York: Basic Books, 1972).

41 In an interview with Dr John Bynner about the Plowden Committee research, Radio Broadcast 1, 3 March 1979, for the Open University course DE 304, *Research Methods in Education and the Social Sciences*, tape available from Open University Educational Enterprises Ltd, 12 Cofferidge Close, Stony Stratford, Milton Keynes MK11 1BY.

42 J. E. Floud, 'Perspectives on Plowden', *The Teacher*, 10 February 1967. Howard Glennerster, 'The Plowden Research', *Journal of the Royal Statistical Society*, Series A, 132 (1969), pp. 194–204. Harvey Goldstein, 'Home and school', *Times Educational Supplement*, 5 May 1972. Henry Acland, 'What is a "bad" school?', *New Society*, 9 September 1971, pp. 450–3 and 'Does parent involvement matter?', *New Society*, 16 September 1971, pp. 507–10. Significantly, the most detailed critique of the Plowden research was done by an American: David K. Cohen, *'Children and Their Primary Schools:* Volume II', *Harvard Educational Review*, 38 (1968), pp. 329–40.

43 US Department of Health, Education and Welfare, *Equality of Educational Opportunity*, prepared for the Office of Education by James S. Coleman (Washington, DC: Government Printing Office, 1966).

44 A seminar at Harvard was devoted to re-analysis of the Coleman data and some of this work is collected in one source: Mosteller and Moynihan, *On Equality of Educational Opportunity* (op. cit.), but this book reflects only part of the extensive interest in the Coleman Report.

45 David K. Cohen and Michael S. Garet, 'Reforming educational policy with applied social research', *Harvard Educational Review*, 45 (1975), pp. 17–43. See also C. E. Lindblom and D. K. Cohen, *Usable Knowledge* (New Haven: Yale University Press, 1979).

46 cf. M. Bulmer (ed.), *Social Policy Research* (London: Macmillan, 1978), especially chs 1 and 15.

Chapter 5

In the Course of Investigation

ANDREW SHONFIELD

In the late 1960s I was a member of the Duncan Committee on British Overseas Representation. Its report, the *Report of the Review Committee on Overseas Representation, 1968–9*, Cmnd 4107, was published in 1969. One of the striking lessons that emerged for me, as a member of this three-man investigation into the instruments of British external policy, was the crucial and unrecognised importance of theory. Since that statement may itself sound more theoretical than informative, let me at once illustrate.

About two-thirds of the way through our exercise, I think we were all three impressed by the evidence that we had received of the failure of the machine that was concerned with the promotion of British exports to formulate a coherent strategy for taking advantage of the opportunities opened up by the devaluation of the pound. Our investigation of individual overseas posts took place more than a year after the devaluation of November 1967, and we naturally included in our inquiries a number of questions designed to elicit evidence of changes of method, specifically those designed to break the depressing postwar trend which had for the past two decades steadily reduced Britain's share of world exports of manufactures. That was, after all, what devaluation was chiefly about. However, we could find no sign that those officers who were engaged in the business of promoting British sales in individual markets abroad were being effectively guided by an overall strategic direction from London, based on appraising the post-devaluation potential of individual British export industries.

It was not that the individual commercial officers were failing to try, or that the British government departments at home did not respond to specific requests for information. There was no lack of energy. What was missing was the sense of any systematic policy rooted in an awareness of the new situation which had arisen from 1967 onwards. All this is mentioned in our report. We were driven to the conclusion that the cause of the trouble lay in the organisation at home.

This part of the system was, strictly speaking, beyond our terms of reference. Still, we felt that we could not leave the problem without some exploration of the Whitehall arrangements which had led to this disappointing outcome. I do not think that any of us felt confident that we had diagnosed the situation fully by the time that we finished; but we had found one or two promising clues. A very significant one for me came when we looked at the important section of the Board of Trade which is called the Export Services Branch.

It was a shock to discover that in the whole of this outfit, whose business is to match the export potential of British industry with the opportunities which are sought out by the government's extensive commercial intelligence system, there was not a single administrative-class civil servant. And when one asked why the operation had been staffed in this way, in view of the hinge position occupied by the Export Services Branch in the British balance-of-payments operation, the answer given by those on the spot was that the manpower requirements of the section were the logical reflection of the fact that it was not engaged in making 'policy' but only in 'servicing' British industry in pursuit of export business.

So here, at the tail-end of our investigation – when we had no time left to pursue the matter in detail – we simply bumped head-on into this major piece of theory about the structure of government. Clearly we should have started with it. With this kind of key at one's disposal, one would be able to decipher many of the underlying structures of government, which might perhaps have made some of our eager questioning of British officers overseas about the detail of their work otiose.

But we were once again the victims of the pragmatic fallacy: just plunge into your subject; collect as many facts as you can; think about them hard as you go along; and at the end, use your common sense, and above all your *feel* for the practicable, to select a few good proposals out of the large number of suggestions which will surely come your way. This method, it seems to me, derives from a view of public affairs which puts the functions of an investigator on essentially the same footing as those of a common-law judge. Such a person is supposed to know all about the underlying theoretical assumptions of those whose affairs he is examining. All he needs is facts.

Now, it seems that the distinction which was so important in this Board of Trade example – between what constitutes 'policy-making' and 'servicing', or the mere execution of policy – is regarded by the civil servants concerned as one which can be readily applied in any given case. I have some doubts about this confident expectation – the spillover between formulation of policy and execution is often very extensive indeed. A body like the Duncan Committee, which does not contain this kind of experience in its membership (there were Sir Val Duncan, Chairman of Rio Tinto-Zinc, and Sir Frank Roberts, former ambassador in Moscow and Bonn, and myself), surely needs expert and subtle guidance by a political scientist on the application of concepts such as these over the whole range of government. This is where there is no substitute for theory – though I hasten to add, in order to avoid any possibility of misunderstanding, that the kind of theory that I have in mind is securely grounded on the prior examination of a mass of empirical data.

The point is relevant to the very formulation of the terms of reference for a committee of investigation such as the Duncan Committee. We were charged to examine *overseas* representation only. Was this in fact feasible? Could we produce a rational and connected set of proposals about the means of conducting British external policy in the 1970s while keeping our eyes deliberately averted from what was going on in Whitehall? Fortunately the Committee twigged this one, and made sure, from the beginning, that everyone understood the interpretation of its terms of reference in such a way as not to exclude the home front. That was as well, because we felt compelled in the end to put forward a number of proposals for reforms in the Board of Trade and the Foreign Office.

But these things were in the nature of addenda to our investigation. Perhaps we would have come to some different conclusions about the best way to organise overseas representation if we had engaged in a critical examination of the central nervous systems of the two or three major departments in London *before* we looked at their overseas arms. Again, the expert guidance of political scientists would have helped.

We had no such assistance, either from political scientists or from the practitioners of any other social science discipline. One of the questions which we were called on to answer was how the change in the balance of objectives in Britain's external policies ought to be reflected in the composition and manning of various kinds of overseas posts, and it would have been useful to be able to obtain some job-analysis data. Nothing of this sort was available. We had to proceed to an estimate of the orders of magnitudes of staff requirements in the 1970s by another route.

We decided that one way of obtaining an insight into the nature of the basic building blocks which compose the Foreign Service was to identify the 'marginal embassy' – that is, a post whose utility was judged to be only *just* sufficient to justify its retention. This would be a post which would be the first to be abolished if the need to cut expenditure became imperative; its present composition, reduced as a result of earlier economy drives, should indicate what the managers or the Foreign Service regarded as a minimum diplomatic resource.

This was our nuclear element. Having found our case, the investigation proceeded to examine the work-load, the premises, the security arrangements, the entertainment and service arrangements on the spot. This could not, it need hardly be said, be a truly professional analysis. But as indicated in the report, we were able to use the device to come to the conclusion that the nuclear element in the Foreign Service structure today was an embassy with a staff of only three British officials, plus a varying number of locally engaged employees.

This was, of course, a theoretical minimum, which could only be reached in places where local staff of the right quality were available at a reasonable price. But it gave us a base from which we could proceed to more complicated calculations of the requirements of a range of different embassy types – stretching from the stripped-down version in places like Central America to the full-scale diplomatic resource required for an embassy like Paris.

But all this was rather rough work, very far from a systematic analysis of the changing requirements of the variety of jobs carried out by British official representatives overseas. We had to operate in this way because the Committee was set up initially without any research capacity at all at its disposal. We had to spend some weeks in discovering the nature of our problems, and only then were we given authority to recruit a research officer. There was no prospect of getting someone in a hurry from inside the service who was versed in the techniques of social science research. An outsider would have presented other problems.

Since time was very short, and our report was required in a matter of months, it was above all necessary to have someone working for the Committee who had the confidence of the civil servants concerned and was familiar with the operations of diplomacy. We were lucky to obtain the services of a diplomatic service officer who had also been an inspector of posts overseas.

Looking back over the operation, it does appear remarkable that the Committee was set up without any investigating arm of its own. It is here that the analogy with the common-law judge really does seem to guide the thinking of those responsible for appointing committees of this kind. Our business is still thought of as being to take a lot of evidence from interested parties, and then to judge the case on the basis of the evidence which the witnesses provide. The notion that we would, as investigators, wish to take the initiative in exploring parts of the field, using our own methods of research, is one that still does not occur naturally to people in government.

Of course it is not exclusively the government's fault. I remember well the delays and difficulties in the Donovan Commission on Trade Unions about the research programme that we needed in order to make informed judgements on the matters before us. There were objections raised initially to the use of sample-survey methods to find out, for example, about the attitudes of workers to shop stewards. Fortunately there was enough time available for the Donovan Commission to be able to build up its research programme gradually.

When work has to be done in some haste, as with the Duncan Committee, which completed its work in nine months, advance planning of research by the government departments responsible for servicing the exercise is acutely necessary. Otherwise one tends to find that by the time one has identified the relevant problems, it is often too late to get any thoroughgoing research completed for the guidance of the Committee. I imagine that the answer from the government side to such a proposal would be that many committees would object if they were presented with a ready-made research team and an outline of its initial programme of work. Surely, it would be argued, the decision must be left to the committee itself and not be foisted on it by the government.

The truth, however, is that committees do begin with a secretariat supplied from the staff of the departments chiefly concerned, and such secretaries often exercise a powerful influence both on the direction taken by the investigation and on the formulation of the conclusions reached. They are, after all, generally chosen because they are expert drafters; and if they know their stuff they will be adept at finding the phraseology which expresses some of the common ground between conflicting viewpoints that any individual member of the committee would frequently be unable to do himself. Moreover, they are also the only full-time workers among a gang of part-timers.

Pretty soon a draft paragraph which has managed to avoid attracting clear-cut opposition from any one member of a committee develops some of the qualities of a sacred text. Do not touch it, one is told anxiously, because if you move one word someone else is bound to start messing about with other bits of it. This mood is most noticeable in the work of a large body like the Donovan Commission on Trade Unions (twelve members), especially in the later stages of its work, when it is clear that there are a number of positions which are irreconcilable on certain matters, and there is anxiety not to spread the area of conflict any further than is absolutely necessary.

In the case of the Duncan Committee, it seemed to me that one of the incidental advantages of having a membership of only three people was that the relationship between members and secretariat was more intimate and informal than in larger bodies. There was no question of the secretariat acquiring subtly some of the attributes of an arbiter in disputes among the members. In a committee of three, the process is one of almost continuous confrontation, and there seems to be much less scope for an outsider to act as a broker with a formula which skilfully evades the implicit differences among the principals. The odds are that the important differences become explicit early on, and then have to be thrashed out between the participants in a face-to-face encounter.

Indeed I must declare a strong prejudice, which I have developed as a result of my experience on the Duncan Committee, in favour of a threesome as a device for serious argument among a group charged to make agreed recommendations on an issue of public policy. I need hardly say that the success of the threesome is predicated on a number of other conditions – an able and energetic secretariat responsive to the committee's arguments, an articulate and uninhibited style of discourse on the part of the members of the committee, and finally an underlying friendliness and desire to find the maximum area of agreement among them.

These conditions were generously fulfilled in the Duncan Committee. I came to the conclusion that the peculiar dynamics of a committee of three people would be worth closer study. When it works, members become very aware of their changing roles in different phases of a continuing discussion stretching over a period of months. One may be cast in the role of a vociferous minority in the morning; in that of the moderate supporter of a view more strongly held by a colleague in the afternoon; and in the evening deliberately hold back in a dispute between one's two colleagues in order to offer at some appropriate moment a resource of arbitration or compromise between them.

Once one has grown used to playing a variety of roles, and also observed each of one's colleagues doing the same sort of thing in relation to oneself, a certain kind of intimacy and confidence in argument seems to be readily established. At its best the process is like a personalised version of Hegelian dialectic – with each member in turn acting his part in the threefold role: thesis, antithesis, synthesis.

Of course, it is not always as nice or as neat as that. Because of the sharpness of the process of direct confrontation, there is always a risk that a situation may become explosive. It is possible that the knowledge that this is so may also, in certain circumstances, reinforce a certain judicial element in each of the characters in the debate. The probability is that they will all of them have the experience at some stage of supplying an element of arbitration between their two colleagues.

A further point is that there is no scope in a committee of three for a minority report; each argument has to be settled, because the members know that the explicit opposition of any one of them to a recommendation will largely destroy its persuasive force.

It may be thought that, in view of the shortness of the time available to the Duncan Committee to complete its task, the large amount of travelling which the members of the Committee had to do, and lastly the fact that they were very busy on other workaday tasks and could not devote more than a limited portion of their energies to the work, the kind of research programme which I have outlined would have been of little use to the Committee. The research workers would have accumulated a lot of new information, but would we have been capable of absorbing very much more? This is a point of substance and it suggests to me the need for a reform of the process by which matters of public interest are investigated by groups of persons who are appointed by the government.

There must, for a start, surely be a period in which members of the committee are engaged full-time in reading themselves into the subject-matter, discovering what up-to-date thinking there is on their problems, and discussing at length with the research director appointed to guide them what are the major issues for investigation and how to set about acquiring the relevant data.

This need not last a very long time. I should have thought that, for the members of the Duncan Committee, six weeks or at the most two months of this kind of work would have been an investment which would in the end have shown a very high return. It is at this stage that the theoretical issues which I noted at the start of this article would be brought into focus. A number of short-term research projects would also suggest themselves; and in view of the necessity of speed, several of these would be farmed out in the form of contracts to university departments or to institutes like Chatham House or the Institute of Strategic Studies.

The kind of problem on which a committee like ours could have done with more guidance – though we did not identify the problem until we were far advanced – was the difference in the qualities that are required of people and institutions once 'multilateral' diplomacy becomes a major element in a country's external relations. This would be so as members of the European Common Market. It is already so in some other important spheres like financial diplomacy, through the International Monetary Fund and the Group of Ten, and commercial diplomacy, through GATT (the General Agreement on Tariffs and Trade). But what kind of diplomat is likely to be required when much of this diplomacy becomes an extra dimension of what is traditionally regarded as domestic policy? And what type of skills will be needed in a multilateral setting where the foreign negotiators are experts in the same kind of work, and in some measure treated as members of the same professional guild, as yourself?

It would also have been useful to relate the problems of training the coming generation of Britain's representatives overseas to the changing requirements of diplomacy in the 1970s. But that would have required, for a start, a systematic analysis of the content of work performed by the different categories of officials in overseas posts; only then would it have been possible to examine the adaptations that might be necessary to meet the new tasks further ahead. We did make an attempt to obtain a breakdown of the work-load in one or two posts, on the basis of estimates of the time spent by various officials on the different activities which they were called upon to perform. But this could provide no more than an impressionistic picture.

What is needed is some serious work on the sociology of administration in the very special kinds of bureaucratic structure which are characteristic of posts overseas. There is, for instance, an inescapable element of ritual in the business of representing one's country abroad – the very context provided by the state to which the representative is accredited demands it – but no one has yet attempted to analyse systematically the changing content of this ritual. It does change; and other things, like the style and content of diplomatic entertainment, should change with it. If there is a cultural lag in these matters, one would suspect that there might well be a tendency on the part of established diplomats to reinforce it.

Perhaps all this may be thought to indicate an altogether excessive concern with what is, after all, the small change of diplomacy. In fact, one needs to identify the small change, and to examine the purposes for which it is spent, if one is ever to build up the larger concept in which the overall purposes of government are measured against the resources devoted to each of them. Only then would it be possible to judge whether the distribution of cash is in line with the relative importance attached to different objectives of policy.

This is the aim of 'output budgeting' in government; and as the Duncan Report shows, a preliminary attempt has been made by a team of civil servants, chaired by the Treasury, to apply the technique to the conduct of British external relations. This was one bit of research which we found was already in progress when the Committee was established. The appendix to our report which describes this work explains why it has not got very far. The central problem is to define the different purposes of policy in such a way that particular inputs of resources can be identified with each one purpose unmistakably – so that in making up the budget one avoids counting the same expenditure several times over in different categories.

I must myself confess to some doubt as to whether this will ever be feasible – though I have no doubt that it is worthwhile trying to do so as a means of achieving clarity about one's objectives.

I came to think, towards the end of our exercise, that the more promising way of proceeding would be to start at the other end, by examining something which people actually did – an activity like political reporting or cultivating certain social relationships in a foreign country – and then asking in detail what specific British interests a series of moves taken over a period of time were intended to serve, and how far they had succeeding in doing so. Once again, therefore, one comes back to the need for detailed analysis of job content, backed by a knowledge of the system of communication and the informal group relations in an overseas post, as well as the formal structure of command.

It is evident that this kind of investigation would require high professional skills. It is not a serious complaint that these are not available ready-made in the British Foreign Service. I doubt if the Foreign Service of any other country in Europe could do much better. The real point is that, under the British system of government, it seems to be left usually to committees of outsiders to identify the long-term problems which can be tackled only on the basis of extensive research – and then to leave the committee to improvise any odd bits of research work that it can get done in the time at its disposal.

It is as if there were still a reluctance to recognise that giving advice on public affairs is not a part-time activity of people with an ability to apply common-sense rules to common-sense problems. It ought to be treated, in my view, as something which requires some whole-time attention, at least at the beginning and at the end of an investigation – which means that government must assume responsibility for paying the normal remuneration of the people concerned during these periods – and needs to be backed from the start by a fully professional research team.

Chapter 6

The Seebohm Committee and the Under-use of Research

PHOEBE HALL

The Seebohm Committee on Local Authority and Allied Personal Social Services[1] made very little use of specially commissioned research when arriving at its conclusions,[2] despite the fact that it was reviewing a particularly under-explored sector of social policy. Why then include a chapter on Seebohm in a collection examining the role of research in the deliberations of commissions? The reasons for this are that the genesis, composition and functioning of the Committee can perhaps throw light upon circumstances which render research of little use and may at the same time, by implication, suggest situations where its role can be more central.

This chapter dwells at some length upon the background to the appointment of the Committee, since its very existence was contentious and this factor more than any other explains why Seebohm decided against a research programme. Secondary reasons for its choice of approach can be found in the selection of the chairman and membership, the terms of reference within which it worked, the poverty of the research capital upon which it could draw, the political environment within which it worked and the nature of the report the group wished to produce. We examine first the general background leading to the formation of the inquiry and then the more precise political manoeuvres which resulted in its appointment in December 1965.

ADMINISTERING WELFARE SERVICES

The Seebohm Committee was asked 'to review the organisation and responsibilities of the local authority personal social services in England and Wales and to consider what changes are desirable to secure an effective family service'. The rationale for its appointment dates back to the immediate postwar period when the legislative framework for administering our welfare system during the 1950s and 1960s was established. From the beginning of the century, views about the best way of organising welfare services have swung back and forth: from the belief that they should be integrated under a single administrative structure, to the opposite opinion that separate organisations specialising in meeting the needs of different groups were desirable. Early nineteenth-century Poor Law legislation reflected the former view; both positions were adopted by the majority and minority reports of the Poor Law Commission in 1909, and, by the 1940s, specialisation and division was a firmly established principle.

The administrative machinery for delivering welfare services established after the last war was divided at central and local levels. The services for children were the responsibility of the Home Office and the local authority children's departments; services for the elderly, the mentally handicapped, the mentally ill and other groups was that of the Ministry of Health and local welfare and health departments (sometimes combined).

PRESSURES FOR CHANGE

The inquiry of 1965 was brought about by the fundamental changes which had taken place in social work and the personal social services during the previous twenty years. The considerable unplanned growth of the services put a strain upon the administrative machinery then operating. This, coupled with the development of a professional identity among social workers and changing beliefs about the causes of social ills and their appropriate remedies, led to requests for a reappraisal of the system. Moreover, the growth of social work and allied services meant that they were no longer insignificant in financial terms and hence there was a greater premium upon making them more efficient. These pressures for change are discussed in turn.

THE EXPANSION AND CHANGING NATURE OF SOCIAL WORK

As social work and residential care expanded during the 1950s and early 1960s, the picture became increasingly complicated. Local welfare and children's departments grew in size while alongside them the health, housing and education departments developed their own welfare provisions. Social work was, therefore, being provided by several local agencies. The standard of care and the resources available varied considerably from agency to agency. In part, this was due to the different central government departments involved; the financial support, training arrangements (there were three training councils) and general professional guidance forthcoming from Whitehall depended upon the branch of the services for which one worked.

The division between welfare provisions at the local level led to some rivalry and confusion. Furthermore, the precise relationship between social workers and other services such as the National Assistance Board (soon to become the Supplementary Benefits Commission) and probation was unclear. It was argued by those giving evidence to inquiries sitting before Seebohm that the expansion of the social work services had resulted in general confusion over the responsibilities of different agencies, an overall lack of resources to meet demand and a complexity which made access for clients difficult.[3] Thus, social work was being provided by disparate groups, in a variety of settings, with different training backgrounds, different degrees of professionalism and different salary structures.

CHANGING ATTITUDES

The two decades following the Second World War saw changes in attitudes towards those in need which called into question the organisational framework governing the delivery of services. Increasingly, the problems of individuals were interpreted as arising, at least in part, from the problems of society in general. The old Poor Law assumptions that individual circumstances were entirely self-created were replaced by the view that the causes of distress were wider and more complicated than had previously been thought.

Such explanations of need raised questions about the adequacy of existing treatment. Complete reliance upon removing individuals with problems from society and placing them in institutions was clearly inappropriate. The individual had to be seen and treated within his societal, community and family context. This changing perspective lay behind the emphasis upon prevention within the children's services and was the driving force behind arguments for community care within the health and welfare sector. Both these policies, in turn, resulted in pressure to reorganise part or all of the existing social welfare structure.

INADEQUATE PLANNING MECHANISMS

As the administrative structure became outmoded so the planning machinery at central government level became increasingly ineffective. The division of responsibility for most social work services between two government departments – the Home Office and the Ministry of Health – had for years obstructed any overview of problems and policy in the welfare services as a whole. An attempt to form an interdepartmental committee, looking at welfare problems across the services, was thwarted in 1956 by bureaucratic jealousies and none of the many narrower inquiries established subsequently was able to make a comprehensive examination of those issues which spanned the entire welfare system.[4]

For these reasons policy development in this field took two different courses. Whilst some issues were seen as important by all involved in planning these services, interesting differences in emphasis emerged. Those working in the children's services, concerned at the significant rise in juvenile crime rates, began exploring the possibilities of prevention, and proposed the development of a 'family service' around the nucleus of the existing children's department. Those planning welfare services were studying the potential of community care and its implications for practice.

THE DEVELOPMENT OF A PROFESSIONAL IDENTITY

The development and expansion of social work was accompanied by a growth in the feeling of common identity between different branches of the profession. From the mid-1930s, when the British Federation of Social Workers was created, attempts were made to draw together, for example, the psychiatric social worker, the medical social worker, the family caseworker and the probation officer. This movement accelerated during the 1950s when it became clear that, whether social workers were helping the elderly, the handicapped, children or the homeless, many of the tasks involved were similar, and this realisation led to demands for a common core to their training. The definition of universal skills called into question the boundaries separating social workers. If they practised a universal art, was it sensible to maintain the structural barriers then in operation?

THE FINANCIAL IMPLICATIONS OF EXPANSION

Finally, in explaining the pressures for change, it must be remembered that the scale of social work activity altered beyond all recognition in the twenty years following the war. The amount spent upon the care of children in need, the aged, the handicapped and the homeless increased by almost 180 per cent (at constant prices) between 1952 and 1968. This growth was particularly rapid in the local welfare services for the elderly and handicapped but both child care and welfare expenditure far outstripped the general rise in total public expenditure.

CO-ORDINATION OR REORGANISATION?

Throughout the 1950s, Committees of Inquiry examining aspects of the welfare services called for a more effective co-ordination of these activities rather than for the fundamental recasting of the agencies involved.[5] Such an upheaval was considered to be either unnecessary or impractical. However, the concern over rising juvenile crime rates,[6] combined with the recognition that an assault upon the problems of certain families might help to reduce this phenomenon, led to the promotion of ideas for reform through reorganisation – more specifically, for the creation of a 'family service'.[7] Such a service was to be formed by enhancing the powers and resources of the existing local authority departments. A committee chaired by Lord Longford,[8] established by the Labour party in 1964 to examine the treatment of young offenders, argued for the enlargement of the children's department in order to form an effective family service. Meanwhile, the Kilbrandon Committee,[9] considering the law relating to juvenile delinquency in Scotland, suggested that the education committee should be given greater powers to establish a 'social education department'. Both reports were recommending structural changes which emanated from the problems of children and centred around services for them.

The policy to create a family service became the overriding interest for most of those involved in the children's services and reached an advanced stage before being challenged. Six members of the Longford Committee took ministerial posts in the new Labour government of autumn 1964.[10] One of these, Alice Bacon, became a junior minister at the Home Office and was thus in a position to plan the children's services along the lines proposed by Longford. By the spring of the following year her civil servants had drafted a White Paper – *The Child, the Family and the Young Offender*[11] – which had as its cornerstone the family service and which the department were determined to publish as soon as possible. Meanwhile, in an attempt to overcome some of the problems of the fragmented administrative system for the social services, a 'Co-ordinator' had been appointed. Douglas Houghton, the first incumbent, was anxious to find a role for himself and yet had difficulty selecting the appropriate project. The 'family service' idea suited his purposes admirably as it embodied a new and broader perspective upon welfare provision. Quite independently of the Home Office, therefore, he too was interested in this policy and put forward an embryonic version of it to the Cabinet. In Scotland, similar developments were taking place. Judith Hart, a junior minister at the Scottish Office, began planning on the basis of the Kilbrandon proposals.[12]

THE CALL FOR AN INTERDEPARTMENTAL INQUIRY

The pressure to form a family service generated a powerful

reaction, one which resulted in the postponement of the existing policy proposals in favour of an inquiry. The frustration of this planning process helps to explain the Seebohm Committee's difficult start in life. By the end of 1964 a number of prominent academics and practitioners within the social services, some closely connected with the Labour Party, became alarmed at the shape the 'family service' proposals were adopting and at the powerful political impetus there seemed to be behind them. Their concerns were that the policy was too child- and family-centred. Many of the needs of the community were not ones which arose directly from families or from people living within them. The concept of a family department was, therefore, too narrow. Departments of social service encompassing both the existing welfare and children's provisions would be more comprehensive in their coverage of needs and have the advantage of drawing all social workers employed by local authorities together under one roof.

By late May 1965 the group had produced a memorandum[13] which was circulated to the principal social services ministers. Both Richard Crossman, who was Minister of Housing and Local Government, and Kenneth Robinson, Minister of Health, were lobbied by members of the group who knew them personally. Accepting that there was a good case for a wider reappraisal of welfare services, these ministers made their opinions known to Douglas Houghton and Alice Bacon. Understandably, both champions of the family service were surprised about and antagonistic towards any suggestion that their policy should be postponed. The issue had to be resolved at Cabinet level. As a result, Miss Bacon was asked to redraft parts of the Home Office White Paper to exclude reference to a family service and to include the announcement that a committee would be established to examine the organisation and structure of the welfare services in general.[14] Similarly, Douglas Houghton was requested to suspend his planning and await the results of the inquiry.

Thus, the creation of the Seebohm Committee was a contentious political decision. Although outward appearances suggested that the Home Office wished to see such an inquiry established, the reality was very different.[15] The Committee's formation removed the initiative for developing the social welfare services from the Home Office and the Co-ordinator of Social Services. As we shall see later, this politically hostile environment helps to explain the way in which the Committee planned and executed its work.

THE FORMATION OF THE COMMITTEE

Since the Seebohm Committee was an interdepartmental inquiry, the process of reconciling competing interests was delicate and time-consuming. Its parentage was complicated, involving the Home Office, the Ministry of Health, the Department of Education, the Ministry of Housing and Local Government and the Co-ordinator of Social Services. The last of these had no powers to establish the Committee so the Home Secretary, Sir Frank Soskice, who was the senior minister involved, was asked to appoint it in conjunction with the other relevant ministers. This meant that the Home Office was in a strong position to exert its influence and it was anxious to ensure that the Committee's composition, brief and mode of working minimised the disruption to its departmental planning.

Lord Seebohm (then Sir Frederic), who was invited to be Chairman, combined a concern for social welfare with successful commercial and banking interests. He had been a Director of Barclays Bank since 1947 but had, at the same time, had a long-standing association with the Family Service Units and the National Council for Social Service. He was Chairman of the York Community Council and the National Institute for Social Work Training and a trustee of the Joseph Rowntree Memorial Trust. It is important for our purposes therefore that his interests, though wide, were not academic ones and his background contained no history of research.

Amongst the nine members, however, four were officially described as 'academics' – a doctor, a lecturer in social administration, a lecturer in social work and an expert in the training of social workers. They were respectively, Professor J. N. Morris, Professor of Social Medicine at London University, Director of the Medical Research Council's Social Research Unit and a member of the Royal Commission on the Penal System; Dr R. A. Parker, Lecturer in Social Administration at the London School of Economics and a former social worker with research interests in the fields of child care and housing; P. Leonard, Lecturer in Social Work at Liverpool University with social work experience in Family Service Units, as a child care officer and psychiatric social worker; R. Huws Jones, Principal of the National Institute for Social Work Training, formerly Vice-Chairman of the Younghusband Committee on Social Workers in the Health and Welfare Services, and a member of the Williams Committee on the Staffing of Residential Accommodation.

Three members of the Committee hailed from the world of local government – one from a county, one from a county borough and one from London. They were Sir Charles Barratt, the Town Clerk of Coventry, W. E. Lane, the Clerk of Lindsey County Council, and Baroness Serota, formerly Chairman of the London County Council's Children's Committee, Deputy Chairman of the Inner

London Education Authority, a member of the Longford Committee, the Royal Commission on the Penal System, the Latey Committee on the Age of Majority and the Central Advisory and Training Councils on Child Care. Both Sir Charles Barratt and Mr Lane had been closely involved with the Local Authority Associations as advisers; the former to the Association of Municipal Corporations and the latter to the County Councils' Association. One member was included for his experience with voluntary organisations – M. R. F. Simson, Secretary of the National Corporation for the Care of Old People. Lady James of Rusholme was selected for her interests in the field of education and voluntary work, as a magistrate, as a manager of an approved school, and to provide the Committee with a second woman.

It is clear from discussions which the writer has had with members of the Seebohm Committee that at least two of the 'non-academic' group were conversant with processing and using research material. Thus, of the ten, a majority could be expected to consider seriously the case for a research contribution to the Committee's deliberations. Yet an examination of the background of the members leads one to suspect that the differing interests brought to the Committee might well have resulted in difficulties over the interpretation of any research findings. In terms of probable government department affiliations the Committee was, perhaps predictably, fairly balanced. Their previous concerns and published work available at the time suggest that two members could be closely associated with the interests of local government, two with those of the Home Office, two had close contacts with the Ministry of Health and one had a more tenuous link with the department but was still primarily concerned with the health and welfare services.

The terms of reference within which Sir Frederic was asked to work called for a 'review' of services and the Committee was requested to 'consider' changes which would secure a more effective 'family service'. (Ironically, the label 'family service' remained in the terms of reference, though Sir Frederic made it clear that this would be widely interpreted.) There was little official encouragement to delve deeply into the subject; no request to analyse, explore or evaluate, and quite deliberately so. The Chairman was specifically asked by Alice Bacon in January 1966 to complete his work within six months. Clearly, some of its initiators saw the Committee merely as a short-term advisory group, expected to deliberate and produce conclusions without any collection of evidence, let alone any research. Sir Frederic refused to be bound by this injunction but it meant that the important decisions upon how the Committee undertook its task and particularly whether it commissioned a research programme were taken in an atmosphere of uncertainty. When the group had been working for some months they were asked again by Miss Bacon in July 1966 to complete their report quickly in order that their deliberations could be taken into account in drafting legislation based upon the White Paper *The Child, the Family and the Young Offender*. The Committee resisted once more and, soon after, the pressure to report ceased when Roy Jenkins became Home Secretary in December 1966. He decided that opposition to the White Paper had been too great to allow policy for young offenders to develop along the lines then being proposed. By that stage, however, it was too late for the Committee to change course and initiate useful research projects.

The Seebohm Committee was established in July 1965, began meeting in January 1966 and published its report in July 1968. It thus took two and a half years to report, a period some felt was too long but, as the Chairman pointed out in his introduction to the report, the members all had full-time jobs and the additional effort needed to attend meetings, process the evidence, visit local authorities and write the report was considerable.

STYLE OF WORK

The Committee decided early in its proceedings to concentrate upon discovering the opinions of those involved in the services concerned, to explore the working of existing local authority structures and to draw upon the knowledge and information already available. Indeed, the first of these tasks was an onerous one – the inquiry received a mass of written and oral evidence, the processing of which was a time-consuming exercise.

Ostensibly, the reason for undertaking no research programme was that 'this would have delayed publication perhaps for another year or two'.[16] Clearly, the pressures from the Home Office to report quickly contributed to this decision. Reinforcing these were the Chairman's own views upon the importance of speed. He was particularly conscious of the fact that while inquiries were under way it was impossible to immobilise all policy developments within the Committee's sphere of interest. In his foreword he argued:

> Government Committees are today usually composed of people in full-time occupations, examining an important subject which calls for urgent action. While I hope that the system of appointing independent committees to study problems of national importance will continue, there is always the risk that unless they are able to work rapidly their report will be overtaken by events. The interval between the appointment of the committee and the

> publication of the report can also be a period of speculation and considerable disturbance for those whose future may be at stake. I hope therefore that serious study will be given to ways of meeting the burden that members carry, so as to ensure that the reports are produced as quickly as possible.[17]

In its report the Committee refers to the many parallel policy considerations taking place at that time, all of which could have had serious implications for the personal social services. There were likely to be changes in the structure and working of local government, following the report of the Committee on the Management of Local Government[18] and the Royal Commission on Local Government in England,[19] which was sitting at the same time as Seebohm. Similar considerations were taking place regarding Welsh local government. The structure of the National Health Service was under review during that period and changes were planned within the education system, namely, the raising of the school-leaving age and the extension of comprehensive education. Furthermore, of considerable importance for Seebohm were the plans of the Home Office for young offenders; the White Paper *Children in Trouble*[20] was published while the Committee was deliberating. As the inquiry points out, 'decisions must be taken soon which will set the pattern for many years to come'.[21]

Apart from the need for speed, the Committee saw 'grave and overriding objections' to research as a basis for decision.

> First there is the difficulty of setting up and evaluating true experiments in such a major and complex field; second, the time required would only prolong the uncertainty about the future which has followed the setting up of this enquiry. This is damaging morale in the services and discouraging progressive development. Third, we doubt whether such experiments in this particular field would produce clear and reliable results.[22]

Quite obviously the Committee felt that inquiries were inappropriate vehicles from which to launch major research programmes. Its particular set of problems (which are discussed in the next section) were especially difficult to evaluate. Moreover, it felt that it did not have the time, for the reasons set out above and for further reasons not alluded to in the report. If decisions upon the organisational pattern of the future personal social services were not taken quickly, some local authorities might pre-empt the inquiry and adopt their own structures. Finally, in predicting that clear and reliable results might not be forthcoming, the Committee members were possibly voicing their uncertainty as to whether they could agree among themselves upon the *interpretation* of any research findings.

The Committee made it plain that, despite its rejection of any immediate research programme, it placed great importance upon the usefulness of social inquiry and evaluation and it outlined the role it thought research should play in this particular field of policy.

> Ideally it [research] should precede change; practically it becomes possible only when problems are identified and investigated sufficiently early and machinery exists for continuous research to be undertaken. Since these conditions do not prevail in the personal social services, we believe that organisational change should be so designed that the changes themselves are evaluated and the sensitive flexibility of the services encouraged.[23]

On the last point the Committee was right. It had very little past research to call upon and only a small number of ongoing projects. There were few good researchers interested in the subject and, therefore, the research network, impetus and investigative enthusiasm to which some committees can turn did not exist. Instituting new research would have required a major initiative on the part of the Committee and considerable expenditure. (Ironically, financial resources would not have been a problem since the Joseph Rowntree Memorial Trust was prepared to provide any research funds which could not be raised through the normal departmental channels.) There were few analytical studies on any aspect of the personal social services, structural or otherwise.[24] The available work was mostly descriptive in character, for example, Rodgers and Dixon's *Portrait of Social Work*,[25] Parker's *Local Health and Welfare Services*[26] and Jeffery's *An Anatomy of Local Welfare Services*.[27]

Precisely why research in this field had been so sluggish is difficult to explain. Many Committees of Inquiry had pointed to the lacunae in our knowledge. Both the Ingleby Report on Children and Young Persons (1960)[28] and the Younghusband Report on Social Workers in the Local Authority Health and Welfare Services (1959)[29] had called for research into aspects of social work, but to little effect. Following the latter committee's recommendation, the National Institute for Social Work Training was established in 1962 and a research capacity was slowly developed there. The Younghusband Inquiry suggested too that legislation should be introduced to enable government departments and local authorities to incur expenses and assist other bodies to carry out research into aspects of social work. No such Act was passed. The Committee's primary focus was not upon the organisational and structural considerations of the welfare services but upon the practice of those working within them. It saw the importance of discovering more about the needs of the community, for example, the activities of social workers, of exploring the size of caseloads, and examining the role and value of case conferences and co-ordinating committees. Research into some of these areas was started but by 1965 the hard evidence relevant to Seebohm was thin. Social work research has developed significantly in the fifteen years since 1965 but, despite a considerable increase in the resources spent in this area, it still remains relatively underdeveloped. Attracting good researchers continues to be a problem; moreover, most practising social workers do not have the skills, the time or the interest to devote to research.

THE CONTRIBUTION OF NEW RESEARCH AND ONGOING PROJECTS

The most important issue upon which the Committee had to make a decision concerned whether to form one unified social services department. This decision was taken fairly early, followed by the contingent questions of how to draw the boundaries around the newly proposed structure, who should head the organisation, its relationship with central government and with other social service agencies such as the education and housing departments, the Supplementary Benefits Commission and the probation service. Such decisions could be informed by the approach the Committee chose, namely, to study existing agencies, their working relationships, efficiency of co-ordination, and so on. Some of those giving evidence to the inquiry felt, however, that experimentation with different structural patterns and different local authority officers in charge of the new departments might be the best means of arriving at a conclusion. This experimentation could have taken place prior to the general reorganisation of local government being considered then by the Maud Commission.[30] One member of the Committee, the doctor, supported this view but was overridden by the majority who felt that, whilst it was in the interests of the medical profession to delay a decision as long as possible, it was in the interests of the social welfare services that a decision should be reached quickly. In the event, it is clear from the Committee papers that the decision to unify welfare agencies had been taken within the first nine months of the Committee's lifetime – the real debate concerned the implications of, and issues which followed from, that initial decision.

The only new evidence sought by the Committee was tapped from an ongoing project headed by Dr Bleddyn Davies. He was studying the relationship between local authority needs and resources in order to examine in more detail and explain variations in the standards of provision of the health and welfare services.[31] In particular, the Committee was interested in the question of whether combined health and welfare departments were more or less effective than separate ones. A clear answer to this question might have helped it to decide on the importance of keeping these two services administratively linked but unfortunately the results were difficult to interpret and ultimately inconclusive. Notes on the research findings were circulated to members of the Committee with an attached comment from the Secretary admitting defeat in his attempts to summarise the results. The members of the Committee found it no easier, and even though this was the only small piece of commissioned evidence, they finally decided not to publish the tables and details of the work. To do so would, they argued, have held up publication and increased the cost of the report. This evidence was, therefore, of little use to the Committee because it provided no precise answers. Had those answers been forthcoming, however, it is doubtful whether the Committee could have used them because the results were submitted so late in the Committee's deliberations – only eight months before the final report was published.

In examining the effectiveness of existing services, the Committee could have initiated some evaluative studies but to do so would have involved a formidable pioneering effort. Even today only one or two projects have attempted this[32] and the methodological problems are considerable. In an effort to gauge how far short of meeting certain defined needs the existing services fell, the Committee asked Dr Jean Packman and Mr Michael Power to bring together certain information already available on the number of children suffering from mental, physical and social handicaps of various kinds. These figures were compared with the number of children known to be receiving help and on this basis the final report concludes that provision fell sadly short of need. However, the Committee missed the chance to make the most of this information since it gave no adequate definition of need.

A third research project which could possibly have been of some help to the Committee was not fully utilised either. The National Child Development project, a follow-up study of children born in the same week in March 1958, had produced some interesting data[33] on the education, behaviour, health and environment of the cohort. The implications of this research for the Committee's deliberations might have been more comprehensively explored had the Committee given the researchers prior warning of its requirements. It requested information at such short notice that a few descriptive statistics and tables were all that could be provided.

A FULLER PICTURE OF THE PERSONAL SOCIAL SERVICES

Despite the Committee's failure to initiate research or capitalise fully upon existing material, in some chapters of the report, and particularly in the appendices, it provided a wealth of information on the personal social services never previously put together. Much of it was provided by government departments and needed little processing but the bringing together of information never hitherto juxtaposed gave students of these services a new slant upon aspects of welfare provision and some opportunity to compare its different branches. The Committee's Secretary, Mr Philip Wolf, was primarily responsible for contacting government departments to obtain the data and for assembling the appendices. Appendix F provides a particularly useful historical picture and furnished the members with a background of information against which to set their ideas. Each of the main services employing social welfare staff was described in some detail; the legislative responsibilities of different statutory agencies, their administrative structure, the services provided, the staffing levels, voluntary organisations and their role, advisory bodies in different service sectors, and so on. For those interested in analysing the personal social services, broad comparisons across service boundaries were possible but, as the statistics had been compiled by different government departments, more sophisticated exercises were not.

THE DRAFTING OF THE REPORT

The drafting process is an important part of any committee's work and the first draft an especially vital stage. The form in which ideas are first committed to paper often crystallises the committee's view. Particularly when members are overworked and their contribution to the committee's tasks is largely taking place in marginal time, it is all too easy to allow others to formulate the arguments and convey them in writing.

Hence, the members with the time, the clarity of thought, the ability to write and the confidence of other members of the committee can make their mark upon a report at this point. Sometimes, as in the case of the Seebohm Committee, those members will be academics and researchers. Dr (now Professor) Parker used his sabbatical leave from the London School of Economics to write first drafts of some chapters and modify others; his role varied from author to editor. It was necessary to create a structure and order within certain chapters where the basic ideas were present, whereas in other cases the ideas themselves required reformulation.

Writing and redrafting a report is a politically sensitive exercise and one which some members will be better equipped to tackle than others. In the experience of this Committee, part of the academic or research contribution was made in this way. A member from an academic environment could be seen as reasonably neutral politically – he was not closely identified by the rest of the group with a particular sector of the services under review – he could analyse the issues and convey clearly in writing the Committee's views to others. This is not to suggest that valuable inputs were not made by other members of the group but the balance of contribution at this stage favoured the academic members.

THE PACKAGING OF THE REPORT

The Seebohm Report itself conveys a somewhat false impression of the extent to which some of the deeper philosophical and sociological concepts underlying the Committee's work were discussed and utilised. The Chairman was most concerned that his report should be clear and unambiguous, containing a direct and forceful message which could be readily understood by politicians, practitioners and the general public. In doing so he decided, with the Committee's support, that some of the more complex background material should be omitted from the final publication. Several interesting papers were produced upon, for example, the function of social work,[34] the concept of a personal social service,[35] co-operation[36] and prevention,[37] but these were excluded. Moreover, the delicate question of precisely how much the report's proposals would cost were not discussed in any depth. Research could have been devised to explore this aspect of the Committee's work much more fully but it was decided that it was politically safer to leave the financial implications deliberately vague. In other words, the inquiry felt that its report would have a greater impact upon those working within the services involved, upon the general reader and, above all, upon politicians, if the social science component was kept to a minimum.

CONCLUSIONS

The Seebohm Committee felt unable to commission any substantial new research programme to help it reach its conclusions but there were fairly compelling reasons why this was so. Although they were a group most of whom could be expected to value the contribution of well-planned and carefully executed research, the circumstances within which they were placed severely limited its potential.

In particular, the group were constrained in planning their approach by the knowledge that, throughout their early proceedings, there were political pressures for them to provide a report quickly. The request from the Home Office that they should produce conclusions within six months could have debarred them from considering an ambitious research component. However, even if the Committee ignored these pressures, the members themselves felt the need to work with speed. They wished to reduce the uncertainty for those working within the services in question, and they were anxious to minimise the extent to which changes in other parts of the social services undermined the case they were preparing.

Many of the problems to which this inquiry addressed itself were not amenable to small-scale research projects. Substantial programmes would have been necessary and the Committee was sceptical that these would produce unambiguous results. Indeed, its only piece of commissioned work failed to deliver clear conclusions. Moreover, it had no solid tradition of social inquiry, particularly evaluative work, within the personal social services upon which to call and hence the initiation of research would have required a major pioneering effort.

Although there were good reasons for rejecting large-scale research studies, the Committee could undoubtedly have utilised ongoing projects more fully. It failed to capitalise upon some of the evidence being produced at the time and it deliberately omitted from its report discussion documents which might have strengthened its case in the eyes of some critics. There were aspects of its work, for example, the financial implications of its proposals, which could have benefited from limited research investigations. However, the inquiry saw its role as monitoring and moulding opinion, its primary function being to sift the evidence of groups involved in the personal social services and draw its own conclusions. Finally, it placed a high premium upon the presentation of a clear, campaigning report, uncluttered by the complexities of research findings.[38]

NOTES: CHAPTER 6

1 The background, working and impact of this inquiry are discussed more fully in P. K. Hall, *Reforming the Welfare* (London: Heinemann, 1976), and in R. Chapman (ed.), *The Role of Commissions in Policy Making* (London: Allen & Unwin, 1973), ch. 6. This chapter is based upon interviews which the author had with members of the Committee, those who gave evidence, civil servants, politicians and others involved in this inquiry.

2 Its report was published in July 1968. *Report of the Committee on Local Authority and Allied Personal Social Services* (Seebohm Report), Cmnd 3703 (London: HMSO, 1968).

3 See, for example, evidence to *The Royal Commission on Local Government in Greater London 1957–1960*, Cmnd 1164 (London: HMSO, October 1960), and that to the *Committee on Children and Young Persons* (Ingleby Report), Cmnd 1191 (London: HMSO, 1960).

4 Examples of the reports of such inquiries are: *Report of the Committee on Health Visiting* (Jameson Report) (London: HMSO, 1956), *Report of the Committee on Social Workers in the Local Authority Health and Welfare Services* (Younghusband Report) (London: HMSO, 1959), *Report of the Royal Commission on Mental Illness and Mental Deficiency, 1954–57*, Cmnd 169 (London: HMSO, 1957) and *Report of the Committee on Children and Young Persons*, op. cit.

5 The two most important ones are the Younghusband and Ingleby Reports, op. cit.

6 The issue of juvenile crime and its role in achieving wider social reforms is discussed in P. K. Hall, *Reforming the Welfare*, pp. 19–33.

7 The Ingleby Committee had received evidence to this effect from, for example, the London County Council's Children's Committee, the Council for Children's Welfare and the Fisher Group.

8 *Crime – a Challenge to Us All* (Longford Report), Report of a Labour Party Study Group, (London: The Labour Party) June 1964.

9 Scottish Home and Health Department and Scottish Education Department, *Children and Young Persons in Scotland* (Kilbrandon Report), Cmnd 2306 (London: HMSO, April 1964).

10 For details of these ministerial offices see P. K. Hall, op. cit., pp. 19–20.

11 Home Office, *The Child, the Family and the Young Offender*, Cmnd 2742 (London: HMSO, August 1965).

12 The Scottish planning process proceeded rather more quickly than that of England and Wales. The Social Work (Scotland) Act was passed in July 1968.

13 This memorandum is reproduced as Appendix 2 in P. K. Hall, op. cit., p. 142.

14 Planning for young offenders continued within the Home Office quite separately from the consideration of the other services for children. It resulted in the White Paper *Children in Trouble*, Cmnd 3601 (London: HMSO, April 1965), and the Children and Young Persons Act, 1969.

15 The Seebohm Committee's own report contributes to the myth that the formation of the inquiry was a Home Office initiative; see the Seebohm Report, p. 17.

16 Seebohm Report, p. 21.

17 ibid., p. 3.

18 *Report of the Committee on the Management of Local Government* (London: HMSO, 1967).

19 *Report of the Royal Commission on Local Government in England, 1966–69*, Cmnd 4040 (London: HMSO, June 1969).

20 See above, Note 14.

21 Seebohm Report, p. 20.

22 ibid., p. 20.

23 ibid., p. 20.

24 R. A. Parker, *Decision in Child Care* (London: Allen & Unwin, 1966).

25 B. Rodgers and J. Dixon, *Portrait of Social Work* (London: Oxford University Press, 1960).

26 J. Parker, *Local Health and Welfare Services* (London: Allen & Unwin, 1965).

27 M. Jefferys, *An Anatomy of Social Welfare Services* (London: Michael Joseph, 1965).

28 Ingleby Report, p. 5.

29 Younghusband Report, pp. 274–5.

30 *The Royal Commission on Local Government in England*, op. cit.

31 This work was later published. See B. Davies, *Social Needs and Resources in Local Services* (London: Michael Joseph, 1968).

32 See, for example, E. M. Goldberg, *Helping the Aged* (London: Allen & Unwin, 1970).

33 Information from this study was published in M. L. K. Pringle, N. R. Butler and R. Davies, *11,000 Seven Year Olds* (London: Longman, 1967).

34 A Seebohm Committee Paper, formally called Family Service Committee Papers (FSCP), 381, available in the Libraries of Bristol University and of the National Institute of Social Work.

35 FSCP 337.

36 FSCP 380.

37 FSCP 580.

38 This chapter was completed before the author joined the civil service and the views expressed are those of the author alone writing in a personal capacity.

Chapter 7

A Commission and a Cost-Benefit Study

A. D. J. FLOWERDEW

> And it came to pass in the twentieth century, in the three score and eighth year and in the fifth month, that the Almighty One who hath His Seat in the Courts of Justice was asked, 'Appoint to thyself men, for I have decreed that there shall be no further place near our chief city for the comings in and the goings out of the birds of men except thou recommendest a site and a time'.

The Almighty One referred to was the Honourable Mr Justice Roskill, now the Right Honourable Lord Justice Roskill, and his Commission was officially the Commission on the Third London Airport. It was appointed by Anthony Crosland, then President of the Board of Trade. At the time of its appointment the need for a third London airport was considered urgent, with rapid growth of air traffic and existing airports in the London area nearing saturation, especially Heathrow and Gatwick, the two owned by the British Airports Authority. The government had tried and failed, after local protest, to make Stansted the third London airport. Hence the need for the Commission; hence too the scale of its operations. Mr Justice Roskill's colleagues were Professor (now Sir Colin) Buchanan, planner, and himself author of a famous report, *Traffic in Towns* (HMSO, 1963), Mr Alfred Goldstein, engineer and transport consultant, Mr Arthur Hunt of the Planning Inspectorate, Professor David Keith-Lucas, expert in aircraft design, Mr (now Sir Arthur) Knight, a businessman, and Professor Alan Walters, an economist.

The Commission's work lasted two and a half years, cost over a million pounds, and is documented in a *Report* (HMSO, 1971) and nine volumes of *Papers and Proceedings* (HMSO, 1969, 1970). It was path-breaking in three separate ways. It was, I believe, the first commission to employ a really substantial in-house research team, rather than merely asking for evidence from the public, or commissioning academics or consultants to carry out research for it, or relying on research carried out within the civil service. The

Commission did all three of these things as well, but the existence of the in-house research team enabled the evidence, the commissioned research and the civil service work to be organised in a framework specified by the Commission, and provided the Commission with the means to carry out research that these other sources would have been unwilling, unable or incompetent to carry out, and within a specified timetable.

There were twenty-three members of the Commission's research team, which was directed by Frank Thompson, an economist in the Ministry of Transport, whose release was only secured when the astronomical market price of the 'next best' alternative leader, an American expert, had been named. About half the team came from the government service: they included economists, engineers, statisticians and planners. The remainder were recruited from industry, local government and universities. The team was organised into five groups: the Director's Group, responsible for statistical and economic work and the crucial task of co-ordination and control; the Central Operational Research Group, headed by the author, which was responsible for work on air traffic control, noise, safety, defence, systems analysis and optimisation; the Surface Access Group; the Planning and Amenity Group; and the Civil Engineering Group. It was nearly eight months after work began before the team neared its full strength, and many left before the Commission's work was over. The Commission also employed, directly or indirectly, a large number of consultants in engineering, town planning, air traffic control, not to mention the Essex University sociologists familiarly referred to by the Commission as the 'drugs and sex lot'.

The framework of analysis chosen was cost-benefit analysis, and this is the second way in which the Commission's work broke new ground. The third London airport study was the most ambitious cost-benefit study which had been carried out at that time and probably since: it required new developments both in methodology and in techniques, and it has as a result become part of the syllabus for many different social sciences courses in universities throughout Britain and overseas – sometimes used to illustrate diametrically opposed points of view in different degree courses in the same university and, in at least one case, in the same degree course. The methodology has been briefly described in Flowerdew (1972), which relates to the choice of sites. The analysis of timing of the need for the new airport is discussed in more detail in an article with a colleague from the research team in Abelson and Flowerdew (1972). The influence in government of the cost-benefit approach developed for the Commission has been less strong. Methodology deriving from Roskill's is used in airport planning and in closely related areas, but there have been few advances in the state of the art, especially in applications of techniques for environmental evaluation, as noted in the *Report of the Advisory Committee on Trunk Road Assessment* (HMSO, 1977). Even in airport planning cost-benefit analysis is perhaps on the retreat – see Frank Thompson's paper 'Investment planning: is airport cost-benefit analysis dead?' (1978). Undoubtedly cost-benefit analysis was seen in Whitehall not only as a useful tool for analysing decision problems, but also as a potentially dangerous one, threatening, perhaps, to put the expert on top rather than merely on tap.

But it was Roskill's third innovation on which most time and money was spent, most hopes were placed and which has apparently been most firmly rejected by the government as a permanent feature of the policy process. This was public participation. This chapter is not primarily concerned with public participation as such, so the discussion of this issue will be brief, though the interplay between research and public participation was important and is discussed below.

At the Stansted inquiry, both through the operation of pressure groups and in other ways, the public had shown an ability to contribute to the decision-making process which seemed to be an improvement on Whitehall. Hence the major reason for introducing a concept of public participation far more ambitious than the local inquiry was not, I believe, to improve the quality of decision-making, but to improve the acceptability or saleability of its findings. For Stansted had failed on both grounds: it was not supported by an adequate technical argument, and it was not able to command public support. The first ground *could* have been responsible for the second, but it seemed plausible to suppose that any further studies, however technically sound, would attract the same suspicion as the Stansted exercise, if carried out without the widest possible public scrutiny.

Whatever the reasons, the degree of public participation in the Roskill Commission's work was unprecedented. The Commission's programme of work, with its five stages, is depicted in Figure 7.1. In Stage I the Commission invited evidence and held hearings, in which cross-examination was allowed, on the methodology it should use. Suggestions were also invited for possible sites. When its shortlist had been chosen, details of the effect of each potential airport were published and further local inquiries were held at each of the four shortlisted sites (Stage II). The Commission's proposed research methodology was also published early in 1969, and comments were invited. The Commission published at the beginning of 1970 the findings of its research team and consultants during Stage III (Commission on the Third London Airport, *Papers and Proceedings,*

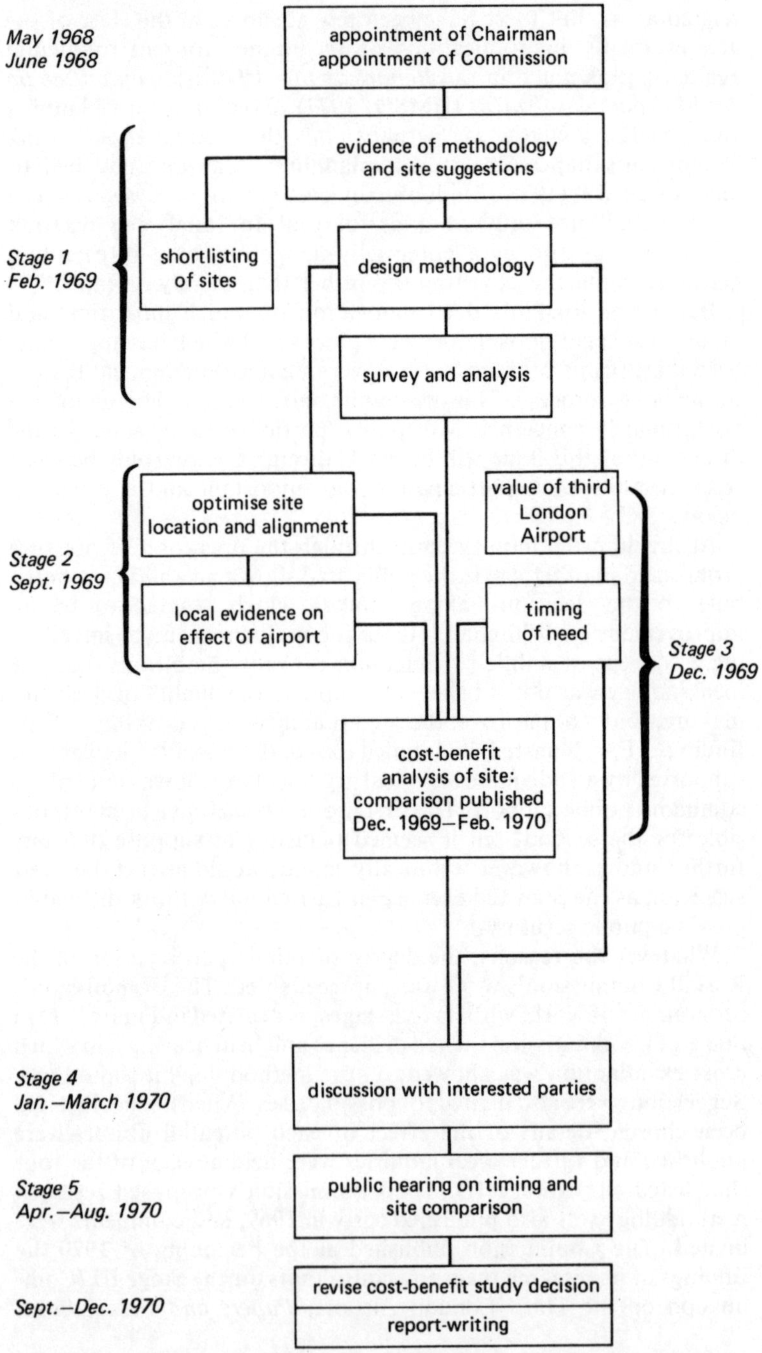

Figure 7.1 *The Stages of the Roskill Commission work programme*

Volumes VII and VIII, HMSO, 1970). Other bodies, including local authorities, pressure groups and the British Airports Authority, submitted evidence at the same time, as they had been invited to do. During the early part of 1970 a number of meetings were held to clarify these documents (Stage IV); then, in the spring, a final series of public hearings provided the opportunity for each group to cross-examine the research team and each other on the details of their case (Stage V). Only after this did the Commission reach its conclusion: Cublington was recommended and a date of 1980. This was not a unanimous decision. Professor Buchanan, in his Note of Dissent, preferred Foulness.

Of the matters considered by the Commission, only the shortlisting of potential sites was not reviewed publicly. (It is true that some defence issues had to be heard in camera, but special arrangements were made for the parties to the inquiry to be represented.) Should – could – shortlisting have been tested publicly? Roskill started with seventy-eight sites: if local evidence had been presented on each Roskill would be sitting still. And the shortlisting had to be done quickly, in order to leave time for the local inquiries and all the detailed work at each shortlisted site. Without public participation the time available for shortlisting could have been much greater, with a consequent improvement in methodology – the shortlisting methodology, described in Appendix 5 of the Commission's report, was inevitably crude.

The public participation exercise was in many ways a great success. The Commission got what it wanted out of it, including an exhaustive survey of effects, even down to the threatened extinction of the last remaining habitat of the broad-leaved nettle-wort in North Hertfordshire and the incompatability with an airport of organ-tuning in Buckinghamshire, cockle-gathering in Essex and radio astronomy in Cambridgeshire. More important, they got an extremely wide discussion of the issues, technical, economic and philosophical.

THE COMMISSION AND ITS RESEARCH

In days of yore when planners scanned
Their crystal balls alone
At least a town or two was planned
Before the need had gone
But now they're so weighed down by all
Their own semantic twaddle
That though the airport's long been built
They're building still – a model.

The research that the Commission wanted involved both the

collection of data, including factual data and expert opinion, and the analysis of the data to provide the basis for forecasts of the effect of alternative airport locations. The Commission was very clear about the need for a comprehensive approach to data collection, since it felt the gaps in the information considered had contributed to the failure of Stansted. The inclusion in the Commission of experts in a number of relevant fields, plus the forensic skills imparted to his colleagues by the judge, enabled the Commission to be critical as well as comprehensive in its approach to data, especially in the weighing of expert opinion. Most experts needed careful interrogation to induce them to provide information in a usable form – that is a form in which it could be analysed for future use. It is salutary to observe that there are far more people to say that something is unthinkable/disastrous/should be avoided at all costs on aeronautical/commercial/planning grounds than there are people prepared to say exactly why. The concept of the 'fatal flaw' used by the Commission proved the critical key for unlocking this particular door. Since all sites had grave disadvantages, all disadvantages which were not insurmountable would have to be explained in detail, tested and quantified where possible. Fatal flaws would have to be defended as such. Since few experts could do this successfully, most disadvantages were explored in detail.

It should be noted here that Buchanan was subsequently to claim that all the inland sites suffered from a 'fatal flaw' (Note of Dissent, in the Commission's *Report*). He did not argue this at the time, however, preferring to wait for the official regional planning evidence to reveal it. In the event, this official evidence stated that regional planning arguments (as distinct from local planning considerations) could not be regarded as very strong in any direction, since there was no reason to believe the chosen South-East regional plan was appreciably better than any other, but that one of the sites would require some revision to the plan, while of the remaining three Foulness was slightly more likely than the other two to cause problems if growth associated with the airport was greater than expected. Not all regional planners would agree with this, and Buchanan's Note of Dissent makes much of regional arguments hardly tested at the Stage V hearings.

The most important functions of the research team during Stage III, however, were design and model-building. Both aspects are required to forecast the effects of different airport locations. The design work is to provide the basis for a comparison of all the effects of the airports: it includes not only the design of the airport itself, but also access links, new towns to house the airport staff, design of flight paths and also choice of policies, for example, for allocating airlines to airports or for pricing public transport access links. Some of the work was done by the Commission staff, some by consultants working for it. Since the design of these facilities can easily influence the choice of site it needs to be done with care, lest a site is unfairly burdened with a penalty it need not carry. I would say this could not have been done without a research team. Consultants can be more committed to a solution than to an approach: one of the Commission's own consultants, whose work revealed a substantial cost penalty against Foulness because of conditions for building, told the Commission the difference was not significant and should be ignored – and when the Commission reported, wrote to *The Times* opposing the recommendation and advocating Foulness. Public bodies can be too inflexible: British Rail's preferred method of calculating fares made the rail link to Foulness so expensive that the research team's traffic model predicted that passengers would choose a complex bus and rail journey using existing track in preference to the new line. The Commission did not accept this fare policy which would have been highly detrimental to the site.

Some aspects of design work must be controversial. The Commission's 'optimal' Foulness lay close to shore, and it was assumed that Luton Airport would continue in operation. Both these factors reduced the overall costs of Foulness in cost-benefit terms, but increased the overall noise effect of the Foulness choice to something not greatly distinguishable from Cublington or Thurleigh. (Luton has quite a serious noise effect for a small airport, but it is a lot more convenient for air travellers than Foulness, while parts of north Kent are affected by noise from a close-in Foulness site.) The result of this decision makes it difficult to justify Foulness as a site even if the noise costs were weighted much more heavily. In fact where the Conservative Government picked Foulness-Maplin they moved its site out to sea, which greatly increased its costs (see *Maplin Airport, Choice of Sites for Runways*, Department of the Environment, 1972). They also said they would shut Luton: and these decisions in turn probably contributed to the economic case against Maplin when it was abandoned.

Design work as shown above can be controversial but is relatively easy to understand: model-building presents both a lay audience and the lawyers who run the public inquiries with enormous problems because of its mathematical basis. But it proved impossible to do without models and in fact the most difficult problems probably arose where the Commission relied on the somewhat unsatisfactory state of the art rather than developing models themselves.

The kinds of models involved were very varied: for instance, a model to relate growth in demand in terms of annual passengers to

Table 7.1 *Research Organisation*

	Research team	*Govt departments other public sector*	*Consultants*	*Other parties*
FORECASTS – PASSENGER	Business and British leisure only	Foreign leisure passengers: British Tourist Authority Others: Board of Trade Working Party	–	BAA Airlines
– AIRCRAFT	supervision	Board of Trade	–	
– AIRPORT CAPACITY	✓	Board of Trade	–	
PLANNING – LOCAL	supervision		4 major studies (employing subconsultants)	
– REGIONAL	—	SE Joint Planning Team	–	some
– ENVIRONMENT	in-house	Counties	sociological consultants	most
– AGRICULTURE	supervision		✓	NFU, etc.
NOISE – HOMES	✓			BAA Counties
– OTHER	supervision	Counties	–	–
AVIATION ISSUES – AIR TRAFFIC CONTROL	✓	National Air Traffic	✓	Counties resistance groups
– SAFETY	✓	Board of Trade	–	Airlines
– METEOROLOGY	supervision	Met. Office	–	Airlines
AIRPORT DESIGN – DESIGN	✓	Public Building Works	–	some
AND CONSTRUCTION – CONSTRUCTION	✓	Public Building Works	–	Foulness airport consortium
– SEAPORT	methodology	National Ports Council	–	Consortium

Table 7.1 *Continued*

	Research team	*Govt departments other public sector*	*Consultants*	*Other parties*
SURFACE ACCESS – ROAD INFRASTRUCTURE	supervision	Transport	(to Transport)	some alternative routes
– RAIL INFRASTRUCTURE	supervision	British Rail	(to BR)	some alternative routes
– TRIP DISTRIBUTION	✓		Computing work	after Stage V
DEFENCE	supervision	✓	–	—
COST-BENEFIT ANALYSIS	✓	Evidence on safety and time from Transport and Technology	–	BAA, Counties, resistance group etc.

Notes: County Planning Departments assisted the Commission by providing information on the distribution of population, schools, hospitals, and so on. They also, quite independently, submitted research at Stage III, carried out by their own consultants.

There were a few areas in which consultants were employed, for example, unconventional transport systems, which do not fit into the above categories.

growth in demand in terms of peak hour aircraft movements; a model to predict the pattern of surface movement to/from homes and offices and from/to airports; a model to verify the feasibility of runway and airspace utilisation in terms of the load placed on air traffic controllers and a model to forecast the reactions of local residents to aircraft noise.

The object of these models is to replace arguments which, while simple, can, and often did, give misleading results. For example, the growth of peak hour aircraft movements is much slower than growth in annual passenger demand, which is largely why the Roskill Commission felt able to recommend a much later date for the new airport than that which the British Airports Authority had been asking for, although the figures on which the timing was based were not very much altered. The pattern of movement to a system of airports is complex: it is not just a matter of assuming each traveller uses the nearest airport, as some airports will have restricted capacity and the schedules will vary; nor is it sufficient to consider merely nearness to London as the criterion: Foulness was nearer than Thurleigh, but the latter airport was much better situated for the bulk of the passenger demand, and surface access costs were thus much lower with Thurleigh as the third London airport than with Foulness. A simulation model was the only way that the Commission could get a positive view as to the feasibility of operation of a route pattern. At shortlisting, house price depreciation was used as a basis for costing noise, but it was clear that some people would be much worse off than this indicated, as they might not only lose part of the value of their homes but also have to consider leaving a home and neighbourhood to which they were strongly attached – this factor could only be disentangled with a model.

Most of the work of the research team and the Commission's consultants was taken up with data collection, design and model-building of this kind, very little in proportion with the cost-benefit analysis itself, though this did provide the framework within which the research was done. Thus Peter Self's attack (1970) on the Commission for having wasted resources and distracted attention from the more humble but useful factual studies for the sake of the 'absurdity' of the cost-benefit analysis is singularly poorly founded. Table 7.1 lists the topics covered by the research team, by government departments and by consultants respectively, and also indicates the main topics on which alternative or complementary evidence was preferred by other parties in Stage II, to be tested at Stage V.

COST-BENEFIT ANALYSIS

> Oh Commissioners may sing
> Of the value of a thing

Such as quality of living or disturbance due to noise
And we justify each figure
With considerable vigour
On the basis of our models and our pretty little toys.
But no matter how we try
We can never quantify
Those poor dark-bellied Brent geese (if we leave them in the lurch)
So we cancel as we wish
These sad geese against the fish
Or a thoroughbredded gee-gee or a Stewkley parish church.

The purpose of cost-benefit analysis is to assist decision-makers by providing an account, quantified where possible, and so far as possible in terms of a common unit such as money, of all the positive and negative effects (benefits and costs) of a decision on all those who are affected both in the short and in the long term. The Commission was instructed to consider the use of cost-benefit analysis by Mr Crosland, who was undoubtedly influenced by the fact than a simple cost-benefit study carried out by John Heath and his colleagues in the Economic Services Division of the Board of Trade had showed that the argument that Stansted was the only realistic choice did not stand up.

Considering the use of a tool is not the same as deciding to use a tool and it is interesting to examine why the Commission chose to follow the cost-benefit route so vigorously. This can be depicted, I think, as a multi-stage decision, and is illustrated in Figure 7.2.

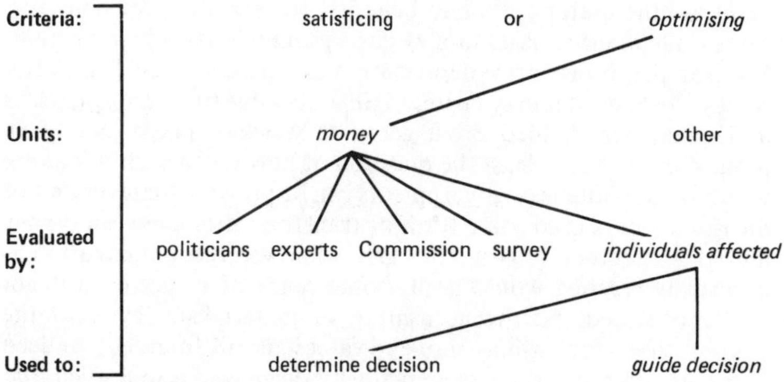

Figure 7.2 *Decision-making methodology*

Satisficing is a fancy term introduced by the recent Nobel prize-winner H. A. Simon to describe a method of decision-making which consists in establishing criteria, for example, for a new home, and then searching until you either find something which satisfies (satisfices) the criteria or you give up, in which case you re-examine the criteria to see if you can relax them. The approach is essentially what was used to produce the Stansted decision and is quite a familiar one within bureaucracies: each site is evaluated, subjectively or objectively, on a number of 'grounds', for example, defence, noise, surface access, construction, air traffic control and regional planning, and a decision made as to whether it is or is not satisfactory on each ground. A useful organisational feature of such an approach is that one departmental representative can often be used to make the decision on each ground; for example, the Ministry of Defence chaps can provide the authoritative view of whether a site is OK for defence. The Ministry of Defence did exactly this and ruled out Foulness during the process of reaching the Stansted decision: the fact that Foulness was later to be their favourite site illustrates the fragility of this approach.

In the Commission's view, no site could possibly be regarded as satisfactory on all grounds; had that been possible there would have been no need for it. It preferred to establish only minimal standards on each set of grounds, so that a large number of sites could be regarded as possibles, and then to find some methods of comparison which would recognise that, for instance, a site with serious access or construction disadvantages might have countervailing noise or air traffic control advantages. It thus chose the 'optimising' path in Figure 7.2.

To compare across different grounds requires a common unit of measurement. Money is a relatively convenient measure: for some of the effects of an airport money costs or receipts to the government are the major costs and benefits, for example, for construction, while in other cases money costs to individuals are important, for example, house price depreciation and access costs. It may not be easy, or indeed it may be impossible, to value time savings, peace and quiet, dark-bellied Brent geese or Stewkley parish church in money terms, but at least the question of how much such things are worth to individuals or governments can be posed. Whatever unit of measurement is used some form of transformation between money and these factors is required: and whatever recommendation is eventually reached would imply some range of values even if not explicitly stated. So the accusation of materialism levied at the Commission for using money values is ill-founded, indeed peculiarly inappropriate when made by those who also argued that people are over-influenced by what is quantified. For the use of money to measure the social value of non-marketed benefits and costs enables these less material factors to be used to influence those decision-makers who are alleged to be easily swayed by numbers. (The experience of the Commission, supported by many other studies, would suggest that these weak-minded people, if they exist, hardly exercise a dominating sway over events.)

This is not to say, however, that there are no problems with the use of money as a common denominator, both practically and philosophically. Practically there were great difficulties: in the end the Commission did accept that time savings and noise could be costed, but only within a wide margin of error, while they refrained from valuing either the birds or the churches. There was, however, a perhaps unfortunate public relations failure on the issue of the churches. The Commission thought, reasonably enough, that it would be useful to have evidence on the pros and cons of valuing the churches, so it arranged to have included with the research team's evidence to the final hearing some proposals stemming from a Church of England Working Party. One day I hope to write the definitive paper, 'How to value a Norman church', but for the present it will have to be sufficient to point out that a historic church can be valued from an aesthetic, a historical or a religious point of view and that it may be looked at as a local, a regional or a national asset. It appeared that from the religious point of view the older type of parish church is not regarded as desirable because of the cost of upkeep and lack of flexibility in use – nevertheless local religious feeling often requires the upkeep and even replacement of parts of the building accidentally destroyed. It was this train of argument that led to the notorious valuation at fire insurance cover proposal, which the Commission rightly rejected, although it has frequently since been criticised as if it had accepted it.

One of the most difficult philosophical questions raised by the money measure of value is that of distribution: is it correct to add costs and benefits in money terms no matter to whom they accrue: is not a pound's worth of benefit to a poor man somehow more important than it is to a rich man; how far should benefits and costs to foreigners, who form such a large part of air travellers, be counted; and should gainers and losers be treated the same? The Commission did not attempt to resolve these issues, preferring to reassure itself by sensitivity analysis that whatever view it took over a wide range would be unlikely to disturb the ranking of sites.

At the third stage of the decision the Commission opted for valuation by individuals affected, the principle of consumer sovereignty, as a general rule, though there were inevitable exceptions, of which defence was probably the most obvious. Individual valuation of defence contributions to the country would be impossible to assess, even if NATO would agree to everyone being informed enough to judge. In effect, defence costs were evaluated by the Commission assuming that money would have to be spent as economically as possible to maintain the country's current defence posture. There was one minor instance of degradation of posture, as the jargon had it, but it was luckily held to be of trivial importance.

However, the replacement cost approach had some profound consequences, of great interest to the student of policy formulation. Broadly, the Cublington site required large-scale rearrangement of RAF facilities, the Thurleigh site likewise for USAF. Naturally, an American air base is a costlier item to shift than a British air base, so Thurleigh accumulated a much higher defence cost, large enough to have influenced the Commission's preference for Cublington. But it would be the Cublington site which would make life most difficult for the RAF and so it was that site which they opposed most strongly – and that was an important issue in the government's decision-making, since the Ministry of Defence had the largest representation in the interdepartmental committee which ultimately advised the Cabinet. This is a very clear indication of the possible divergence between cost arguments and political clout arguments, which must not be overlooked by those who wish not only to make good recommendations but also to see them adopted.

The Commission was frequently advised that in order to make the comparison across grounds it should get political guidance or expert guidance or even rely on its own good sense to evaluate the different factors – anything, it sometimes seemed, rather than find out from the people really affected. To ask politicians to supply the values would, in the view of the Commission members, have been abdicating their responsibility – most of them at least taking the view that their job arose just because the political decision-making system had foundered. A good example of a study adopting just this approach is that of Mexico City Airport (R. de Neufville and R. L. Keeney, 1972). To a degree, the Commission behaved as though it believed that its role was to advise the country, not just the government of the day – if that was its belief it might be thought at variance with the way it reported, an issue to which I shall return. I have already indicated why the Commission might not have wished to rely on expert valuation; all too often there was no argument to justify the expert's view. The suggestion that the Commission should value things itself might seem both tempting and flattering, but the temptation was resisted, except on one occasion, in private. The idea of a survey of local opinion to assess relative values has been much advocated for transport policy recently, but the trouble is that only some of the costs and benefits fall locally – there is no reason why local people should be especially careful of the interests of air travellers, or even of the taxpayers' interests.

But perhaps the most important reason for wanting to use the values of the individuals affected was the concept that this would be justiciable, that is, would be open to challenge by evidence on which judgement could be exercised to reach a conclusion. Justiciability was highly valued by the Commission, perhaps because it provided a link between the ideas of lawyers and of social scientists. Perhaps it was valued for the practical reason that if the Commission's recommendation could be backed up by evidence and argument it would be more easily accepted. This proved to be over optimistic. Another important reason was, I think, a matter of political/moral philosophy: the philosophy of liberalism, as expressed alike by the Joseph-ite wing of the Conservative Party and the Social Democrats following Crosland. A central proposition of this kind of liberalism is that people should do what they wish if it does not adversely affect the interests of others – from which it is a short step to asserting that people should normally be the judges of their own welfare.

The technicalities of the work resulting from this choice by the Commission do not need to be described here: they are extensively documented in the Commission's *Papers and Proceedings* and elsewhere. I might however mention that for reasons of time and for reasons of perhaps ill-judged prudence, the innovative research was confined to areas which had not previously been studied. Thus the research team estimated noise costs, which had not been done by anyone previously: but values of time and accident costs were taken from those currently in use by the Ministry of Transport. Possibly it could have been easier to defend the methodology had it been developed more directly in the context of airport planning – but it is important not to underestimate the difficulty of the task that would have faced the research team in setting up a new methodology for valuing time or safety from scratch. Still, a lot of unnecessary criticism was attracted by the Ministry's rather arbitrary method of calculating the value of a human life – which was in practice almost an irrelevant issue, since all sites were to be made as safe as they could be and the theoretical advantage of Foulness as an offshore site with a consequential diminution of risk to third parties was offset by the inconclusive evidence which suggested that a higher proportion of fatalities would be expected from ditching in the North Sea.

This leaves one stage of the decision-tree. Should the Commission's choice be dictated by the numbers, or should it use its judgement to reach a conclusion? The report goes to great lengths to make it clear that the Commission preferred to use its judgement – but since its judgement agreed with its numbers many commentators preferred not to believe it. Some indeed argued, absurdly, that since the preferred site was also that with the least access cost, the Commission had been swayed by access costs alone. Peter Walker was not among those commentators: he said that the government merely wished to put a higher value on the environmental factor than the Commission, thus implying that the government accepted the numbers but not the judgement. The members of the Commission believed that many important factors had not been quantified: they also, individually, held varying beliefs about the accuracy of the quantified values or the assumptions on which these should be based. On the occasion referred to above six of the Commission members tried their hand at providing their own best guesses of values of both quantified and unquantified items. It is interesting that the values ranged widely and in many cases were very large – but all six conclusions were the same. Commission members were very clear that this was an exercise and not a decision-making procedure; but it was an impressive exercise and must have influenced them.

PUBLIC PARTICIPATION

Sing a song of sixpence
Cost or benefit
Four and twenty wise men
Picking at a nit
When the costs are counted
They weight them or they fudge
Oh isn't that a dainty dish
To set before a Judge.

Can mathematics and economics form the basis for a useful public discussion of issues? And can a good piece of research be done when it is thus exposed to public view? These questions, while inward-looking, are significant and may be discussed before raising the outward-looking issue of the effectiveness of public participation in the Commission's work.

There seems little doubt that the type of public participation which took place was influenced strongly by the type of research carried out. Put crudely, at Stage I the Commission heard the actual interest groups, at Stage II it heard the local people and at Stage V it heard from economists and modellers. Not everyone represented at Stage V brought in these high-powered consultants to defend their alternative cost-benefit studies or to shoot holes in those of the research team, but plenty did, notably the 'Essex' group of County Councils, the 'Buckinghamshire' group, the Wing Airport Resistance Association, the British Airports Authority and the Thames Aeroport Group.

One might have expected, and I must admit I did expect, that it would be easier to reach agreement on a technical level with these technical chaps. Not a bit of it. The evidence put up and defended by them frequently seemed even more amazingly at variance with the theories as understood by the research team or the facts as we believed them. The Buckinghamshire group's noise costs were nearly nine times those of the Commission. Professor Lichfield, for the 'Essex' group and others, thought 6d (2½p) an hour an appropriate value for leisure time. A trip generation model produced by two groups of county councils and the Thames Aeroport Group suggested that the Foulness system would generate more trips than the Cublington system for every zone except Cornwall. The Thames Estuary Development Company thought that aggregates at Foulness would be £1·25 cheaper than at an inland site as against the research team's estimate of 50p – which incidentally tends to reduce one's faith in the argument, put up among others by Peter Hall and Peter Self, that construction costs were more likely to be accurate than the 'softer' non-marketed costs and benefits.

Did these marked differences suggest special pleading to make a case for their clients – or does it represent a reasonable difference between professionals? No one argued at the time that the research team was biased, though some, notably George Stern (1976), did later, while Professor Parry Lewis argued that the retention of the research team and their ability to make further calculations to advise the Commission following the Stage V hearings was unfair.

From the research team's point of view, maintenance of an unbiased position presented a rather different problem. Inevitably during a process of evaluation of argument many points were made, some good, some bad. The good ought to be adopted, clearly, and the bad rejected. Yet, since the Commission's own commissioned research at Stage V was clearly pointing towards an inland site and against Foulness, the most expensively and strongly argued cases presented by other parties were in favour of Foulness. So inevitably there were more points of all kinds, both good and bad, favouring Foulness and if the good ones had to be accepted there was the strong danger of the Commission's final report 'leaning over backwards' at least to some extent, to favour Foulness. This danger was not totally overcome.

The Commission's timetable included at Stage IV an informal exchange of views between interested parties. It had been hoped that this would be the stage for hammering out disagreements between experts, establishing the possible alternative bases for modelling and reaching a consensus on some of the issues. This was only partially successful. Just a few issues were made less controversial, many became more so over this period. Probably the most successful use of Stage IV was briefing counsel for the parties to understand the models and the basis of cost-benefit analysis – a process in which I acquired considerable respect for the legal mind and for the power of their main tool, Aristotelian logic, when applied with persistence and with flexibility. Of course there was considerable difficulty in understanding the often heavy mathematical content of the models – it was indeed necessary for the Chairman to define the new offence of 'practising numeracy', which is, however, legitimate if carried out in private by consenting adults.

Stage V presented other problems for researchers – both the research team and those employed by other parties. If issues are to be debated and if possible resolved in public, people cannot keep coming back for another round, since all other parties should be given time to reply to each new point raised, and the inquiry would never terminate. The Commission has to cry enough – and it is just tough if in the researcher's view there is still some useful research to be done. Also if nobody challenges a particular issue it does not get debated. Since as it happened there was no serious disagreement at Stage V with the proposition that a new airport was required, there was very little additional work done on this topic, a matter for which the Commission was afterwards criticised, especially by economists (see, for instance, E. J. Mishan, 1970).

I think there is an institutional lesson too. The research team consisted mainly of practising researchers, drawn to a large extent from outside the university and used to having to make assumptions to get results. By contrast several of the economists giving expert evidence were academics, trained to pull holes in other people's work, not necessarily skilled in providing a substitute. An exception was Professor Lichfield, whose work as a consultant in this area is well known and distinguished, but whose main presentation tool, the Planning Balance Sheet, is designed to provide for a good deal of flexibility of interpretation, which did not find favour with the Commission. In the end Professor Lichfield was unable to find an analysis to support his client's case. Application of economic work in the public sector might be less controversial and more widely used if there was more interchange between academia and Whitehall, and more acceptance by the former of the need to be constructive and of the latter to provide an adequate theoretical basis for their arguments. There is also a real dilemma for the expert witness, who may accept an invitation to give evidence for a client and be drawn gradually into defence of a case in which he does not really believe. Academics, used to presenting several sides of an argument, may find this all too easy, yet the ultimate result can be that the public loses faith in the value and impartiality of the expert witness.

One final point on the question of the effectiveness of Stage V for discussing research. The cost-benefit framework turned out to be an excellent framework for structuring the debate since its comprehensive nature together with its need for clarity in assumptions makes the issues to be resolved much clearer in principle. Perhaps this may be why many of the lawyers – not forgetting the legally untrained but natural forensic genius Councillor Derrick Wood of the Action

Committee against Foulness – seemed able to grasp the logical structure of the study better than their expert witnesses. On the other hand there may be some doubt as to how far they were really convinced by the numbers in the evaluation tables.

I now turn to the second issue of this section. How did the public inquiries work as an exercise in public participation? I think the answer must be that Stage II was pretty successful, but Stage V much less so. The public had disappeared, to be replaced by its lawyers and its experts. At the end of Stage V the lawyers seemed to me to be reasonably happy that 'justice would be done'. The experts, as I have indicated, seemed less happy: some would only perhaps have been happy if their models had been adopted in entirety. But the public did not know what had happened. Interested parties were quick to spot this, and to provide their own version of events, in easily digestible form. The media, who might have provided a watchdog role, were 'turned off', not by the complexity of the issues so much, I believe, as by the detail and depth. No planning correspondent could have been expected to sit through the ninety-odd days of hearings at the Piccadilly Hotel, fascinating, instructive and occasionally hilarious though they were.

To have solved this problem would have required a positive approach on the part of the Commission to managing the media, or more generally managing its public relations. This it did not do, and deliberately did not do, believing that it was not its job to sell its solution. This was a matter of principle, not of dignity; the principle being that judicial independence can be jeopardised if decisions have to be made 'acceptable'. Certainly trial by television could have seemed a trivialisation of the issues – though as it turned out it was a presentation by Jack Saltman on BBC TV which went furthest of the media towards presenting a balanced view. Perhaps the Commission believed that the government should be free to make up its mind on the report, without added pressure from the Commission. But the government, faced with an enormous selling job to the electorate on joining the Common Market, was not likely to relish also having to sell Cublington to an alliance ranging across a good deal of the Establishment from the *Daily Telegraph* to the environmental lobby. If one single factor could explain the failure of the Commission to get its recommendation implemented, perhaps it was its not using the media to put across the Commission's assessment of the evidence. Months after the Commission had reported, my well-informed next-door neighbour thought that Foulness would be the worst site for weather because of the coastal fogs – yet all the inland sites had poorer visibility on account of low-lying cloud. And there were singularly few issues which, although firmly resolved at the hearings, did not become used again as part of the subsequent debate. The very depth and detail of the analysis was thus to some extent its downfall.

IMPLEMENTATION

> They're going to build an Airport on the sands at Shoeburyness,
> They'll build a score of motorways – the cost you'll never guess,
> They'll subsidise the railways as the fares grow less and less
> But they'll never get the passengers to fly!

Frank Thompson, in a paper given to an International Symposium on Airport Location Methodology in 1971 pointed out the significant differences in the decision-making process of the two stages of deciding on a location for the third London airport. Each stage can be thought of as consisting of analysis and decision-making. In the first stage analysis was carried out by the Commission's research team and by experts engaged by other parties: the Commission made its assessment based on the analysis and evidence submitted to it. The first stage ended with a recommendation to the minister.

In the second stage government departments took over the analytical role, using as raw material the Commission's report and other papers together with any further material submitted or available to them. They were not usually able to question witnesses or evidence. The Cabinet became the final decision-maker. Thompson's next point is worth quoting verbatim.

> One peculiarity of the formal procedure may be noted in passing, namely, the fact that while in each of the two stages analysis and decision-making are closely intertwined, there are virtually no significant linkages between the two stages themselves. On presentation of its report, the work of the Commission Members and their Research Team is complete, their Members then dispersing, and playing no role in the second stage, that is to say, the Commission does not have the opportunity of defending its report against criticism, or of rebutting criticism from those engaged in the second stage of the process.

Most writers on the problems of implementation, or how to improve the effectiveness of research, have suggested that success or failure depends to a significant degree upon the extent of interplay or feedback between decision-makers and analysts. This feedback would normally include such things as an exchange of views and eventually a consensus on decision criteria, an explanation and acceptance by decision-makers of the methodology before the results are known, and the ability of decision-makers to ask and receive answers to supplementary questions in the form of sensitivity analysis or otherwise.

In its role of decision-maker, the Commission followed this pattern just about perfectly: not surprising therefore, on the theory, that the Commission's report followed closely the analytical work carried out. But in its role of analyst for the government, the Commission was unable or unwilling, or both, to adopt the same line. In doing so it was not being wilful or foolish, nor, I think, was the government: it was following a precedent reflecting an attitude to the separation between analysis and decision-making which is deeply entrenched. Analysts are technicians, doing what they are told. Commissioners are men of judgement invited to express a responsible, authoritative view, which in part derives its authoritativeness from the supposition that no attempt is made to influence them by government. So the analogy was a false one.

Unfortunately, false analogy or not, it seems there may be valid implications for the effect of Commissions. Of course one case does not make an argument, and anyway governments will always, and for very well-understood reasons, want sometimes to undertake activities against the advice of the most dispassionate and objective weighing of the pros and cons by Commissions of judgement. In a democracy they cannot be prevented from doing so except in constitutionally pre-defined areas.

Still, it is at least arguable that Commissions ought to want their recommendations to be implemented and so ought to make it easy, not difficult, for governments to do so. Men of judgement and standing might be expected to want this both in terms of the national interest and of their own job satisfaction – there may be some bitter satisfaction in saying, now that Stansted once again looks like being the third London airport, 'I told you so'; but surely small compared to seeing one's recommendations accepted. Would not the trouble, expense and indignity of a positive, even aggressive, public relations policy have been worthwhile?

When the Commission reported in December 1970, Mr Crosland was in opposition and John Davies was at the Department of Trade and Industry which had taken over from the Board of Trade. It was, however, Peter Walker, Secretary of State of the newly formed Department of the Environment, who announced the government's acceptance of the Commission's recommendation on timing, 1980, and the rejection of their recommendation on site, Cublington, in favour of Foulness, the site recommended by Professor (now Sir Colin) Buchanan in his Note of Dissent. The Heath government had departed, and Crosland was back in office, when the plan to construct a third London airport at Foulness, now re-christened Maplin, was finally dropped, inevitably postponing the timing of the introduction of a third airport to, at the earliest, the mid-1980s.

This might suggest an association of the Commission's work with a political slant and a naive explanation of the rejection of its site recommendation could be that the methodology used by the Commission for airport planning was associated with a political ideology more congenial to the Labour than to the Conservative Party. This conclusion would be mistaken in my view. The ideology of ministers was important, but not just in terms of a left/right distinction. The ideology of the civil servants involved was also significant, and so was the method of presentation of the Commission's findings to the public and the role of pressure groups of many different kinds.

Whitehall mandarins distrusted the Commission's work; the experts were claiming to go too far in resolving the issues – and in so doing they were revealing one of the, in the mandarins' view, familiar drawbacks of experts, namely, that there were rival experts who disagreed hotly. Powerful departments like Defence were being asked to swallow their least favourite site. An ambitious minister with a new and ambitious department could claim the choice of Foulness was an indication of the government's concern for the fashionable cause of the Environment with a capital E. (It was said that Peter Walker regretted that the cost of Foulness was not even more in excess of Cublington, since if it had been the government could claim to be placing an even higher value on the environment – forgetting, or pretending to forget, that many of the environmental factors were already taken into account and that Foulness carried serious environmental costs as well as the inland sites.) Mr Heath himself, though still in his 'Selsdon' phase, was more of a pragmatic free-enterpriser than an old fashioned liberal, as subsequently proved by his famous volte-face; besides, he played the organ at a church near Cublington. It was left to Tory liberals like Nicholas Ridley and social democrats like Bill Rodgers to argue the Commission's case in the Commons. And even they did not get a chance to do so until the House of Lords had fulfilled its familiar role as a front for all the major establishment pressure groups in the country. The mauling that Roskill got in the Lords would have been difficult for any report to survive.

Whether the Commission got what it wanted for decision-making from the hearings, the public participation was far from de-fusing the issue once the recommendation was made. Buchanan was not the only person who had only to help himself from the vast array of material to construct his own partial case. Possibly the representatives of pressure groups who sat in the Piccadilly Hotel during Stage V of the Commission's hearings and listened to the evidence being tested were convinced of the fairmindedness of the decision-making process. But those they represented were certainly not – or if they had been would it have made any difference? After all the location of an airport stands to benefit some and harm others. Should the losers cease to protest just because they are told their losses have been outweighed by others' gains? Maybe if the Commission's compensation proposals had been immediately adopted by the government the blow would have been softened, but the anti-Cublington lobby was a powerful body and had interests which would not be consoled by compensation. So many came to think, following the Roskill experience, and other similar experiences, that perhaps research combined with public participation is a way of providing the maximum ammunition for your opponents, who will not necessarily be dedicated to obtaining the best solution in the interests of the community as a whole.

Some people have argued that the Commission's work must have been wrong, since the government failed to accept it. I have tried to say the (very limited) sense in which I believe this to be true and the more basic sense in which I believe it to be false. In the end three propositions, not provable, appear nevertheless to be probably correct: that the Conservative government of 1970–4 would always have chosen Foulness; that the development of this site would have been an enormously costly failure; and that Roskill's work ensured that it would eventually have to be dropped. So, except for some unlucky residents near Stansted, perhaps it was a success after all.

ACKNOWLEDGEMENTS

The passages heading each section are taken with gratitude from the anonymous unpublished Technical Appendix to the Roskill Commission's Report.

I am deeply indebted to the Right Honourable Lord Justice Roskill, to Professors Alan Day, John Heath and Peter Self, to Dr Christine Whitehead, to Martin Bulmer and to Frank Thompson for quick and penetrating comments on the first draft of this chapter. None of them is responsible for its errors.

APPENDIX: RELEVANT OFFICIAL PUBLICATIONS

(a) Publications of the Commission on the Third London Airport 1969–72

Papers and Proceedings, Volume I, Stage I: Public Hearings part 1, Written and oral evidence.

Papers and Proceedings, Volume II, Stage I: Public Hearings part 2, Other written evidence.

Short List of Sites and Site Information for Stage II Local Hearings

1 Foulness (offshore)
2 Nuthampstead
3 Cublington (Wing)
4 Thurleigh (Bedford)

Papers and Proceedings, Volume III, Stage II: Local Hearings Foulness (offshore)

Papers and Proceedings, Volume IV, Stage II: Local Hearings Nuthampstead

Papers and Proceedings, Volume V, Stage II: Local Hearings Cublington (Wing)

Papers and Proceedings, Volume VI, Stage II: Local Hearings Thurleigh (Bedford)

Papers and Proceedings, Volume VII, Stage III: Research and Investigation, Part 1, Assessment of the Short-Listed Sites: Proposed Research Methodology.

(All the above published in 1969 by HMSO.)

Papers and Proceedings, Volume VII, Stage III: Part 1 as above and Part 2, Results of Research Team's Assessment.

Papers and Proceedings, Volume VII, Stage III: Part 3, Maps, Diagrams and Design Study Drawings.

Papers and Proceedings, Volume VIII Stage III: Part 1, specially commissioned studies (Airport City).

Papers and Proceedings, Volume VIII, Stage III: Part 2, Section 1, specially commissioned studies (various).

Papers and Proceedings, Volume VIII, Stage III: Part 2, Section 2, specially commissioned studies (airspace factors).

Papers and Proceedings, Volume VIII, Stage III: Part 2, Section 3, specially commissioned studies (various).

Papers and Proceedings, Volume VIII, Stage III: Part 2, Section 4, specially commissioned studies (sociological study).

Papers and Proceedings, Volume IX, Stage III: public evidence.

(All the above published in 1970 by HMSO.)

Report of the Commission on the Third London Airport 1969–72 (London: HMSO, 1971).

(b) Other government publications

Traffic in Towns (London: HMSO, 1963).

Report of the Interdepartmental Committee on the Third London Airport, CAP 199 (London: HMSO, 1964).

Report of the Inquiry into Local Objections to the Proposed Development of Land at Stansted on the Third Airport for London (London: HMSO, 1967).

The Third London Airport, Cmnd 3259 (London: HMSO, 1967).

Maplin Airport, Choice of Sites for Runways (London: Department of the Environment, 1972).

Report of the Advisory Committee on Trunk Road Assessment (London: HMSO, 1977).

REFERENCES

P. W. Abelson and A. D. J. Flowerdew (1972), 'Roskill's successful recommendation (with discussion)', *Journal of the Royal Statistical Society*, series A, 135, pp. 467–510.

B. Abrahams, A. D. J. Flowerdew and J. U. M. Smith (1978), correspondence on 'SOSIPing, etc.' by G. J. A. Stern (see below), *Operational Research Quarterly*, 29, pp. 173–9.

Rt Hon. Lord Boyd Carpenter (1976), 'Airport planning in the UK: past, present and future', *Fifth World Airports Conference* (London: ICE).

R. de Neufville and R. L. Keeney (1972), 'Use of decision analysis in airport development for Mexico City', in W. Drake, R. L. Keeney and P. M. Morse (eds), *Analysis of Public Systems*.

A. D. J. Flowerdew (1972), 'Choosing a site for the third London airport: the Roskill Commission's approach' in P. R. G. Layard (ed.), *Cost-Benefit Analysis* (Harmondsworth: Penguin).

C. D. Foster, *et al.* (1974), *Lessons of Maplin*, IEA Occasional Paper 40, (London: Institute of Economic Affairs).

P. Hall (1970), 'Roskill's felicific calculus', *New Society*, 19 February, pp. 306–8.

J. B. Heath (1977), 'Roskill revisited' in M. Posner (ed.), *Public Expenditure-Allocation between Competing Ends*.

N. Lichfield (1971), 'Cost-benefit analysing in planning: a critique of the Roskill Commision', *Regional Studies*, 5, pp. 157–83.

D. McKie (1973), *A Sadly Mismanaged Affair* (London: Croom Helm).

E. J. Mishan (1970), 'What is wrong with Roskill?', *Journal of Transport Economics and Policy*, IV, 221–34.

J. Parry-Lewis (1971), *Mis-Used Techniques in Planning No. 4*, Parts I and II, Occasional Paper No. 11 (Manchester: University of Manchester Centre for Urban and Regional Research).

P. Self (1970), 'Nonsense on stilts: the futility of Roskill', *Political Quarterly* (July).

P. Self (1975), *Econocrats and the policy process. The politics and philosophy of cost-benefit analysis* (London: Macmillan).

G. J. A. Stern (1976), 'SOSIPing or sophistical obfuscation of self-interest and prejudice', *Operational Research Quarterly*, 27, pp. 915–29.

F. P. Thompson (1971), 'The final framework for the assessment of the analysis. Commission on the Third London Airport' in *International Symposium on Airport Location Methodology* (London: Planning and Transport Research and Computation Co. Ltd).

F. P. Thompson (1978), 'Investment planning: is airport cost-benefit analysis dead?', *Symposium on financial aspects of the UK airport industry* (London: Polytechnic of Central London).

A. Williams (1973), 'CBA: bastard science and/or insidious poison in the body politick?' in J. N. Wolfe (ed.), *Cost-Benefit and Cost Effectiveness Analysis* (London: Allen & Unwin).

Chapter 8

The Younger Committee and Research

GERALD RHODES

The Committee on Privacy under the chairmanship of Mr K. G. (later Sir Kenneth) Younger was set up early in 1970 and reported in July 1972. Under its terms of reference it was required to consider the need for legislation to give further protection to individuals and commercial and industrial interests against intrusions into privacy, but an important restriction was that it was to consider only intrusions arising from the activities of private individuals, organisations and companies. The Social Science Research Council, with its general interest in the problems of research for government Committees of Inquiry, secured agreement to attach an observer to the Younger Committee who, with proper safeguards for the confidentiality of its proceedings, would be able to see papers and attend meetings in order to assess how members of the Committee viewed the need for research, how they set about getting research done, the problems they encountered and the use they made of the research findings. The following account is the report of myself as observer.

THE NEED FOR RESEARCH

Before the Younger Committee was appointed various proposals had been made to create a statutory general right of privacy, and one of these, Mr Brian Walden's Right of Privacy Bill which was debated in the House of Commons in January 1970, was the immediate occasion of Mr Callaghan's announcement of the appointment of a committee. The framework of the Committee's deliberations was therefore set by the basic problem of whether the threat to privacy was one which could be met by specific remedies in the different areas in which it might arise or whether in addition there should be statutory provision conferring a general right of privacy.

The Committee had little in the way of information or guidance when it began its assessment of the problem. Most subjects investigated by committees have at least a nucleus of accepted opinion from which investigation can begin. For privacy there was not even an accepted definition, and intrusions into privacy seemed to mean anything from neighbours peering over the fence to sensational stories of industrial espionage. Right at the start of the Committee's proceedings the Home Office identified four main areas of public concern: the increasing use of computers; the use of electronic devices such as concealed microphones; intrusion by the press and broadcasting; and commercial and industrial activities including the activities of private detectives, the sending of unsolicited circulars, particularly those advertising manuals of sexual techniques, and industrial espionage. The identification of specific areas of concern in this way was of importance right through the work of the Committee, not least in connection with its use of research. But it was clear that, whatever decision the members of the Committee eventually came to on the general right question, they would have to examine a considerable number of disparate topics falling within their terms of reference.

Why did the Committee decide to commission a survey of public attitudes to privacy, and what did it hope to get from a survey? Given the nature of the Committee's subject of inquiry and the lack of any firm information about the meaning and importance of privacy, it was natural that it should wish to establish whether there existed widespread anxieties about intrusions into privacy, or whether perhaps certain particular developments, such as the possibility of misuse of computerised personal information, were largely responsible for the undoubted increase in discussion of the issue in recent years. These questions were important both to the Committee's treatment of individual aspects of the privacy issue and to the argument about a general right. The difficulty was to find a way of getting reliable information about public attitudes. A certain amount of information was available about complaints which had been made; for example, there had been a number of complaints to the Press Council about intrusions into privacy by newspapers; again, the Home Office reported that they had had many complaints from people who had received through the post circulars advertising sex handbooks. But these in themselves did not indicate how far there was genuine and widespread anxiety about invasion of privacy.

This problem was evident in July 1970 when the Committee did not feel that it justified commissioning a survey; it did however agree then, in accordance with normal practice, to issue an invitation to the general public to put in evidence, and an advertisement to this effect appeared in the press in the middle of August. The total response from members of the public resulting from this and other publicity was 214 letters, over half of which fell outside the Committee's terms of reference; all the members of the Committee agreed that this represented a very small response. And indeed it was this small response that prompted the Committee to give consideration in September 1970 to commissioning a survey of public attitudes.

It is important to stress the negative element in the chain of events which led to the decision to commission a survey. On the face of it, the response to the public advertisement seemed to indicate very little public concern over the question of privacy; and this in turn was a factor influencing some members of the Committee to believe that concern which had been expressed elsewhere might be exaggerated. But in view of the lack of other direct evidence it seemed doubtful whether the Committee would be justified in taking this view simply on the basis of the response to a public advertisement. A public attitudes survey would be one way of testing whether this apparent lack of concern truly represented public feeling.

More positively, a survey might provide a means of checking against independent evidence some of the claims and assertions which the Committee would receive from the evidence of organisations and other interested parties; it might also throw up areas of concern of which the Committee would otherwise have been unaware. However, it was recognised that the nature of the subject would make it difficult to devise a survey which would be expected to yield reliable positive information of this kind.

The lack of response from the general public to the Committee's publicity is stressed in the Committee's report as a major reason for undertaking research in the form of a survey of public attitudes. But perhaps public reaction or lack of it is best seen as something which alerted the members of the Committee to the importance of a problem which had been there from the beginning but to which hitherto they had not really directed their attention. When they did seriously consider it in September 1970, they were all agreed that they ought to try to get information on the views of the general public, and that a sample survey was the way to do this. It might only confirm what some members already suspected, that there was not a widespread concern with intrusions into privacy, but this in itself was an important and necessary piece of information for the Committee to have.

GETTING THE RESEARCH DONE

Once the decision had been taken in September 1970 attention was concentrated on practical problems of getting the research done. The first task was to decide on the scope of the survey, but the Committee soon had to face the familiar twin problems of time and money which condition all research work.

At its meeting on 23 September the Committee considered and approved an outline scheme for the public attitude survey drawn up by the Secretary. The scheme had two main objects: first, to see how important the concept of privacy was to people interviewed, and, secondly, to test the strength of their reactions to particular examples of intrusions into privacy. A further aim was to see how attitudes varied with age, sex or social class. To carry out the first of its main aims the Committee proposed that people should be asked what they understood by privacy, and then how they regarded protection of privacy in relation to fundamental rights such as freedom of speech, or to current issues such as reducing unemployment. The second aim was to be achieved by asking whether people had suffered intrusions into their privacy by specific means such as the activities of private detectives or press publicity, and whether they thought that the law should be strengthened to deal with these and other specified examples of intrusion.

Armed with this outline scheme, the Secretary next had to try to get it put into operation as quickly as possible. This involved negotiations with, first, the Home Office Research Committee, which has the important task of co-ordinating the Home Office programme of requests for social surveys for submission to the Office of Population Censuses and Surveys (OPCS) and, in particular, indicating priorities among them. OPCS likewise, when it receives programmes of requests from the various departments, has to decide priorities according to its resources.

The Secretary accordingly wrote to the Home Office Director of Research and Statistics on 24 September asking him not only to put the proposal for a public attitudes survey to the Research Committee, but also to give it the highest priority, perhaps even so that it could be started before 1 April 1971. The reason for the urgency was that the Committee was aiming to prepare its report in the summer of 1971, and it therefore needed the results of the survey by early summer if it was to give them adequate consideration.

At their meeting on 21 October the Research Committee agreed to make the Younger Committee's proposed public attitudes survey the first priority in the Home Office's 1971–2 programme for submission to OPCS. On the basis of past experience this assured the survey of an early start in April 1971. The survey, although by no means negligible in size – it was to cost £15,000 – did not present any great financial problem in terms of the OPCS's annual budget for surveys of £820,000 in 1971–2.

The outcome of this meeting seemed to be highly satisfactory to the Younger Committee. But there was one snag, and it concerned the timetable. In the course of discussions it had emerged that even if the survey began on 1 April 1971 the results would not be available at least until September, and would thus be too late to be taken into account if the Committee maintained its provisional timetable. In the event, the Home Office took up the Committee's request with the Treasury who agreed that the relatively small amount of money required to begin preliminary work on the survey should be made available on OPCS's 1970–1 vote, thus enabling work to start in January 1971.

The Committee's attitude was that if the survey was to be of any use the results must be available about the middle of 1971; it therefore supported the attempt to get the starting date brought forward. At no time did it consider that it should alter its own timetable and postpone production of its report in order to permit adequate discussion of the survey findings if it finally transpired that they could not be available until the autumn. Rather it was prepared to abandon the survey if the results could not be ready earlier.

Thus the first and more formidable hurdle had been cleared with comparative ease. Following discussions with the Home Office Research Unit and OPCS the Secretary then put proposals to the Committee at its meeting on 25 November. These elaborated the outline discussed earlier, providing for the survey questions to fall into four groups: what people understood by privacy; how important they thought it was; whether they had experienced intrusions into their own privacy and what they had done about them; and whether they thought that there should be a legal prohibition on each of a number of specific but hypothetical examples of intrusion to be put to them.

The Committee endorsed the Secretary's proposals with only minor modifications. From this point onwards the arrangements for the survey were largely in the hands of the experts, particularly at OPCS and Research Bureau Limited (RBL), the private organisation engaged by them to carry out the work. Early in 1971 the latter carried out a pilot survey, in the light of which they proposed certain modifications to the questionnaire, including the omission of a group of questions designed to find out how fast people thought privacy was being eroded. The Chairman and Secretary of the Committee discussed these proposals with the Home Office Research Unit, OPCS and RBL on 23 February 1971, and they were later put to the whole Committee on 18 March with an invitation to members to approve the final form of the questionnaire. This was the first occasion since November on which the Committee had discussed the survey, although it had been kept informed of progress meanwhile. The constraints of time and expert knowledge which operate in this field of research are well illustrated by this March meeting. Some members were not happy about the fact that RBL had decided to frame the questions dealing with hypothetical intrusions into privacy as if they had happened to those who were being interviewed. These members wanted the questions expressed impersonally. The Chairman, although pointing out that to make any substantial alteration to the questionnaire at that stage might jeopardise the timetable of the whole survey, agreed to put this point to RBL. The latter replied politely but firmly rejecting the request mainly on the grounds that it would unduly lengthen the interviews. The Committee had to be content with this answer.

THE RESEARCH FINDINGS AND THEIR IMPACT ON THE COMMITTEE

One problem which faces all committees which commission research is that during the interval when they are awaiting the results their work is continuing and may result in somewhat changed perspectives on the problems which have been remitted to them. In the case of the Younger Committee, nearly nine months elapsed between the time when the survey was given the go-ahead in October 1970 and the presentation of the preliminary findings by Research Bureau Limited in the middle of July 1971. Before discussing these findings it is therefore essential to indicate briefly how the work of the Committee had been going during those nine months.

It was agreed at an early stage that discussion of the question of whether there should be a general right of privacy should be postponed until progress had been made in discussing measures to deal with specific aspects of intrusion into privacy. Naturally, a good deal of the time of the Committee was taken up with consideration of evidence, both written and oral, but increasingly its attention focused on a small number of important issues which linked up closely with the areas of concern originally identified by the Home Office. They included: were the safeguards against intrusion into privacy by the press, radio and television adequate? Did the increasing use of computers pose an actual or potential threat to privacy? Ought the activities of private detectives to be more carefully controlled? What, if anything, could be done about the use of 'bugging' and other devices for observing people's activities and listening to their private conversations?

Apart from the evidence which came from such diverse bodies as the British Computer Society and the Church of Scientology, Worldwide, the Committee relied chiefly on two other sources of information; the activities of the secretariat, and the reports of two sub-groups of the Committee. The secretariat produced a series of papers reviewing the literature and evidence on individual aspects of the Committee's work, and calling attention to the areas where decisions would be needed. All this was a normal secretarial function but especially important in this case because of the wide range of topics to be examined. Of the two sub-groups set up, one was concerned with the technical legal question of the extent to which existing law gave effective protection against certain forms of intrusion into privacy. The other was asked to examine 'alternative means of controlling the handling of information by computers'.

This latter group was important not only for the influence which it had on the Committee's recommendations in one of the more difficult areas of inquiry. It also contributed to the Committee's thinking on some matters relevant to the public attitudes survey. In particular, the sub-group argued that fears about the invasion of privacy by computers had been exaggerated, and related more to potential future use than to existing use; moreover, these fears were particularly concerned with the public sector, which was outside the Committee's terms of reference.

It may be said then that by the middle of July 1971, on the eve of receiving the preliminary results of the public attitudes survey, the members of the Committee were already fairly clear about which areas of inquiry were the most important; moreover, they had not read or heard anything which inclined them to move away from their first tentative view that intrusion into privacy was not a subject of widespread anxiety on the part of the general public. The question was whether the findings of the survey would confirm or rebut these views.

Protecting people's privacy was rated as only moderately important by those interviewed in the survey when compared with general issues such as keeping down prices and reducing unemployment; on the other hand it was rated as the most important of a group of social isues which included improving race relations and protecting the freedom of the press. Less than half of those interviewed said, even after prompting, that they had themselves suffered an intrusion into their privacy during the previous year. Among those who had, the largest area of complaint was about interfering neighbours, followed closely by callers at the door, especially Jehovah's Witnesses, and unwanted material through the post, such as advertising for *Reader's Digest* or for sex manuals. Few mentioned intrusion by the press or private detectives or in connection with computers.

Those taking part in the survey had been given thirteen examples of possible intrusions into privacy. In each case they were asked to say whether they thought there was an intrusion, whether they would be annoyed or upset if the incident happened to them, and whether they thought such activities should be prohibited by law. The most decisive response in favour of legal prohibition arose from a question concerned with computers, but this is not surprising given the nightmarish possibilities conjured up by the form of the question.[1] Large majorities were also in favour of banning by law postal advertising of manuals of sexual techniques, and the publication in newspapers of details of wills and proceedings in minor court cases. Some activities which were strongly regarded as intrusions into privacy (for example, prying neighbours and religious canvassers) were nevertheless not thought to require prohibition by law to anything like the same extent.

The findings briefly summarised above were in line with the Committee members' expectations; they saw them not as providing much in the way of new information but as confirming the views to which they were already tending. This was especially true in relation to the large general questions of the meaning of privacy and how important people felt its protection to be. In the report they did not commit themselves to a definition of privacy, believing that it was a concept which could not be satisfactorily defined. It is not therefore surprising that Research Bureau Limited in their report on the survey commented that most people had found it an extremely difficult question, and their replies could not easily be reduced to neat categories for analysis.

On the importance of privacy the Committee noted in its report that the survey and other evidence confirmed 'what a few moments' intelligent reflection makes obvious' (para. 105); for example, that everyone needs some privacy, that the more you have the more you cherish it, and so on. Certainly the survey indicated that 'people who have become accustomed to privacy prize it the more highly' (para. 79), but it was not possible 'to state in general terms how much or how little privacy is necessary' (para. 113). Again, the fact that protecting privacy was ranked highest in the survey among a number of social issues was not viewed by the Committee as being of any great significance. For one thing, protecting privacy appeared in both lists of issues and some people might have guessed that the interview was about privacy and therefore given it a higher rating. Secondly, the survey seemed to indicate that many people were valuing privacy in relation to the dangers of interference with personal liberty by a totalitarian government and this may have helped to give it an importance which it would not have had if a more restricted definition had been chosen.

Given this general view of the Committee, it is interesting to see how it treated some of the findings relating to specific examples of intrusion into privacy. The Committee recognised that the form of the question on computers at least partly accounted for the very strong response in favour of strengthening the law, but it also thought that: 'the response suggests that the idea of easy access to personal information is regarded as objectionable by the vast majority of people' (para. 576). This reflects the fact that at a very early stage the members of the Committee had concluded that the use of computers would be among the most important issues with which they had to concern themselves, and that it was apprehension about the future rather than what was happening at present which was the main concern. The survey findings fitted in with this approach.

On the question of postal advertisements for sex manuals the Committee's attitude was rather different; in spite of the relatively large volume of complaints about this practice and the confirmation of public attitudes by the survey, it was doubtful whether to regard this as an intrusion at all (para. 421). Even if it was, it did not think it sufficiently serious to justify further legal protection (para. 425).

Similarly, on the question of publication of proceedings in minor court cases, the Committee took the view that it would be wrong to impose a ban by law. Here, however, much more than in the case of sex manuals, it was influenced by evidence from other sources, and by the need to weigh conflicting principles. The Magistrates' Association, the police and the press all argued strongly that it would be wrong to suppress the identities of those involved in court cases; and the Committee agreed that the 'free reporting of defendants' identities in ordinary proceedings in magistrates' courts' should be maintained (para. 174). It dealt more briefly with the question of publication of wills, mainly because it did not fall within its terms of reference to discuss information made available by law by a public authority.

By contrast, in two cases where a large majority of those interviewed in the survey were against local restrictions (private detectives and credit rating agencies) the Committee, as a result of its deliberations and of other evidence, concluded that there were serious problems and that some strengthening of the law was desirable. There were in addition other areas of investigation which were of great concern to the Committee but scarcely touched on in the survey, particularly industrial espionage and the use of technical devices for watching or listening to other people's activities.

Nothing in the survey of public attitudes to privacy caused the Committee to change its views. Its report would have reached essentially the same conclusions and used the same arguments even if there had been no survey. The significance of the survey lies in two other directions. First, its status was that of a piece of rather special evidence. True, it was a relatively minor piece in terms of its effect on the Committee's thinking; but it was the only evidence which came neither from interested bodies nor from individuals with a grievance. It was, within the normal limitations of sample surveys, unbiased and objective. Secondly, and arising from this, its chief function was to give reassurance to the members of the Committee. Without the survey they would have felt uneasiness at the possibility that there might be some area of public anxiety about protection of privacy which other sources of information had not disclosed. With the survey findings they could state with more confidence where public anxieties lay. To say this is to say that the survey fulfilled a marginal but nevertheless useful role in the Committee's activities.

CONCLUSIONS

Time and money, but especially the former, are the main practical problems for Committees of Inquiry which intend to commission research. Most research which goes beyond analyses of existing data is time-consuming, whereas committees are frequently under pressure to report quickly. David Donnison suggests in Chapter 2 that it is not really possible to reconcile these differing time-scales, and that committees may have to rely chiefly on whatever research is already being done in their field of inquiry.

The problem of time-scale must, however, be related to the committee's basic attitude to research. It is most acute for those committees which regard research as vital, and which would find it difficult if not impossible to do their work without it. There are other committees, however, where research is not seen to be quite so important. It is rather a means of filling what would otherwise be gaps in the sources of information. In its absence the work of the committee would not be so adequately done as the members would like but the loss would not be disastrous. Clearly the Younger Committee falls into this second group.

Conditions were favourable to the Younger Committee. It had good liaison with the sponsoring department, perhaps the most important condition for success in commissioning research. It was helped by the fact that the Home Office Research Unit and Committee, with a relatively long tradition of research in the social sciences, were both alert to the possibilities of research and responsive to the requests made to them. The result was that questions of time and finance were resolved as satisfactorily as they are ever likely to be. Yet even so it was by no means certain that research would go ahead, because the Committee would have abandoned the attempt to carry out a survey of public attitudes rather than modify its timetable if it had not been possible for the results to be ready by the middle of 1971. If it had felt that the research was indispensable it might have been faced with a very difficult choice in such a situation.

This suggests that one should look at possible ways of dealing with the time problem where committees regard research as a vital part of their work, other than relying on whatever work happens to be in progress, as David Donnison proposes.

There are two approaches, one general and one specific. In general, it can be argued that committees are often set up to consider issues which over a period of time have become matters of increasing public concern; government departments, therefore, might do more to try to anticipate the need for an inquiry, and themselves engage in or commission research in areas of growing public concern. This is already done to some extent. The fact that the Home Office Research Unit was largely set up as a research unit in criminology reflects a conscious need for more reliable information in this field. But perhaps research units in departments need to be strengthened and their scope broadened. This question was touched on by the Heyworth Committee, although it made no very positive recommendation about it.[2] Such a development might benefit many committees. The Younger Committee, for example, found that there was a dearth of information in Whitehall on the subject of privacy, and its task might have been easier if some research had already been done on it.

There are obvious difficulties in the way of extending the scope of departmental research, not least in deciding priorities where resources are scarce. Moreover, there would still remain specific questions which a committee set up to investigate a particular problem might want to examine more closely. Hence it has been suggested that sponsoring departments might themselves plan research for a particular committee in advance of its appointment, so that presumably once the committee was in being it would be presented with a programme and timetable of research already in progress. It is argued by Sir Andrew Shonfield in Chapter 5 that this would help to ensure more effective use of the limited time available to committees, and that this advantage would outweigh the limitation on the traditional freedom of committees to decide their own procedures.

These suggestions raise wide issues about the purposes which Committees of Inquiry serve and the nature of the research appropriate to them. It might be thought, for example, that extending the scope of departmental research would bring less need for committees since the research could point to the solution of certain problems which otherwise might need to be examined by a committee. There are, however, other purposes which committees may serve, such as providing reassurance after some particular incident has aroused public concern, or focusing public attention on the complexity of the issues involved in a particular problem. Perhaps then this suggestion, although it may be valuable in relation to committees, is best seen as helping more generally to contribute to informed discussion of matters of public concern.

Again, advance planning of research for a particular committee may be useful where the committee's main function is to produce a quick answer along lines which can be fairly well predicted; and where the research is on a relatively limited scale. But sometimes the matter is not so urgent, possible lines of action more open and thorough analysis of the problem is the all-important consideration. A committee which is in this situation and which is not content simply to accept whatever research is already being done independently may have no alternative but to commission further research. If so, the consequential effects on the committee's timetable must be accepted. These questions cannot be answered simply from the experience of one committee with the problems of research.

NOTES: CHAPTER 8

1 The question was: 'In a few years' time from now, it may be technically possible for details of your life such as family circumstances, financial situation, political views and so on to be recorded on a big central computer, with any of the information being available to anyone who asks for it; would you regard this as an invasion of privacy etc.?' The questionnaire and the report on the survey by Research Bureau Limited are reproduced as Appendix E of the Committee's *Report*, Cmnd 5012 (London: HMSO, 1972).

2 *Report of the Committee on Social Studies*, Cmnd 2660 (London: HMSO, 1965), paras 128–40.

Chapter 9

Research for the Royal Commission on the Press, 1974–7

JEREMY TUNSTALL

ROYAL COMMISSIONS ON THE PRESS: HOW TO MAKE POLICY IN A NON-POLICY FIELD?

As a field for commission investigation, the press has a number of unusual characteristics. In the press, the traditional policy is of not having a policy. 'Press freedom' is seen as requiring minimal policy interference. Secondly, in the press, politics is inevitably salient. The British press historically is the offspring of party politics; and now that the formal links between party and press have almost entirely been dissolved, the salience of politics within the press is, if anything, heightened. Press Commissions are set up for party political reasons; consequently if their proposals are to achieve wide acceptance they must appear non-partisan.

Thirdly, any Royal Commission on the press is confronted with an industry whose mythology and ideology are (compared to those of industries of similar public importance) remarkably free of challenge. Some of the core mythical assumptions of the press industry survive only because they are so little and so unsystematically examined by that main public challenger of assumptions – namely, the press itself.

Press Commission chairmen, members and staff have – compared with many other Royal Commissions – been remarkably lacking in previous knowledge of the subject. Because the subject is regarded as a non-policy one, there is no single Whitehall department with expertise over the broad field of the press; consequently the staff of civil servants have no departmental tradition of expertise upon which to rely. Because the field is so politically charged, both politicians and the leaders of the press industry are excluded from membership. The members of Royal Commissions on the Press have relatively little previous systematic knowledge of the subject. Moreover academics with press research experience nevertheless lack experience of policy-oriented press research.

The third Royal Commission on the Press (1974–7) was, in addition, extremely unfortunate in the death of its original

Chairman, Sir Morris Finer, seven months after his appointment. This Press Commission was unusual also in the quantity and variety of research which it undertook. The July 1977 report tells us that the cost of 'investigation and research work' was £242,027. The Commission's thirteen published volumes included 2,241 pages of research findings and 404 pages devoted to two reports, though none of the written and oral evidence appeared in print.

Also unusual was the crescendo of public controversy surrounding the press during the life of the Press Commission. The Commission was set up in 1974 in the midst of rapid inflation and the related economic difficulties which affected the press especially severely. The economic crisis affecting the press was the focus for one of several linked controversies. A second was the vexed question of 'new technology' – the electronic revolution in the press. Third was the controversy over the issue of a 'closed shop' journalism. Fourth was the transformation – by takeover and by diversification – of the British press into an industry consisting largely of subsidiary press companies within oil, paper, banking and other companies. Fifthly, throughout the 1974–7 life of the Press Commission the popular Fleet Street national newspapers (all four of them tabloid, after the *Daily Express* switch to the smaller size in January 1977) were engaged in a ferocious sales war to the death.

These various press controversies received massive press coverage which largely overshadowed press coverage of the Royal Commission itself. Some of this coverage of the press – especially over the journalists' 'closed shop' issue – reached a quantity and level of passionate self-justification not previously seen in the British press since 1945. Any press commission is in a delicate position, in that the press holds the potent sanction of being able to drown its report at birth. This Press Commission's own public relations were, in my view, badly handled and it received a substantial amount of hostile news coverage. A tendency inside the Commission to dismiss almost any policy proposal as 'politically impractical' rested partly on the fear that the national press might drown at birth not only a particular proposal but the entire final report.

Two polar opposite assessments of the 1974–7 Royal Commission on the Press (and of the contribution of research to it) seem possible.

Paul Johnson – an active member of the Commission – wrote an approving account of its work. In his view[1] the Commission's report was an intelligently conservative, realistic and efficient document, which sagely dismissed all the various schemes for intervention in the affairs of the press. Johnson also thought the eleven volumes of research findings stood as a solid and impressive achievement in their own right.

A second, and radically opposed, assessment is that the Commission's report was a doctrinaire and brazen justification of a press industry now corruptly dominated by monopoly profit and international capitalism. The research programme is seen as the ineffectual victim of a profoundly reactionary report.[2]

THE POLICY CONTEXT

There have been three Royal Commissions on the Press in Britain – the Ross Commission of 1947–9, the Shawcross Commission of 1961–2 and the McGregor Commission of 1974–7. Despite significant differences in their terms of reference and methods of approach, a strong family resemblance exists between all three Commission reports. This resemblance partly derives from their common dilemma – policy-making in a non-policy field. The 1974–7 Commission had to confront the Press Council and the press monopoly legislation which were the main consequences of the first and second Commissions respectively. The two earlier reports were about the only two documents it could safely be assumed everyone – staff, members, witnesses, researchers – had all read in common. The earlier reports were also the best two post-1945 repositories of facts about the press. A benchmark in many subtle ways, they were the most persuasive indications of how such a slippery subject-matter should be subdivided into topics and issues which could eventually be turned into chapters in the final report. The earlier reports were benchmarks also in the sense of a standard to be surpassed: 'We must at least do better on this than Shawcross.'

The first, 1947–9, Royal Commission was set up by the Attlee government after pressure from National Union of Journalists members both inside and outside Parliament. It had a slightly unreal existence because, under newsprint rationing, papers were still extremely thin and many accusations (for example of 'black lists') were poorly substantiated and relatively trivial. The terms of reference were wide – encompassing free expression and accuracy as well as ownership and control. This Commission largely rejected the criticisms which lay behind its being set up. Its main recommendation was the Press Council – a proposal which the press only finally accepted six years later (and then in watered-down form) after a government threat of legislation. The Ross Commission's concern with editorial performance was also reflected in its pioneering research efforts; its civil service staff did some crude but useful content analysis mainly of the press in 1946–7. The Ross Commission nevertheless had some severe weaknesses; it failed to grasp the a-typicality of the times in which it existed, and ignored television.

The Ross Commission also mis-read a slight reduction in concentration of ownership in the 1930s. The Commission said that it would regret further concentration in national, or provincial, newspapers, magazines or newsagencies, but thought such further concentration improbable. It was soon proved wrong in each case. A final weakness was the Ross Commission's overwhelming concern with national newspapers.

The second Royal Commission (1961–2), appointed by a Conservative government, was intended as a relatively quick investigation with terms of reference largely restricted to the finance and ownership of the press. This Shawcross Commission had only five members (against seventeen for Ross) and lasted only a year and a half (against just over two years for Ross). In the mid-1950s newsprint rationing had ended, commercial television had appeared, and a wave of closures and takeovers had swept through the press. The closure of the *News Chronicle* and a mammoth three-way merger (which resulted in the *Daily Mirror* and a large slice of the magazine industry merging into what became IPC) were the main precipitating events. The Shawcross Commission once again reported that the existing level of concentration was not excessive but recommended monopoly legislation to prevent any more major mergers between large press companies. This fairly modest proposal was enacted in somewhat watered-down form in 1965. The Shawcross Commission's main 'research' effort consisted of a management consultant's report which found Fleet Street production to be heavily overmanned. Shawcross favoured (again implicitly) the retention of a dominant national press in Fleet Street. It also favoured strengthening of the Press Council, and rejected various schemes for market 'interference' and the re-distribution of advertising revenue. The Shawcross Commission's strategic failure was in not recognising that the events of 1955–61 were only the beginning of a long press adjustment (especially to television). For example, the very next year, 1963, was a record year for closures of competing provincial dailies.[3] The Shawcross Commission, in recommending legislation against major press mergers, failed to anticipate the future focus of concentration on to local *weekly* newspapers and a tendency for press companies in trouble to seek survival as subsidiaries of non-press companies. Most remarkably the Shawcross Commission failed almost entirely to consider the profound consequences for the press of the emergence of television.

When the third Press Commission was established in 1974, the weaknesses of the Ross Commission and especially of the Shawcross Commission were easily understood. In the first year of this third Commission, members and staff seemed agreed that they would have little difficulty in doing better than the Shawcross Commission.

Nevertheless the McGregor Commission devoted much attention to the chief consequence of the first Commission, the Press Council, and (like the second Commission) called for it to become stronger, but without teeth. The McGregor Commission also devoted much attention to the chief consequence of the second Commission – the press merger legislation – and called for some tightening up there. McGregor re-emphasised Shawcross's concern about Fleet Street production overmanning. The McGregor Commission's Interim Report was entirely concerned with the plight of national newspapers, and it saw salvation in reducing manning, plus new (electronic) plant. Finally McGregor wanted to preserve the dominant British press in Fleet Street. While McGregor differed from its predecessors in saying this explicitly, there was no explanation as to why London (along with Tokyo) should retain its dominant national press – despite the strong trend in virtually every other Western democracy (including France and West Germany) towards a stronger *provincial* press pattern.

While considering the 1974–7 Commission in the context of its two predecessors, some further points may be made.

First, there was a *political* failure – a failure to recognise that the press is an industry like no other primarily because of its political importance. Any analysis which concentrates on more 'objective' financial factors is inevitably ignoring the central issue. The third Press Commission was, like the others, set up for political reasons – especially Labour Party anxiety over Rupert Murdoch's bare bosoms approach with the *Sun* (which not only replaced the old pro-Labour *Daily Herald*, but also threatened the *Daily Mirror*). The more immediate Labour Party initiative was a policy booklet called *The People and the Media*, which demanded several kinds of state intervention. These proposals were indeed poorly (or not at all) thought out; but the Commission in rejecting them failed to acknowledge a worrying political reality – a major reduction in all-party support for the established press order.

Secondly, there was – as with earlier Commissions – a failure to explore the full implications for the press of radio, television and other electronic media. As with its two predecessors, the 1974–7 Press Commission ran concurrently with a Broadcasting Committee (the Annan Committee, 1974–7). This arrangement should have made monitoring of the development of the other media both convenient and easy. But there was no attempt even to keep abreast of evidence submitted to the Committee on Broadcasting. There was only one joint meeting of members and occasional contact between the two Chairmen. This was strange in view of the

McGregor Commission's faith in the press electronic revolution – a revolution which brings 'press' and 'broadcasting' ever closer. There was no attempt even to estimate the likely sum of lost advertising which would result from another advertising-financed television channel.

A further weakness was the tendency to segment the subject-matter into watertight compartments/chapters, without noticing major inter-chapter inconsistencies. For example the 'new technology' already means in other countries that journalists keyboard their own words into print; any fairly inclusive British journalists' trade union must thus become much more powerful, (in effect a journalist–compositor union). This rather strategic point is not considered in the chapter on the 'closed shop' in journalism.

Another failure to make obvious connections is as follows. The McGregor Commission strongly favoured the survival of Fleet Street's eighteen newspapers (nine morning, seven Sunday, two evening). However, it rejected 'state subsidies' (or favoured such a minimal form as to amount to rejection). But loss-making is predicted to remain common. Thus a non-state source of subsidy is required. By default this becomes an implicit endorsement of Fleet Street newspapers as loss-making prestige subsidiaries of mainly non-press conglomerates.[4]

Finally the McGregor Commission, despite some pleasant nineteenth-century quotations, was remarkably a-historical. Although not a great deal of policy-relevant literature on the British press did exist, the Commission largely ignored some which did, including two important historical studies.[5]

While the two previous Royal Commission reports carried excessive influence, developments between 1949 and 1961 and between 1962 and 1974 remained by comparison *terra incognita*. No attempt was made, for example, to acquire a back-run of the trade press, and it was surprising to find as far as two years into the inquiry that some of the major press events of the mid-1960s were unknown to Commission staff and members.

GENESIS AND CHRONOLOGY

The Royal Commission's account of its own genesis appears in the Final Report (pp. 2–3):

> We were set up in May 1974, and began work in September . . . In announcing his intention to appoint the third Royal Commission, the Prime Minister [Harold Wilson] referred to the problems of the Beaverbrook newspaper group, which had just closed its Glasgow printing plant, and to the dangers of a further

> restriction on the public's choice if other papers were to close. A debate on 14 May, initiated by the Opposition, cast light on the preoccupations of the Government in resorting to a Commission, and of members on all sides of the House of Commons.
>
> References were made to the economic and production difficulties of the press, often attributed to overmanning, and to the dangers to diversity of choice arising from further concentration of ownership. Apart from this, there were two main themes: the balance between ensuring for the press 'as much freedom as possible on matters of public interest while leaving the individual better protected from harmful intrusions into his privacy', and the insistence of Labour members that the general political tendency of the national press was hostile to the Labour Movement . . .
>
> In the debate, the Opposition took the view that all the facts were known and that enquiry could only delay the action needed to modernise production . . .
>
> In July 1974, the Labour Party published a discussion document, *The People and the Media* . . . Later on, in evidence to the Commission, the Party adopted the main proposals in the document as their official policy . . .
>
> Our appointment was not widely welcomed . . . most newspapers, both editorially and at management level, were at best lukewarm and suspicious of the Government's motives in establishing the Commission. Of the unions in the industry, only the NUJ welcomed the Commission.

The timetable of the Press Commission – with particular emphasis on its research programme – is set out in Table 9.1. The key precipitating event was the general election of February 1974, which marked the end of the 1970–4 Conservative government; the minority Labour government inevitably meant another election soon (it occurred in October 1974) and the Prime Minister may have seen the setting up of a Press Commission and a Broadcasting Committee as a means of exerting pressure on the media. In the February 1974 election the *Sun* had editorially supported the Conservative Party, giving the Conservatives better than two to one support on a circulation basis among the national daily newspapers.

Immediately after the February election, transparently inspired press stories began to forecast both a Press Commission and a Broadcasting Committee. Canvassing within the government and the Parliamentary Labour Party took place over the terms of reference and the membership. The setting up of the Royal Commission on the Press was announced on 2 May; the Chairman was to be Sir Morris Finer, a personal friend of Harold Wilson. Finer, a judge in

Table 9.1 *The 1974–7 Royal Commission on the Press and its research timetable*

Timetable of the Royal Commission and major events in the press	*Research timetable*
2 May 1974 RCP (Chairman Sir Morris Finer) announced by Prime Minister	
25 June 1974 Ten members of RCP announced	
July 1974 RCP Secretary appointed	18 July 1974 First research proposals made to RCP
	23 Sept. 1974 First RCP research meeting
7 Nov. 1974 'Topics for Consideration' (in written evidence)	
15 Dec. 1974 Death of Sir Morris Finer	
Mar. 1975 Professor O. R. McGregor as new RCP Chairman	
Apr. 1975 NUJ ADM	
	May 1975 ACAS industrial relations studies commissioned
	July 1975 Q to provincial newspapers
18 Sept. 1975 Interim inquiry requested into National Newspaper Industry	Sept. 1975 Q to wholesalers
	Sept. 1975 Financial Q to national newspapers
	Sept. 1975 Mail survey, journalism recruitment
	Sept. 1975 Fieldwork, public attitude survey
	Oct. 1975 Fieldwork, influentials survey
	Oct. 1975 Q on employment and earnings in national newspapers
Sept.–Nov. 1975 First main round of oral evidence	Oct. 1975 Newspaper content analysis began
Mar. 1976 Second main round of oral evidence	March 1976 Mail survey, editors and journalists
17 Mar. 1976 *Interim Report* published	
April 1976 NUJ ADM	
	June 1976 Q on 'related holdings'

Table 9.1 *Continued*

Timetable of the Royal Commission and major events in the press	*Research timetable*
	July 1976 Supplementary Q to selected provincial newspaper centres
Nov. 1976 The *Observer* bought by Atlantic-Richfield	
19–21 May 1977 *Daily Mail* 'slush fund' story	
1 July 1977 Trafalgar House buys Beaverbrook Newspapers	
7 July 1977 *Final Report* published and some research volumes	
1 Sept. 1977 Remaining research volumes published	

the Family Division of the High Court, was unusual among judges in being of Jewish working-class background.

Seven weeks later ten members for the Commission were announced. This group was criticised both in the press and in Parliament as being too pro-Labour and three new members (Bishop, Chorley, Silbertson) were soon added. The appointment of the Commission's Secretary was announced in July.

Meetings of the Commission members did not commence until September and Sir Morris Finer died suddenly (of cancer) in December. The new Chairman, Professor O. R. McGregor, was only appointed (again after the personal involvement of Prime Minister Harold Wilson) in March 1975, although he had been elected as temporary Chairman by his colleagues immediately after Finer's death. Professor McGregor was a personal friend of Sir Morris Finer and had recently served under his chairmanship on the Committee on One-Parent Families.

The chairmanship of Sir Morris Finer thus lasted for four preliminary, relatively inactive, months and for only three months of active work. In terms of research, however, he showed an active interest. The first research proposals were made in a letter (from myself) dated 18 July 1974; the first meeting (attended by Finer, McGregor and Chorley for the RCP, and by Colin Seymour-Ure, Oliver Boyd-Barrett, James Curran and myself) to discuss research was on 23 September. Further memos and discussions followed and the RCP was broadly (but vaguely) committed to conducting some research by the time of Finer's death.

The only 'research' activity of any significance to occur in this phase was the compilation of a list of 'Topics for Consideration' mailed out on 7 November as a guide to potential providers of written evidence. This document was composed by Finer and the Commission's Secretary and inevitably reflected their early relatively high degree of unfamiliarity with the field.[6]

Phase two (roughly 1975) was marked by a quiet opening period, during which the RCP had its first major series of meetings. A number of inquiries and research proposals were also discussed, the first major ones to be commissioned dealing with industrial relations. The autumn of 1975 also saw the launching of the main phase of a range of research projects – financial inquiries, sample surveys and content analysis. It was during this autumn also that several academics (having previously worked one day a week) became for a year three-day-a-week consultants to the Commission. Cynthia White, Denis McQuail, Colin Seymour-Ure and Jeremy Tunstall all worked on approximately this basis for academic year 1975–6. We thus all worked as academic consultants on a part-time basis and each of us contributed just under one year of full-time work equivalent. The Commission had no Director of Research.

In September 1975 the Commission was asked by the government to produce an Interim Report on the National Newspaper Industry. This request arrived just as the Commission was involved in its first main phase of oral evidence.

The major event of 1976 was the appearance in March of this Interim Report. McGregor as Chairman, supported by two members (Chorley and Hunt) worked on a nearly full-time basis – first assembling the Interim Report and secondly becoming involved in an intensive series of meetings with employers and trade unions in Fleet Street. These meetings resulted in the establishment of a Joint Standing Committee intended to introduce the 'new technology' for which the Interim Report argued. The Interim Report thus constituted not only a financial/industrial relations report, but also represented a highly complex piece of industrial relations negotiations as well. The Interim Report inevitably had a great impact on the whole Royal Commission exercise. It concentrated the minds of the Commission once more upon the *national newspapers* and led the Commission into – in my stated view at the time – a quite mistaken view of the 'new technology' as *the* solution to *the* problem. It thus had the indirect consequence of making other problems and other solutions less central. After this point the Commission largely closed its ears to any new ideas whether from the evidence or the research. The request for an Interim Report had been predictable[7] and, with hindsight, probably the government's request should have been rejected.

The original suggestion for an Interim Report came from Lord Goodman, who (as well as being on friendly terms with the leading members of the Labour government) was Chairman of both the Newspaper Publishers' Association and the *Observer*. This latter was the most vulnerable of all the Fleet Street newspapers. The Interim Report provided no direct help and after discussions with many possible buyers – including several in Fleet Street and in the international oil industry[8] – the *Observer* was in November 1976 bought by Atlantic-Richfield, one of the twenty largest companies in the United States.

Also during 1976 the bulk of the research studies were completed, and the latest of the research studies initiated.

The Final Report was published in early July 1977, meaning that the first half of 1977 was taken up mainly with writing, agreeing and publishing the report. About half of the research volumes were published with the Final Report; the remainder were delayed for a few weeks by industrial action at the printers and their publication was further deliberately delayed until 1 September. A point here (which presumably affects other Royal Commissions) is that the printing and publication occur at great speed – in days rather than in months. At least as far as the research volumes are concerned this speed of publication contains hidden dangers – allowing the research volumes to reach final form only a few weeks before their publication and that of the report. An accidental consequence of this timetable is to allow research to miss its deadlines without hazarding the final publication deadline.

The publication of the Final Report was somewhat overshadowed by two further events. First a particularly blatant and untrue story in the *Daily Mail*, which the Prime Minister (James Callaghan) asked the RCP to discuss in its report; the Commission chose (as usual) a compromise – agreeing to look at the case, but more briefly than the Prime Minister wanted. The RCP was seen once again to exhibit the twin bad habits of bowing to obvious political pressure and itself indulging in instant journalistic coverage of day-to-day controversies.

The second closing event was the takeover (again after much speculation and takeover bidding) of the *Daily Express, Sunday Express* and *Evening Standard* by Trafalgar House – a construction, shipping and real estate conglomerate. The RCP report had nothing to say about who should or should not be allowed to take over the group in question (even though the financial troubles of the *Daily Express* had contributed to the RCP's being set up). The timing of the Trafalgar House takeover – a week before the publication of the Final Report – made cruelly clear what Fleet Street (and to some extent the government, which was consulted) thought of the third Royal Commission on the Press. It also provided one more instance which could be quoted as evidence that this Commission's entire timetable was dogged by misfortune.

Certainly the timetable of the Commission was marked by unforeseen events. The greatest of these was the death of the first Chairman, Sir Morris Finer; but to my mind it is unlikely that the Press Commission would have done better under his chairmanship. The various political-economic events which undoubtedly affected the Commission can only be claimed to have blown the Commission off course if some previous and wiser course could be discerned. The request for an Interim Report could still have been accepted, but in my view the Interim Report itself should have said that the basic problem in Fleet Street was not overmanning, but over-subsidisation (for reasons of prestige and power) of an over-dominant national press – to which the solution is fewer titles. In this light the crises of the *Observer* and the Beaverbrook Press could have been met with a consistent policy. They should both have been allowed to die – a free market solution – in preference to being purchased by wealthy conglomerates whose motives were of a diffuse prestige (that is, power) kind, by a Press Commission whose terms of reference called for knowledge and examination of just such motives.

TERMS OF REFERENCE, MEMBERSHIP, STAFF

The terms of reference for the 1974–7 Press Commission were wider than for either of its two predecessors:

> To inquire into the factors affecting the maintenance of the independence, diversity and editorial standards of newspapers and periodicals, and the public's freedom of choice of newspapers and periodicals, nationally, regionally and locally, with particular reference to:
>
> (a) the economics of newspaper and periodical publishing and distribution;
> (b) the interaction of the newspaper and periodical interests held by the companies concerned with their other interests and holdings, within and outside the communications industry;
> (c) management and labour practices and relations in the newspaper and periodical industry;
> (d) conditions and security of employment in the newspaper and periodical industry;
> (e) the distribution and concentration of ownership of the newspaper and periodical industry, and the adequacy of existing law in relation thereto;

(f) the responsibilities, constitution and functioning of the Press Council;

and to make recommendations.

The terms of reference for the Interim Report were also quite lengthy, although they pointed much more narrowly: 'to examine urgently the financial situations and immediate prospects of the national newspapers'. Also specifically mentioned were 'new technologies', and the need to introduce change 'in a socially acceptable way'. These interim terms of reference showed every sign of being a compromise negotiated between the Fleet Street employers and trade unions, as well as the Department of Trade and the Royal Commission itself.

The membership of the Royal Commission (after Sir Morris Finer's death) was as follows and this is how they described themselves – to givers of oral evidence – in September 1975:

Chairman:
Professor O. R. McGregor Professor of Social Institutions, London University, and Head of Department of Sociology, Bedford College. Director, Centre for Socio-Legal Studies, Oxford University and Fellow of Wolfson College, Oxford.
Members:
Mrs Elizabeth Anderson Freelance writer, Past President, Church of Scotland Women's Guild. She represented that organization on the Women's National Commission from 1971–3.
Mr David Basnett General Secretary, General and Municipal Workers' Union.
Mr G. S. Bishop Chairman, Booker McConnell Ltd. Served in the Ministry of Food (later Agriculture, Fisheries and Food) from 1940 until he joined Booker McConnell in 1961.[9]
Mr R. R. E. Chorley Chartered Accountant. Partner in Coopers & Lybrand. Acted as accounting adviser to the National Board for Prices and Incomes from 1965 to 1970, and as consultant to the Post Office Users' National Council. Member of the Finance Committee of the National Trust and member of the Tribunal set up under the Finance Act 1970.[9]
Mr Geoffrey Goodman Industrial Editor, *Daily Mirror*.
Professor L. C. B. Gower Vice-Chancellor of Southampton University. Professor of Commercial Law, London University 1948–62; Law Commissioner, 1965–71. Trustee of the British Museum.[9]
Mr Malcolm Horsman Deputy Chairman and Joint Managing Director, the Bowater Corporation Ltd.

Lord Hunt Leader, British Expedition, Mount Everest, 1952–3. Chairman, Parole Board for England and Wales, 1967–74.
Mr Paul Johnson Author. Editor of the *New Statesman*, 1965–70.
Mr John Eilian Jones Managing Editor, *Caernavon Herald Group*.
Mr Ian Richardson City Editor, *Birmingham Post*.
Miss Eirlys Roberts Deputy Director, Consumers' Association.
Mr Z. A. Silbertson Official Fellow in Economics since 1971 and Dean since 1972, Nuffield College, Oxford. Courtaulds Ltd from 1946 to 1950, and University Lecturer in Economics at Cambridge from 1953 to 1971. Member of Monopolies Commission 1965–8 and appointed a member of the British Steel Corporation in 1967.[9]

The point most widely noted in the press was that four members were journalists. But these particular four had little else in common. Ian Richardson's dissenting note to the Interim Report and Geoffrey Goodman's signature of the Minority Report in the Final Report made this abundantly clear. Paul Johnson's views on the press were – in conventional political terms – more similar to his currently hostile views on trade unions than to the socialism he had favoured when the editor of the *New Statesman*.

More significant probably was that nearly all of the members were men aged in or around their fifties and resident in the south-east of England. There was one Welshman and one Scotswoman. As usual the Commission was strong on legal, academic, economics and business backgrounds. Easily the strongest area of expertise was in finance/accountancy/economics and general management.

There was no single power behind the Chairman's throne on this Commission. The nearest person to this role was probably the accountant Roger Chorley – who was the key specialist in the three-man group (including Professor McGregor and Lord Hunt) which produced the Interim Report. Chorley also was the dominant force behind all of the Commission's numerous financial inquiries and questionnaires; however, he made little effort to push his views in other areas and he was not, for instance, a regular attender at oral evidence sessions.

McGregor was very much the most active member of the Commission. After him came a loose group of Chorley (specialising in finance), Lord Hunt (journalist's training), Aubrey Silbertson (monopoly, economics) and Paul Johnson. Then came an outer ring of other members, also concerned mainly with specialist topics.

Two members of the Commission could be said to be pro-Labour politically, and among the other twelve members there was a fairly identifiable consensus which stretched from Lib-Lab views across several shades of Conservatism; this political consensus overlapped with the main financial-economic expertise of the Commission. My impression was that most of the members were readers of *The Times*. There was – not surprisingly considering the weight of financial expertise – a noticeable inclination to leave financial questions to the experts. The issues which carried the widest interest among all the membership were broadly questions of editorial content; the Press Council attracted the largest single turnout of members for an oral evidence session.

The staff were of course mainly civil servants – although an accountant was also drafted in. But this was less of a shoe-string operation than some have been; the Commission's total expenditure was £731,533, some of which paid for an adequate back-up force of executive grade and clerical civil service staff. The Commission staff were responsible to the Department of Trade, but – because Harold Wilson and James Callaghan each took a special interest – the staff were also aware of watching eyes in Downing Street.

There were three senior members of the staff, two administrators and one economist. None had any previous experience either of the press or of Royal Commissions, and only one of the three had any obviously relevant expertise. Two of the three had Oxbridge degrees in English literature. One consequence of these backgrounds was that the overwhelming weight of recognisable expertise resided not on the staff but among the membership.

The consequence of this staff/membership balance was that neither seemed to view it as their function to develop policy ideas. The membership (with their economic/financial expertise and experience) and the staff (with their civil service experience) both sat there waiting for someone else to shoot up proposals which they could then shoot down.

This put the policy onus mainly upon the givers of evidence and the researchers, but neither of these groups did much in the way of proposing policies – most of the evidence-givers preferred to defend their particular corner of the status quo and most of the researchers were hesitant in offering policy proposals on the grounds that this would be trespassing on the members' preserve.

Thus, while this Royal Commission received a great deal of evidence and set up lots of research, at the centre of the operation – the more active members and the senior staff – there was an atmosphere of shoulder-shrugging and occasionally of somnolence. The work of the Commission was dominated by the Chairman and the Secretary and by their concern to run a tidy ship with the minimum of untidy dissent and minority reports. The Final Report was largely written by the two senior staff members.

STYLE OF APPROACH

During the first year, it was conventional wisdom in the Commission that the formal evidence would probably not reveal a great deal. Although this expectation was reflected in the decision not to publish any evidence, the evidence did strongly influence the outcome.

Written evidence was the most important single source of material available to the Commission in its first year. The best and most thorough evidence was produced by the largest press groups: Times Newspapers' evidence was perhaps the best argued, Mirror Group Newspapers' evidence was the most detailed and the Liverpool Post and Echo was about the best of the provincials. The industry-wide bodies – the trade associations, the trade unions and bodies like the Press Council – were in most cases rather lightweight in both quantity and quality. The Labour Party, the Trades Union Congress and the National Union of Journalists were all extremely weak.

Oral evidence was provided on invitation (and usually after further questions via correspondence) by forty-five bodies. Newspaper and magazine groups, and industry-wide associations and unions provided most of the oral evidence. The commonest number of Royal Commission members present was four (out of fourteen); only rarely was any kind of research data used as a basis for questioning.

Visits were made by Commission members and staff to a number of press organisations in London and the provinces, including a visit to Dundee. Most such visits were extremely brief. Also very brief were visits paid to West Germany, France, the Netherlands, Sweden and the United States. Only sketchily prepared, these foreign visits produced only brief and impressionistic reports back to the majority of members. The present writer argued for the deliberate choice of three regions of Britain where research could have been focused; my advice was also in favour of sustained visits to a smaller number of countries such as France and Japan.[10] Despite two short visits to France, the Commission's information on the French press remained superficial; no detailed attention was paid to important questions such as new press technology in France or the decline since 1950 of the Parisian press (relative to the provincial press) and the lessons for Fleet Street.[11]

Meetings of the Royal Commission members usually took place on Friday afternoons – not perhaps the most wide-awake time of the week. There were four two-day meetings, and fifty-three half-day or full-day meetings. (The Interim Report three-man group had twenty-one separate meetings). This total of sixty-one days or half-days of full meetings was very similar to both the Ross and Shawcross Commissions. Both of those, however, lasted for shorter periods. The McGregor Commission averaged only about twenty meeting days per year.

It takes, in my view, at least six months for even a quick and intelligent mind to read, talk and think itself into a subject as subtle and complex as the British press. Initially the academic consultants were the only people who had already invested this degree of attention in the subject. Potentially, therefore, the influence of the researchers was probably greatest before any research had been done. The first people to achieve the 'six months full-time' level of knowledge were the senior staff members, followed by the Chairman, followed by some of the more active members. The bulk of the members were only achieving this level of knowledge during the closing flurry of meetings in the third year.

Well into the second year, the full meetings of the Commission (from occasional observation) appeared to be rambling and poorly informed; the visits appeared to be little more than jaunts whose real value was in building morale and consensus in other areas; and much of both the oral and written evidence matched the most cynical early predictions. The Commission was thus inevitably influenced by those few organisations, such as Times Newspapers and Mirror Group Newspapers, which produced intelligent evidence. These large press groups deployed impressive expertise in both management and editorial areas, on legal questions and in presenting their own survey research; they took the trouble to use senior (and politically experienced) journalist talent to get the documents decently written. These few groups produced the only impressive performances at the oral evidence; and they followed up those efforts with informal contacts.

The Press Commission's style of approach ensured by default, in my view, that the information supplied by the major press companies – the replies to financial questionnaires, the written and oral evidence, plus related correspondence and informal contact – was indeed the prime shaper of the final product.

THE RESEARCH PROGRAMME

The main investigations mounted by the Royal Commission and the main related publications are indicated in Table 9.2.

Table 9.2 *Investigations and publications*

Type of investigation	*Publication in which findings appear (All volumes published in London by HMSO for the Royal Commission on the Press)*
(1) *Financial investigations* (mainly by questionnaire, and including management consultants' report)	(a) *Interim Report: The National Newspaper Industry*, Cmnd 6433 (March 1976), 116 pp. (b) Final Report, Cmnd 6810 (July 1977), 298 pp.
(2) *Other research by the staff of the Royal Commission*	(a) *Concentration of Ownership in the Provincial Press*, Cmnd 6810–5 (July 1977), 121 pp. (b) *Periodicals and the Alternative Press*, Cmnd 6810–6 (July 1977), 73 pp.
(3) *Reports by the Advisory, Conciliation and Arbitration Service*	(a) *Industrial Relations in the National Newspaper Industry*, Cmnd 6680 (Dec 1976), 342 pp. (b) *Industrial Relations in the Provincial Newspaper and Periodical Industries*, Cmnd 6810–2 (July 1977), 158 pp.
(4) *Sample surveys* (by Social and Community Planning Research)	*Attitudes to the Press*, Cmnd 6810–3 (July 1977), 380 pp. Part 1: 'The attitudes of the general public', pp. 1–139 Part 2: 'The attitudes of people in influential positions', pp. 141–275 Part 3: 'Postal survey among editors and journalists', pp. 277–380
(5) *Content analysis*	Denis McQuail, *Analysis of Newspaper Content*, Cmnd 6810–4 (July 1977), 364 pp.
(6) *Reports by academic consultants*	(a) *Studies on the Press* (Sept. 1977) 397 pp. *Part A:* Oliver Boyd-Barrett, 'The Collection of Foreign News in the National Press, pp. 7–43 *Part B:* Colin Seymour-Ure, 'Science and medicine and the press'; 'Parliament and government'; and 'National daily papers and the party system', pp. 45–201 *Part C:* Jeremy Tunstall, 'Letters to the editor'; 'Editorial sovereignty' in the British Press; and 'The problem of industrial relations news in the press', pp. 205–397

Table 9.2 *Continued*

Type of investigation	Publication in which findings appear (All volumes published in London by HMSO for the Royal Commission on the Press)
	(b) Cynthia White, *The Women's Periodical Press in Britain, 1946–1976* (Sept. 1977) 85 pp.
(7) *Miscellaneous*	(a) *Appendices*, Cmnd 6810–1 (July 1977), 166 pp.
	(b) Rex Winsbury, *New Technology and the Press* (1975) 59 pp.
	(c) Denis McQuail, Review of Sociological Writing on the Press (1976), 86 pp.

Total pages = 2,645
Total retail price of publications = £39·05

(1) *Financial investigations.* These were conducted mainly by the staff of the Commission, and partly by Coopers & Lybrand (the accountancy firm in which Roger Chorley was a partner). The main instrument used was a mailed questionnaire – one questionnaire was of forty-eight pages, but most were quite short. The investigations provide much of the data for the Interim Report and for the first one-third of the Final Report.

(2) *Other research by the staff of the Royal Commission.* Some of this was further accountancy work done within the Commission's staff; but some – notably the report on the Alternative Press – was the work of non-accountant civil servants on the staff.

(3) *Reports by ACAS.* The Advisory, Conciliation and Arbitration Service was invited to produce reports on the national and provincial newspaper industries; these reports consider the structure of the industry, management and union organisation, the industrial relations set-up and then make recommendations for more efficient arrangements.

(4) *Sample surveys.* Further detail on the programme of sample surveys is provided in Table 9.3. All of the surveys were conducted by the public sector survey research specialists, Social and Community Planning Research.

(5) *Content analysis.* This work was undertaken by Professor Denis McQuail (then at the University of Southampton). The content analysis deals with the year 1975. It covers all national dailies, national Sundays and provincial mornings; a sample of provincial evenings and local weeklies throughout the United

Table 9.3 *Sample surveys*

Time of data gathering	*Subject of survey*	*Type of survey*	*Question-naires comple-ted*	*Response rate %*
Late summer –autumn 1975	Journalist recruits and trainees	National stratified mail survey	1,219	71
Sept. 1975– Jan. 1976–	Attitudes of general public to the provincial press	National sample. Interview survey.	2,401	77
Oct. 1975– Feb. 1976	Attitudes of people in influential positions	Headteachers, council officials, councillors, managing directors, and trade union secretaries in 12 evening newspaper circulation areas	350	87
Mar.–May 1976	Editors	National stratified sample. Mail survey	330	63
Apr.–May 1976	Journalists	National sample. Mail survey	911	43
TOTAL			5,211	

Kingdom; and more detailed content analysis of national daily coverage of three topics – industrial relations, social welfare and foreign news.

(6) *Reports by academic consultants.* These are reports on topics more broadly related to the performance of the press, and deliberately written in a more speculative way. Each of the eight papers deals with an area relevant to policy questions. Oliver Boyd-Barrett's paper covers the declining number of British press foreign correspondents. Colin Seymour-Ure's papers discuss, for example, the weakness of political parties (in contrast to governments) in relation to the press. One of Jeremy Tunstall's papers challenges the notion of the sovereign editor (and thus of the tendency of the serious newspapers to define 'press freedom' as the 'right of the editor to edit'). Cynthia White's paper looks at the market forces underlying the dramatic shifts in women's magazines in recent decades.

(7) *Miscellaneous*. This includes two Working Papers which were published before the Final Report. The Appendices volume includes ownership and financial detail and a summary of the sample survey study of journalists' recruitment and training.

Several additional pieces of research were not published. One was a study originally about local radio already under way at the University of Leeds to which some press questions were added. Another was a report summarising the broad shape of commercial audience survey research data (made available by IPC and other large press groups). Also unpublished was a financial questionnaire inquiry on pensions.

RESEARCH AND THE THIRD ROYAL COMMISSION ON THE PRESS

The main difficulties with the Commission's extensive research programme were its lack of guiding policy ideas or proposals, its lack of organisation and control, and its failure to incorporate much of the research into its Final Report. This may seem an ungenerous comment since the programme of research ultimately published bore quite a close resemblance to the programme of research outlined in my original suggestions of July 1974. This letter (to the RCP Secretary) suggested three types of research:

(1) *Surveys* of 2,000 journalists, 2,000 print workers and 1,000 managers; surveys in three contrasted regions each including 500 members of the public, 100 news sources and 100 advertisers; surveys related to specialised topics (such as the trade unions or crime) and involving journalists, news sources, advertisers and the public; and a survey with executives of publications launched and closed in the previous two years.

(2) *Topics for desk research* (to be done by Commission staff or outsiders) on: press profitability, subsidies in selected countries, Press Councils, recruitment and education of journalists and press managers, the PPITB, the issue of 'other' ownership interests, schemes for reducing local monopolies and their probable consequences, the probable decline of the British national press, the British news agencies, and a long list of questions relating to editorial standards.

(3) *Topics for management consultant/accountancy research*: the performance of press trade unions and managers, the press distribution system, the allocation of advertising between press and TV, and recently launched and ceased publications.

These suggestions did provide the starting point for a series of meetings. However, in these meetings constant demands from the researchers present for the provision of hypotheses, or policy ideas or policy scenarios to be tested, were constantly rejected. At the first research meeting (with Finer, McGregor and Chorley) on 23 September 1974 a two-page memo of my suggestions for the central thrust of the inquiry was read by all present and discussed at some length. It began as follows: 'The central question concerns the present dominance of London-based morning newspapers and magazines and of London-owned provincial evenings.' More detailed points were:

(1) 'Britain is unique among industrial nations in the concentration of morning and Sunday papers . . . '
(2) The exceptional concentration of this national press and of magazines and provincial dailies.
(3) The ownership of monopoly evenings by national groups.
(4) Britain unusual in Europe in not having papers owned by parties, politicians, or trade associations.
(5) Press ownership in commercial broadcasting unusual in Europe.
(6) 'There is now a strong trend for big press groups to be owned by larger companies whose main interests lie outside the media . . . a trend which brings Britain much closer to a pattern previously best exemplified by Italy, Mexico, Brazil and Argentina.'
(7) 'Britain is unusual in its almost total lack of university training in journalism and its complete lack of any university institute or unit devoted to research on the press.'
(8) 'Britain is the only country apart from the USSR which is both the base of an international news agency and has a monopoly national domestic news agency . . . '
(9) 'Finally the British press is unique in the extent of both its export and import links with the press of other countries.'

At this first meeting the four researchers present were asked for specific policy proposals. We deliberately declined to supply any at this point, but in the coming months we did frequently offer policy suggestions and ask for policy proposals upon which we could research.

There were, of course, several layers of factors behind this reluctance of the Commission's two Chairmen and its staff (as well as the members) to satisfy the researchers' demands for specific policy proposals: the tradition of the press as a non-policy field; the high degree of unfamiliarity about its subject within the Commission in its first year; the usual concern for ultimate unanimity and thus a tendency to shy away from anything as controversial as any worthwhile policy proposal was likely to seem.

The standard division of labour – members, staff, researchers – is probably particularly restrictive in a press commission; when the members – whose preserve this is – decline to indicate even very general policy proposals, then the staff and the researchers can only introduce their own proposals by stealth. A premium is thus placed on the maximum possible level of vagueness: 'Yes, I think monopoly looks as if it'll be important'; 'Yes, a question on the Press Council is bound to be useful, we'll have to say something on that'; 'No, old chap, we can't possibly show the questionnaire to the members or we'd waste all day on the first page'.

Despite considerable vagueness as to why the research was being done – and despite explicit awareness among both staff and researchers that research was often conducted and then ignored – nevertheless everyone agreed that research was a thoroughly good thing. It gave everyone a comfortable feeling of positive activity. A large number of separate studies were undertaken – somewhere between thirty and fifty separate inquiries according to definition. At least eight members of the Commission staff (above the clerical level) were involved; eight academic consultants were used; in addition there was the survey programme, the management consultant work and the ACAS reports. Between twenty-five and thirty people were thus involved in the research and other investigations.

The social research was controlled by Professor McGregor and the financial research by Roger Chorley, with the detailed control resting with the three senior staff civil servants. These five individuals could have held regular meetings attended by senior academic research consultants, the staff accountant, and the industrial relations adviser (Professor Sid Kessler of City University, who was deeply involved especially in the negotiations surrounding the Interim Report). This committee, had it met, would, however, have posed a threat to the Commission's authority. An attempt was made to form a Commission sub-committee on social research – but its purpose seemed mainly to be to enthuse two or three of the members; after a few meetings – at which topics apart from research were much to the fore – this sub-committee fizzled out.

The senior social researchers were frequently consulted on a wide range of topics and were shown quite a lot of Commission documents; but in general the research programme was uncoordinated and individual researchers worked in relative isolation – some of them unaware not only of the Commission's policy ideas, but even of other pieces of research on topics relevant to their own.

SURVEY RESEARCH

All of the survey research was done by a single organisation,[12] Social and Community Planning Research. Professor McGregor and the Commission Secretary attended some of the meetings with the survey executives. Nevertheless there was often a remarkable vagueness as to what should go into the questionnaires.[13] There was also very little guidance as to how this research would be written up and what policy ideas should be borne in mind. The most successful survey in terms of response rate was the one on 'Community Influentials'.

The journalists' survey illustrated all the problems – in particular the Commission's indecision as to whether such a survey should be done. First suggested by myself in July 1974, this survey was the subject of much doubt among some Commission members, and the subject of an increasingly exasperated flow of arguments, letters and memos from myself. It took eighteen months for the Commission finally to agree to a (mail not interview) survey of editors, and to another survey of journalists. This highly avoidable delay led to a rushed pilot study and a decision to sample via the National Union of Journalists' and Institute of Journalists' membership lists (against my advice to sample via employing organisations); these lists proved in some cases to be up to twenty years out of date. Following unfavourable publicity in the trade press[14] about the mailed questionnaires, a hostile debate ensued at the 1976 Annual Delegate meeting of the NUJ. The final successful response rate was only 43 per cent.

Reports on the surveys were written by the survey executives and published in *Attitudes to the Press*. The journalists' recruitment survey was completed well ahead of the others (mainly because one Commission member, Lord Hunt, showed an energetic interest) but despite the available year before it went for publication no attempt was made to request additional tabulations or to modify a commentary which to my mind gave a more favourable impression of the training scheme than was justified by the survey data. In my opinion all of the survey reports constitute only 'first draft' skimmings of the available data.[15]

THE ACADEMIC RESEARCH CONSULTANTS

The advantage of being only very loosely controlled or directed was that we were able to negotiate pieces of work which interested us and which we thought relevant. The main frustration was realising in advance that little attention would be paid to what we said. In some respects Denis McQuail's content analysis was the most successful piece of research, partly because it was closely matched to the Commission's terms of reference.

Colin Seymour-Ure's work was potentially the most important – because it dealt with the central dimension of politics and the press. Despite a very full and sympathetic hearing by the Commission members his central theme (that the British press is too much separated from party control) seemed to them not only unfamiliar but also bizarre.

Denis McQuail, Colin Seymour-Ure and myself were each given one long session with the Commission members (and a nearly full turnout of them) in which to discuss our research. We had other advantages – repeated informal access to the Commission secretariat and occasional meetings with the Chairman. We also had a good rough idea of what would and would not be acceptable to the Commission. We learned to put our own ideas somewhat indirectly. This, of course, enabled the Commission to ignore altogether the policy implications.

Two of the academic consultants had the experience of some of their work being in effect ruled out of bounds as involving distinct policy proposals which lay well beyond the broad Commission consensus of minor tinkering with the status quo. One of my requested papers was supplied in first draft form with the title: 'The British Press and its other business interests, or vice-versa'. This sixty-seven page paper argued that the British press was undergoing a crisis of legitimacy, the most serious part of which resulted from the ownership of major press groups by multi-nationals and conglomerates. The paper quoted among other unsavoury precedents the case of Weimar Germany – the control of much of the press by the Ruhr steel industry and Alfred Hugenberg pre-dated and facilitated Hitler's seizure of power. Because the reactions to this paper were so negative, my decision was not to re-write it but to submit public evidence to the Commission.[16]

James Curran had a somewhat similar experience with a paper written for the Commission entitled 'Advertising media planning and the British press 1945–75'. This paper argued, among other things, that advertising favoured newspapers read by middle-class people and penalised those read by working-class people. Only a very brief summary of this paper is published in the volume of Appendices.

RECOMMENDATIONS

In 1974–7 we had the peculiar phenomenon of two concurrent committees on press and broadcasting which not only largely ignored each other but also largely ignored some of the most central communications policy questions – the future allocation of advertising and the merging of press and broadcasting technologies, the rapidly increasing dependence of both on a state agency (the Post Office), and so on. Perhaps the solution might be two concurrent commissions with active liaison between the two inquiries written into the terms of reference of each.

For future Royal Commissions on the Press I suggest the following:

Terms of reference. These should explicitly call for a range of policy options – with one of the functions of a press commission being seen as stimulating debate rather than producing a bland and unrealistic consensus.

Staff. At least one senior member of the staff should have experience in social research, and one other member of the staff should have government information experience.

Members. The 1974–7 Royal Commission was weak on several sorts of relevant expertise, most obviously in management experience of the press, advertising, electronic engineering, broadcasting and academic research knowledge of the mass media. There was also no member from the north of England. In my view the level of political experience was inadequate; too many probably false assumptions were made about what was politically practical.

Research. Any future RCP will have an easier task here in that it will be able to see what the 1974–7 press research looked like and to think about where it went wrong. The central need must be to develop policy ideas or proposals or options or scenarios – to which research can be made relevant.

FINAL VERDICT

What of Paul Johnson's self-congratulatory view of the 1974–7 Press Commission and its research? Or are some of the scathing critiques of both Commission and research which appear in James Curran (ed.), *The British Press – a Manifesto* a fairer estimation?

In my view both accounts are mistaken. Paul Johnson is correct in thinking the Press Commission a 'conservative' body, but surely wrong in believing that only very minor changes in the British press are either desirable or practicable. And Johnson's friendly view of the research only makes sense if you broadly accept his belief that nothing much needs changing.

It does not please me to see Marxist critics apparently sharing with the conservative consensus on the Commission a belief in the inevitability of the British press being owned by oil companies and conglomerates. Nevertheless, the British press in the last twenty years does seem to me to have come in important respects to resemble what was previously a Marxist caricature. But the more ideological pieces in *The British Press – a Manifesto* are surely invalid on several other grounds. In terms of simple scholarly respectability some of the contributions are shoddy – few of the contributors have taken the trouble to read all of the Commission's volumes, and one or two have scarcely read the two report volumes. Some contributors expect the press single-handedly to right all the wrongs of society. And most lack any sympathy with, or insight into, the problems of a Royal Commission on the Press.

In my view the Press Commission had many weaknesses, especially its failure to confront in either of its two reports or in its eleven research volumes so many central questions. Even on the 'new technology' it is surprisingly weak on serious analysis, and blinkered to the medium-term consequences. In my view it has also largely failed even to analyse the central core of the Fleet Street problem – the nature of management and the preponderance of prestige (that is, political power) goals. It has missed also the power of the press to set and maintain an agenda; the radical reduction of Fleet Street is not yet on the agenda of the British press, or of Parliament or of British press commissions. It has failed to see that if you want to maintain Fleet Street, this means subsidies, and that Britain does already have state press subsidies (mainly VAT zero rating). The Commission too easily accepted the conventional wisdom of the press that public policy equals 'state interference', despite the historical fact that even in the 1870s public policy (in the telegraph) was crucial to the evolution of the British press.

The large quantity of research published does at least indirectly challenge much of the mythology of the British press. The reports – except where the language is deliberately ambiguous – are written with great clarity, which makes it all the easier to see their major internal inconsistencies. And compared with many other similar bodies – for example the Annan Committee on Broadcasting – the McGregor Commission on the Press is a paragon of clear thinking, clear expression, practical proposals and high-quality research.

NOTES: CHAPTER 9

1 Paul Johnson, 'Three years on the Press Commission', *New Statesman*, 8 July 1977.

2 James Curran (ed.), *The British Press – a Manifesto* (London: Macmillan, 1978).

3 In 1963 competing evening newspapers closed in Leicester, Leeds, Manchester, Birmingham, Nottingham and Edinburgh – reducing in a single year the number of provincial cities with competing evening newspapers from seven to one (Glasgow).

4 A point which is mentioned just once – in the Final Report, para. 15.31.

5 e.g. Political and Economic Planning, *Report on the British Press* (London: PEP, 1938). This is in many ways still the most important and policy-relevant single document on the British Press. Other works which the present writer tried (largely without success) to bring to the Commission's attention included J. Edward Gerald, *The British Press under Government Economic Controls* (Minneapolis: University of Minnesota Press, 1956); and Graham Cleverley, *The Fleet Street Disaster: British National Newspapers as a Case Study in Mismanagement* (London: Constable, 1976).

6 The present writer was shown this document in draft. My advice (16 October) was that the document was 'slapdash' and inadequate. 'The answers you get to this document will tend to shape the whole of the remainder of the study.' My advice was to take the document through several more drafts; another draft was discussed at a meeting of Finer, the RCP Secretary and myself on 6 November. In the final version, mailed out the next day, eleven of the thirty-three questions were taken wholly or partly from my suggestions.

7 The present writer in fact suggested that the expected Royal Commission should perhaps produce 'an interim report dealing with the immediate problem of certain extremely vulnerable publications'. (Letter published in the *Guardian* in late March 1974, several weeks before the RCP was set up.)

8 See the *Observer*, 28 November 1976.

9 Appointed in addition to the original Chairman and ten members. Professor Gower was appointed after the death of Sir Morris Finer – presumably to fill the legal gap.

10 My letter of 12 January 1975 to the RCP Secretary suggested that Japan was 'the most important single case, and the one which contains the largest number of lessons for Britain'. This letter accompanied a requested paper on the French press; visits were later made to Paris, Lyons and Bordeaux – all suggested in my paper. However, the RCP did not take my advice to look at France in detail.

11 The only more than superficial work on the press of another country was Rex Winsbury's work, *New Technology and the Press*, (London: HMSO for RCP, 1975).

12 My advice from the outset was to split the surveys between at least two survey organisations.

13 My suggested list of questions formed the starting ground for four of the five questionnaires. In the fifth case, the starting ground was a document entitled 'Training and education in, and for, journalism', signed by Oliver Boyd-Barrett and myself.

14 *UK Press Gazette*, 26 April 1976.

15 Repeated questions, when the surveys were being commissioned, as to how they would be written up and re-written, were invariably brushed aside.

16 Jeremy Tunstall, *Will Fleet Street Survive until 1984?*, unpublished evidence to the Royal Commission on the Press, March 1977.

Chapter 10

The Royal Commission on the Press, 1974–7: A Note

O. R. McGREGOR

I am grateful for the opportunity to add a footnote[1] to Professor Tunstall's account of research for the Royal Commission on the Press 1974–7, of which I was the Chairman. I do not propose to debate Professor Tunstall's criticisms of the Commission's conclusions but only to correct some of his inaccuracies and to add a general comment.

The Commission recognised that the effectiveness of its academic advisers would depend on mutual confidence which it did its best to establish within the inescapable restraints of time and procedure upon a body determined to report within three years. The academics were all employed on the footing that, whilst the Commission would have the right to publish what they wrote, they would be free to publish on their own account any work which the Commission decided not to use. As the Commission could not commit itself in advance to publish everything produced for it, this arrangement ensured that none of the work of the academic advisers could be suppressed. Professor Tunstall states that he and Mr James Curran 'had the experience of some of their work being in effect ruled out of bounds as involving distinct policy proposals which lay well beyond the broad Commission consensus of minor tinkering with the status quo'.[2] I do not know what Professor Tunstall means by the phrase 'in effect' in this sentence. He was – and is – free to publish his paper on 'The British press and its other business interests, or vice-versa'.[3] Far from Mr Curran's paper on 'Advertising Media Planning and the British Press 1945–75' 'being in effect ruled out of bounds' by the Commission, it organised a seminar on 'Advertising and the Press', in which Mr Curran participated, and circulated his paper to all who attended as one of the two main contributions for discussion.[4]

It is proper that I should state my belief that Professor Tunstall's essay sets an unfortunate precedent in one particular respect. He accepted a special relationship with the Commission and was taken into its confidence. At no time did he declare a possible intention of publishing his views about relationships within the Commission[5] or of using information gathered, in his capacity as a scholar, in private conversations and meetings. In my view, Professor Tunstall has set an example which may result in the imposition of restrictions on the freedom of academic advisers employed by commissions and committees in the future. I do not suggest that advisers to these bodies should observe a lifelong vow of silence but only that they should follow the ordinary requirements of courtesy and discretion. Perhaps the time has come when it would be useful for the Home Office to consult a representative group of people who have served as advisers, secretaries and chairmen of official Committees of Inquiry, with the object of framing general guidance for conduct in this area.

In the case of the Royal Commission on the Press, the advisers were in regular touch with the secretariat, they saw Commission papers, they had access to members and they came to meetings of the full Commission from time to time in order to discuss what they were doing. Even so, they were not in a position to become familiar with the whole of the Commission's activities or with the reasons for many of the decisions taken. Thus, Professor Tunstall reports that 'an attempt was made to form a Commission sub-committee on social research' which soon 'fizzled out'.[6] The Commission did start off with an *ad hoc* group concerned with research. However, it decided very early in its deliberations that research was too important to be left to a sub-committee, and should always have the attention of the full Commission. Accordingly, it resolved that all proposals for research should be brought before the Commission, and none was undertaken without its consideration and approval. By his misunderstanding of this point of Commission procedure, Professor Tunstall conveys the misleading impression that members of the Commission were so uninterested in research that they allowed their research sub-committee to 'fizzle out'.[7]

Professor Tunstall quotes himself rather more often and writes with rather more inaccuracy and innuendo than is customary in scholarly work; some attention must therefore be paid to these features of his narrative so that readers may judge his reliability as a reporter and commentator. He asserts that Sir Morris Finer, the first Chairman of the Commission, died of cancer and was 'unusual among judges in being of Jewish working-class background'.[8] He did die of cancer and he was Jewish, if these be relevant considerations; of working-class background he was not. He was not 'a personal friend of Harold Wilson';[9] and he did not exhibit a 'relatively[10] high degree of unfamiliarity'[11] about the press. In fact, he was very knowledgeable. In his younger days at the Bar, he had written regularly for several years for the London *Evening Standard*;

he became a confidant of Lord Beaverbrook; and he remained throughout his life on friendly terms with many newspapermen.

Professor Tunstall makes several inaccurate statements about the Commission's attitudes and conclusions. I have selected for comment one example only. He discerns the 'Commission's faith in the press electronic revolution'[12] and notes 'a quite mistaken view of the "new technology" as *the* solution to *the* problem [of national newspapers]'.[13] What the Commission actually concluded was that

> The cost savings,[14] especially for the qualities, are of the greatest importance in helping to offset rising costs. Nevertheless, such savings cannot guarantee the future of every title. Even if all newspapers accomplish the change, competition may still result in some newspapers closing, since the new technology does little to alter the relative position of competing titles, though it does improve the position of quality relative to popular newspapers. But this caution is not an argument against change. If a reduction in labour costs is not sufficient to secure the continuance of every title, it may at least give them the breathing space to find new markets.[15]

Professor Tunstall makes extensive use of innuendo. 'Meetings of the Royal Commission members usually took place on Friday afternoons – not perhaps the most wide-awake time of the week.'[16] 'Well into the second year the full meetings . . . [from occasional[17] observation] appeared to be rambling and poorly informed.'[18] The many visits made by the Commission and its secretariat to press organisations in London and the provinces 'were extremely brief'. Also 'sketchily prepared' and 'very brief' were visits paid to other countries. All 'the visits appeared to be little more than jaunts whose real value was in building morale and consensus in other areas'.[19] '[A]t the centre of the operation – the more active members and the senior staff – there was an atmosphere of shoulder-shrugging, and occasionally of somnolence'.[20] The senior staff in the secretariat are labelled as having possessed no 'previous experience either of the press or of Royal Commissions, and only one of the three had any obviously relevant expertise. Two of the three had Oxbridge degrees in English literature'.[21] Professor Tunstall reports as a sample of their conversation: 'No, old chap, we can't possibly show the questionnaire to the members or we'd waste all day on the first page'.[22] Undoubtedly, the secretariat of a Royal Commission provides a miniature case study in which arguments about the appropriate relationships between generalists and specialists in the civil service can be examined. But Professor Tunstall's caricature of the officials who served the Commission with outstanding intellectual ability and administrative skill is unworthy and untrue. Moreover, he describes inaccurately the constitutional position of the Commission. He states that 'the Commission staff were responsible to the Department of Trade, but – because Harold Wilson and James Callaghan each took a special interest – the staff were also aware of watching eyes in Downing Street'.[23] The Commission was an independent body which, as a matter of convenience, drew pay and rations from the Civil Service Department; they were not responsible to the Department of Trade. Constitutionally, the Secretary was responsible to the Chairman and he was responsible to the Queen. Sir Harold Wilson did take a special interest in the work of the Commission; Mr Callaghan did not; and, as far as I am aware, the secretariat was not conscious of 'watching eyes in Downing Street'.

In a different vein, Professor Tunstall combines inaccuracy and innuendo in his account of the British Leyland 'slush fund' story which appeared in the *Daily Mail* two months before the publication of the Commission's Final Report. The Prime Minister, Mr Callaghan, asked the Commission for an assurance that its report would deal adequately with the issues of principle which arose from that story and the *Daily Mail*'s commentaries upon it. Professor Tunstall relates how 'the Commission chose (as usual) a compromise – agreeing to look at the case, but more briefly than the Prime Minister wanted. The RCP was seen once again to exhibit the twin bad habits of bowing to obvious political pressure and itself indulging in instant journalistic coverage of day-to-day controversies.'[24] I do not understand how the Commission could have refused the Prime Minister the courtesy of taking his request for an assurance seriously, or why this courtesy should be described as 'bowing to obvious political pressure'. The Commission's conclusion, which was not agreeable to members of the Labour Party, was that: 'The question raised by the Prime Minister's enquiry is whether the conduct of the *Daily Mail* provided evidence of abuses which would lead us to re-consider some of the chief recommendations and conclusions in our Report. We do not believe this to be the case.'[25] Professor Tunstall's charge that the Commission indulged in 'instant journalistic coverage of day-to-day controversies' is also untrue. The facts about the *Daily Mail* story were not disputed even by the *Daily Mail*, and the Commission did no more than apply the principles of its report to them in order to demonstrate how it would deal with a particularly shocking instance of irresponsible journalism.[26]

Presumably the other example of bowing to political pressure which Professor Tunstall has in mind by his use of the phrase 'once again' in the passage quoted above, was the Commission's agreement to undertake an Interim Report. Of this, Professor Tunstall observes that the 'request for an Interim Report had been predictable and, with hindsight, probably the government's request should have been rejected'.[27] The circumstances in which the Commission agreed to produce an Interim Report were that Lord Goodman, Chairman of the Newspaper Publishers' Association, wrote to the Secretary of State for Trade requesting that the Commission be asked to act because 'the [national] newspaper industry is currently facing a crisis of unprecedented dimensions and dangers'.[28] The General Secretaries of the trade unions in the industry also expressed to the government their agreement that an inquiry should be undertaken without delay.[29] I cannot apprehend the grounds on which the Commission could have declined the industry's and the government's request for an Interim Report and at the same time have retained its credibility, let alone a prospect of co-operation from the industry in their future inquiries. The two examples which Professor Tunstall cites give no support to his offensive assertion that an independent Royal Commission was in the habit of 'bowing to obvious political pressure'.

I now turn to Professor Tunstall's more general criticism that the Commission failed to produce ideas about policy which could be tested by research. Sometimes, official Committees of Inquiry, like the Committee on One-Parent Families,[30] are appointed in part as a result of the range and vitality of research in the areas covered by their terms of reference. Such committees are likely to have at least several members expert in different parts of their remit, and they may start work with a clear notion of what their policy choices are and along what lines their main recommendations will run. Their chief task will be to draw together and deploy existing knowledge in such a way as to present the politically influential public with the most compelling supporting arguments for their conclusions. The Royal Commission on the Press stood at the other extreme. Over its very wide terms of reference, knowledge was patchy and unsystematic, policy choices were ill-defined and academic study of the press had not advanced far enough to be of much assistance. The Commission had to begin by considering what were the issues with which it had to deal, and whether and how any could be illumined by empirical inquiries within the time available. Certain subjects selected themselves at different stages in the Commission's work. For example, the financial situation of national and provincial newspapers had to be investigated; information about the procedures and state of industrial relations in the industry had to be collected and analysed; data about the earnings and demographic structure of the labour force in Fleet Street had to be obtained; newspaper content had to be analysed; and some knowledge had to be acquired about readers' attitudes to the press. At an early stage, some studies were commissioned in order to provide members with essential background information, and later published as Working Papers.[31]

Nevertheless, there is truth in one of Professor Tunstall's comments on the Commission's research programme. Parts of it did 'lack . . . guiding policy ideas or proposals'.[32] But how could it have been otherwise when much of the time and work of members and staff had to be spent on the formulation of the very policy ideas which Professor Tunstall wished to make the basis of research? Commissions must restrict their research to projects which can be completed in time to influence their reports, and this means that it must be set in train almost at the outset. Further, when Professor Tunstall complains of the Commission's 'failure to incorporate much of the research into its Final Report'[33] he forgets that the report of a Royal Commission is not a suitable place for extended accounts of research findings. The Press Commission's Interim Report was presented in fourteen pages as Part A of the volume in which it was published. The research on which it was based was summarised in Part B which contained nine chapters and seven appendices running to one hundred pages. The Final Report relied upon generalisations from its research which was finally published in six volumes and four Working Papers. Despite this extensive programme of research, the Commission was one of the bodies which did not – and could not – know in respect of many of the problems it had to study what research it should have undertaken until it was too late to act on the knowledge.

I shall not comment on the substance of Professor Tunstall's views about policy for the press. Yet on one fundamental issue of policy, on the desirability and possible forms of governmental intervention in the press and their implications, empirical knowledge could not take the place of social and political judgement. In Professor Tunstall's opinion, however, the members of the Commission were ill-equipped to exercise such judgement because 'their level of political experience was inadequate'.[34] '[T]here was', he writes, 'a *political* failure – a failure to recognise that the press is an industry like no other primarily because of its political importance.'[35] Here again, he pays too little attention to the report of the Commission he is criticising. It refers to 'a recurring theme in our report, namely, that, for some purposes, the press must be regarded as an industry like any other although, from the point of view of its contribution to the maintenance of democracy, it has to be seen as an industry like none other'.[36]

Professor Tunstall's essay is an example of the habit of some newspapers, severely criticised by the Royal Commission, of presenting 'contentious opinions on the basis of inaccurate reports'.[37] His central disagreement with the Commission turns on differences of view about policy matters. Yet he seems unable to accept that the Commission, having heard what he had to say, simply disagreed with him. He documents at painstaking length the number of times he drew his views to the attention of members of the Commission, reaching the conclusion that because they did not accept his analysis, they were wrong; and wrong because they were badly chosen, ill-informed, badly staffed and had adopted slovenly procedures. Whether he or the Commission was right about the policy issues must be for readers of the Interim Report and Final Report to judge.

NOTES: CHAPTER 10

1 This note expresses my own opinions. No member of the Royal Commission on the Press or of its secretariat can be held to have approved any part of it.
2 p. 146.
3 p. 146.
4 A summary of the proceedings of the seminar is contained in Appendix E, *Final Report, Appendices*, Cmnd 6810 (London: HMSO, 1977), pp. 125–30. Mr Curran's paper has been deposited with the Royal Commission's evidence. Professor Tunstall observes (p. 137) that '. . . it was conventional wisdom in the Commission that the formal evidence would probably not reveal a great deal . . . [T]his expectation was reflected in the decision not to publish any evidence . . . ' His statement is misleading. The Commission deposited sets of its evidence in the Public Record Office and in seventeen of the copyright, university and public libraries in the United Kingdom and Eire. The Commission's decision was not taken in the light of the paucity of revelations in the evidence but as a result of the formidable cost of printing it in the traditional way. It was satisfied that the evidence will be easily accessible to scholars. One set was given to Professor Tunstall's own university library (*Final Report*, pp. 251 and 255).
5 I shall not comment on Professor Tunstall's assertions about these.
6 p. 144
7 Professor Tunstall also writes that the Chairman, Mr Roger Chorley, the Secretary and two assistant secretaries 'could have held regular meetings attended by the senior academic research consultants . . . This committee, had it met, would, however, have posed a threat to the Commission's authority' (p. 144). I cannot envisage what the nature of such a threat might have been. In fact, *ad hoc* groups of members, of the secretariat and of researchers met throughout the Commission's existence to plan projects and to receive progress reports.
8 p. 130.
9 p. 128.
10 It is not clear from the text whether the intended comparison is with Professor Tunstall himself or with the man reading the *Daily Mirror* on the Clapham omnibus.
11 p. 131.
12 p. 127.
13 p. 131, *italics* in original.
14 It is essential to distinguish between savings on labour costs resulting from the

introduction of new technology and the savings from reduced manning in the use of existing machinery. The Commission urged both kinds of saving.

15 *Final Report*, para. 5.43, p. 44.

16 p. 137–8.

17 This is accurate. Professor Tunstall attended fewer than half a dozen of the sixty-one half- and full-day meetings of the whole Commission.

18 p. 138.

19 p. 138. Professor Tunstall did not accompany the Commission on visits.

20 p. 136.

21 p. 136. Both had been at Cambridge, like Professor Tunstall himself.

22 p. 144.

23 p. 136.

24 p. 132. Professor Tunstall does not disclose the source of his knowledge of what the Prime Minister wanted. Even if it had wished, the Commission could not have investigated the case as both civil and criminal proceedings were pending.

25 *Final Report*, p. 106.

26 *Final Report*, pp. 105–8.

27 p. 131.

28 *Interim Report: The National Newspaper Industry*, Cmnd 6433 (London: HMSO, 1976), p. 16.

29 *Interim Report*.

30 Cmnd 5629 and 5629–I (London: HMSO, 1974).

31 The publications in the Royal Commission's Research Series are: *Industrial Relations in the National Newspaper Industry*, Cmnd 6680 (London: HMSO, 1976); *Industrial Relations in the Provincial Newspaper and Periodical Industries*, Cmnd 6810–2 (London: HMSO, 1977); *Attitudes to the Press*, Cmnd 6810–3 (London: HMSO, 1977); *Analysis of Newspaper Content*, Cmnd 6810–4 (London: HMSO, 1977); *Concentration of Ownership in the Provincial Press*, Cmnd 6810–5 (London: HMSO, 1977); and *Periodicals and the Alternative Press*, Cmnd 6810–6 (London: HMSO, 1977). In addition, the Commission published four Working Papers: Rex Winsbury, *New Technology and the Press* (London: HMSO, 1975); Denis McQuail, *Review of Sociological Writing on the Press* (London: HMSO, 1976); Oliver Boyd-Barrett, Colin Seymour-Ure and Jeremy Tunstall, *Studies on the Press* (London: HMSO, 1977); and Cynthia White, *The Women's Periodical Press in Britain, 1946–1976* (London: HMSO, 1977).

32 p. 142.

33 p. 142.

34 p. 147.

35 p. 126, *italics* in original.

36 *Final Report*, pp. 159–60.

37 *Final Report*, p. 214.

Chapter 11

The Royal Commission on the Distribution of Income and Wealth

MARTIN BULMER

The Royal Commission on the Distribution of Income and Wealth (RCDIW), set up in 1974, is a standing Royal Commission.[1] As such, it differs from the other commissions discussed in this book, all of which have been *ad hoc* inquiries set up to investigate and report within a set period of time. The standing Royal Commission, with a continuing span of life and continuity in its inquiries, presents several distinctive features, which this chapter seeks to describe.

The RCDIW was set up by the incoming Labour government in 1974, following a pledge in the February 1974 election manifesto to 'establish a standing Royal Commission to advise on income distribution, both earned and unearned, with particular reference to differentials and job evaluation'.[2] This commitment formed part of the Labour Party's social contract with the trade unions, within its overall industrial relations and collective bargaining strategy. The appointment of Lord Diamond (the former Labour MP, Chief Secretary to the Treasury, 1964–70) as Chairman of the Commission was announced by the Secretary of State for Employment (Mr Michael Foot) in the House of Commons on 18 July 1974, as part of a general statement on pay policy.[3]

The Royal Warrant setting up the RCDIW, appointing the Chairman and members and giving the basic terms of reference, was signed in August 1974. It charged the Commission to inquire into, and report on, such matters concerning the distribution of personal incomes, both earned and unearned, and wealth, as might be referred to it by the government.[4] Lord Diamond was initially appointed on a full-time basis, later (April 1978) moving to half-time. The other original Commissioners, who are part-time, included an industrialist, a banker, a representative of the TUC, a leading trade unionist, a building society executive and three academic social scientists – an economist, a sociologist and a social policy teacher.[5] Though there has been some turnover among the Commissioners, and their number has fallen from eight to six,[6] they represent a wide range of interests by including at least two industrialists, two members from the trade union movement and two academics. This diversity is not designed to represent different interest groups, so much as to secure authoritative support for the empirical basis of the RCDIW's work.[7] As the Chairman has observed:

> As you would expect from a Royal Commission, we strive to be impartial and objective. Each of us has his or her own opinions about whether income and wealth should or should not be more equally distributed but we are not asked to report on these opinions. We are all united in wishing to present the facts in ways which are helpful to people whatever opinions they hold.

The work of the Commission, which is governed by its terms of reference, falls into two parts, the Standing Reference, and specific references (of which there have been three up to 1978). The Standing Reference reads as follows:

> To help to secure a fairer distribution of income and wealth in the community there is a need for a thorough and comprehensive inquiry into the existing distribution of income and wealth. There is also a need for a study of past trends in that distribution and for regular assessments of the subsequent changes.
>
> The Government therefore ask the Commission to undertake an analysis of the current distribution of personal income and wealth and of available information on past trends in that distribution . . .
>
> The Commission are invited to consult with the Government Statistical Service on any changes in the official collection of statistics which would help them in their task.[8]

The First Report on the Standing Reference was published within a year of the setting up of the Commission, the Second Report followed in 1976[9] and the Third Report in 1977.[10] Lord Diamond explained the reasons for having a standing commission by the simile of a moving picture.

> What we have to describe is a moving picture and a moving picture consists of a series of snapshots taken over a period of time. What we publish on a particular day may cover only a year, and is only a snapshot. It is then necessary to do another snapshot in a year's time, or whatever the appropriate period may be, to see how the picture has moved. And you don't get the whole story unless you get the movement. It is always very difficult

picking up the past to compare like with like . . . you can never get everything on exactly the basis you would like . . . but as you move on, you can get comparisons which are literally like with like, and trends become clear which underline the accuracy or inaccuracy of earlier trends . . . Moreover, in our particular case, you could not get hold of all the information immediately. So that it enables us not only to show trends by repeating figures, but by digging more deeply into various aspects of the distribution of incomes and wealth, for which the figures weren't available originally, but which are becoming available, as people keep the figures in the way which we ask them to keep them. So as you move on, you get more and more information, you have more and more time to dig into certain things, so a standing reference serves both those purposes.

After the First Report, the frequency of reports on the standing reference is determined by the Commissioners. The Chairman elaborated:

> To report every three months would be silly. You often don't have any new figures. To do it once every five years would be too long a period to wait, because the picture is changing too fast. In fact we find that a year to two years is the appropriate time. We cover a very wide scale, and precisely the same argument doesn't apply to every single set of figures. So it's left to us to decide, and it works itself out. When you come across the facts of the case, a decision is not very difficult.

The *specific* references which the Commission receives from the government, by contrast, require investigation for a finite period, culminating in a report. To date there have been three, on income from companies and its distribution;[11] on higher incomes from employment and self-employment;[12] and on lower incomes (defined as about the lowest 25 per cent of income recipients).[13] The report on the first was published in 1975, on the second in 1976 and on the third in 1978. Specific references are formally sent to the Commission by the Department of Employment (DE)[14], which is the Commission's sponsoring department. They are the outcome of consultation within the government and between DE and the Commission as to the work which the Commission can reasonably undertake. (In its first two years, when dealing with the standing reference and two specific references at the same time, the workload seems to have been excessive, particularly for the Commissioners.) Lord Diamond explained:

> The special references arise when the government want something very specially done. You will see from the manifesto that there was already reference to 'people at the bottom of the pile'. And I think top salaries were also envisaged. So very early on we got a reference on top incomes. That was the government – as represented by DE – which was particularly concerned with the sorts of things which it was envisaged in the manifesto we would be doing . . . The Treasury wanted information about company incomes, in order to inform itself the better before reaching a conclusion on dividend restraint policy. It therefore gave us a reference, through DE.
>
> All the special references have had a time date on them, and this is important in understanding the kind of Royal Commission which we are. We are not the kind which settles down to a four-year review of a whole host of factors, then making a recommendation at the end of it and that fulfilling its function. This Royal Commission is there to help the policy-making body – namely the government – reach a conclusion on the facts which it has not fully got, and therefore wants the Royal Commission to supply it with. We help it by giving it the best answer we can within a certain time.

As Chairman, Lord Diamond has been concerned from the start to make clear that the Commission's terms of reference involve producing reports of a factual nature which would assist and inform policy-makers and those active in collective bargaining. Systematic inquiry therefore plays an extremely important part in its work. In Lord Diamond's own words:

> What we were required to do was to report about the distribution, the spread [of income and wealth], as it was and as it had been and as it was developing. And to give all information to those who might form views as to how it should develop in the future, which was not our job. And the more I have been at it, the more I am satisfied that this was the right approach. First of all, the figures are always wanted. Every policy-maker and every decision-maker always has to reach his conclusions on the basis of inadequate information. Certainly in government you have to, because you have no time to wait for all the information to be collected, because by the time it has been collected it's irrelevant, it's gone by. Secondly, the best persuaders are the facts. It is never very difficult to come to a policy decision once you have got all the facts.

The RCDIW, as already indicated, arose out of the government's 'social contract' with the trade unions. Between the manifesto and the Commission starting work, the 'particular reference to differentials and job evaluation' in the manifesto disappeared, though the preamble to the Standing Reference reads: 'To help to secure a fairer distribution of income and wealth in the community'. At the outset of the Commission's work, there was some divergence of opinion among those giving evidence on the standing reference over what they saw as the role of the Commission. Mr Jack Jones of the TGWU expressed the hope that the Commission would provide practical proposals to fill the gaps in our knowledge, 'acknowledge the gross inequities which existed', and 'indicate the kinds of measures needed to reduce those inequities'.[15] The CBI, on the other hand, expressed concern about the political nature of the Commission's work and argued that 'fairness is not equivalent to equality but to a system of just differentials'.[16]

The Chairman emphasised from the outset the need for 'independence, impartiality and thoroughness' in the Commission's reports. The Commission's role was primarily a factual one.

> Our task is a narrower one than I sometimes feel is appreciated. We have not been asked to assess or propose policies for the *re*distribution of income and wealth. The wealth tax is not a matter on which we have been asked to report.[17] Of course the information in our reports bears on many questions about redistribution and fairness and equality, and that is why our work is so relevant. To the extent that we can provide more and better information, policies and debates about those issues will be improved . . .
>
> Some people, if the facts show that movement is at the rate of 15 m.p.h., will say that's too fast, according to their scales, and other people will say that's too slow. Other people will say that's about right. But what they need to know first is: what was the speed at which the vehicle was moving? 15 m.p.h. And what were the conditions, what kind of road? And how do vehicles of a similar kind move in other countries on similar roads? And what are the circumstances and surroundings which affect such a judgement? And then they will apply their own scales and philosophy to it.

Elaborating this view, Lord Diamond explained:

> What Royal Commissions do who have recommendations to make under their terms of reference is to collect the facts and then, on the basis of the facts, to make recommendations. Fine, but the making of recommendations is the part that, in my view,

interests government least. Recommendations often get filed and left there, because the government and civil service are very good at making decisions – ministers and their advisers combined – if they have got the facts. So in my view the better part of the purpose which a Royal Commission with recommendation powers serves is to collect the information, and it would do three-quarters of its job or nine-tenths of its job if it stopped there, because people reading it would know what conclusions follow. Indeed, not all recommendations of all Royal Commissions are accepted. That is an understatement, simply because in general the facts that have been unearthed are not denied, but governments come to different conclusions on the basis of those facts. It is facts that are wanted, and it is no great restriction that you cannot go on from facts to make recommendations. You have the great advantage that when you have a body of people with diverse views, diverse philosophies, diverse backgrounds, diverse attitudes, coming to a single conclusion about a set of figures, the authority and objectivity which that imparts to their findings is enormous, so long as they don't try to draw conclusions from it . . . The very fact that you are not required to make and do not make recommendations adds to the credibility of the facts which you produce. There is a great tendency for people to say, if somebody produces a set of facts and comes to a certain conclusion on it, well these are the facts which have been selected to demonstrate that conclusion . . . Once there is a recommendation at the end or a conclusion drawn from the figures of that kind, the reader suspects that the facts were garnered in order to lead up to that conclusion. If you do not have that, then I find there is more of a tendency for people to accept the facts just as preparation of authoritative facts.

The reports of the RCDIW are thus predominantly very comprehensive factual statistical accounts of the state of knowledge about particular aspects of income and wealth distribution in Britain, coupled with very careful examination of methodological problems in the measurement of income and wealth. The Commission has also worked closely with the Government Statistical Service, making in its reports a number of specific proposals, for the improvement of official statistics upon income and wealth. (This chapter does not attempt to summarise nor to evaluate the *content* of the RCDIW reports, to which the interested reader is referred.)

The programme of work of the Commission is planned and directed by the Commissioners, who meet on average once a month for a whole day. Research is not undertaken by the Commissioners themselves but by the staff of the Commission. The RCDIW is unusual among the bodies considered in this book in having a relatively large research and statistical capability of its own, with an original complement of forty-four staff, later reduced to thirty-five. The staff consists of a small central secretariat, a statistical support unit and an operational branch for each reference currently being undertaken (usually the standing reference plus one specific reference). Each operational branch forms an interdisciplinary team, headed by an assistant secretary or chief statistician, with at least one economist, statistician and principal plus assistants and support staff. A sociologist was also recruited for the low incomes reference. Some of the staff are civil servants on secondment; others are recruited directly by the Commission itself. This is deliberate, since the Commission seeks neither to be staffed wholly by civil servants (with the risk of becoming an outpost of the Government Statistical Service) nor to rely wholly on directly engaged staff. In mid-1978 the Commission's staff consisted of four senior administrators, seven statisticians, four economists, one research officer and seventeen junior administrators (including statistical support staff and secretaries). This represents a considerable weight and concentration of expertise which distinguishes the RCDIW markedly from other Commissions.

Like other Royal Commissions, the RCDIW takes written and oral evidence. As a Royal Commission, it is obliged to accept any written evidence which may be submitted. Invitations to give oral evidence are issued selectively where the Commission judges that an organisation or individual has particular relevant knowledge and expertise. Some time after the relevant report has been issued, the Commission publishes a selection of the written and oral evidence which it has received.[18]

On the Standing Reference, the Commission took written evidence at the outset and then heard witnesses orally. Much of this latter evidence was methodological, with witnesses telling the Commissioners what distinctions should be drawn and how they thought the Commission should analyse income and wealth. On the specific references, the Chairman explained that:

> Certain witnesses choose themselves to be seen, because clearly they have the authority and the knowledge which is more than can be put into a piece of paper. People like the CBI and the TUC and the Local Authorities' Association can give an enormous amount of information and so they almost select themselves to be seen orally. Others are selected because of the merit of their written evidence and the fact that you can understand it better when you see people orally. We had a very difficult reference with regard to people at the bottom of the pile, because we were

asked in the reference to go into the social and economic factors. If you want to get at factors, you have got to listen to a lot of people explaining what they think are causes, factors and so on, and so you could not do that satisfactorily just by written evidence, so that's another category of witness where you have got to get the witness in front of you.

The taking of written and oral evidence plays a significant part in the RCDIW's work. At certain points in the first two years, the taking of oral evidence in particular placed very heavy demands on the time of the Commissioners, vastly more than one day per month. By comparison with Commissions that will make recommendations, however, written and oral evidence has played a less salient part in the Commission's work, in that the substantive findings of the Commission do not depend heavily on this evidence. The written and oral testimony is important in defining problems, suggesting directions in which to look, clarifying the bases on which measurement be made, and so on. Some of the initial academic evidence on the standing reference, for example, contains very lucid expositions of problems of research into income and wealth, some of which was incorporated into the First Report. On contentious and intractable issues such as the causes of poverty, oral evidence provided an opportunity for exponents of different schools of thought to state their case. But the bulk of the data which are published in the Commission's reports do not derive from the written and oral evidence taken. Most of the data for these reports are compiled by the RCDIW's own staff, under the direction of the Commissioners, with assistance from the Government Statistical Service in particular, and from outside consultants.

The process of responding to references is described by Lord Diamond as follows. The Commissioners are responsible for deciding on the programme of work of the Commission's staff, which they do partly on the advice which they receive from the staff through the Secretary, and partly from their own views as to what they should be looking at. Many of the Commissioners are very much experts in the field in their own right (which is why they were appointed). 'As a Commission, we discuss all these ideas, to see which of these ideas are worth following up. In the light of these ideas the Office then provides the Commissioners with a lengthy document setting out the work which might be done and the sort of benefits that might be obtained from it, and suggesting the way in which this general idea could be implemented in full detail.' The Commissioners will either agree or vary it, a decision is made as to the kind of things to be covered, and a timetable is agreed with the staff as to what is to be done. 'And then in due course a paper is produced, along the lines indicated, showing the sort of information which we asked for, and that would be then amended, or extended, or shortened or whatever the case may be, and it would then take its final form and be ready for inclusion in the next Report.' So the Office produces for the Commission (1) initially, a planning paper for a particular reference (or for further work on the Standing Reference), and (2) their report of the work which the Commissioners asked them to undertake on the basis of the planning paper, which summarises their investigations in the intervening period and is considerably fuller than what is eventually published.

In between stages (1) and (2), the Commissioners and staff agree how the work shall be accomplished, how much internally and how much externally. Most of the work for reports is done by the RCDIW's own staff. Since a high proportion of the matters for report is statistical, they receive assistance from government departments concerned, and particularly from the Government Statistical Service. A good deal of this work is not 'research' in the sense of original first-hand investigations but the collation and refinement of statistical data collected originally by government as the by-product of administrative processes. Given the complexity of measuring income and wealth, moreover, the RCDIW has been able to perform a very important synthesising role as well as securing improvements in the way official series are produced. It has also undertaken original inquiries of its own, for example, the estimates (based on a model) of the relative size of inherited wealth and of lifetime accumulation in Chapter 9 of the *Third Report on the Standing Reference*.

On certain topics, outside consultants have been used and research commissioned. Dr T. Stark and Dr A. J. Harrison have been commissioned to carry out particular pieces of research into international comparisons of the distribution of income and wealth.[19] Mr N. Bosanquet was taken on to the staff while working on labour economic aspects of the lower income reference. A number of specific research contracts have been given to outside researchers: for example, to Professor J. S. Revell to attempt to reconcile balance sheet and estate multiplier estimates of the distribution of personal wealth; to the Policy Studies Institute for Mr J. L. Nicholson to work on income distribution; and to Mr R. Layard and others at the LSE for a re-analysis of income data from the GHS.[20] Outside consultancy firms have also been used, for example, the work done by Hay-MSL for the reference on higher incomes.[21]

The cost of this research and consultancy is met from the RCDIW's parliamentary estimate for the year, which is a subhead of the DE's vote. The cost of outside research has varied from year to year. In 1977/8 it was £43,000 out of a total expenditure of £353,000 (one-eighth of the RCDIW's budget).[22] More outside research is commissioned in connection with specific references than for the Standing Reference. On lower incomes, for example, at least eight separate pieces of work were commissioned from academics.[23] In addition, the Commission received on an allied services basis without payment special tabulations or information from the CSO, DHSS, DE and the Supplementary Benefits Commission, and the OPCS Social Survey Division carried out a special follow-up survey of GHS respondents.

In general, the Commission has tried to do as much of its work itself as it could, and has drawn upon the expertise of academics where it knew that they were already working in the field of income and wealth distribution. It has not attempted to initiate major new programmes of outside research nor to draw into work in their field academics who were not already specialists in it. The expenditure of the Commission on outside research seems relatively modest. Its own large professional staff is much more remarkable and unusual.

An integral part of the Commission's research and intelligence work is its publication programme. This has drawn together a wide variety of statistical data, many of which have never been brought together before, and published them in a lucid manner. This is also true of methodology. The First Report, for example, contains in Chapter 3 a very clear explanation of different ways of measuring income and wealth distribution and trends. The Commission has had some success in disseminating the results of the work. Press coverage of the reports has been considerable, and data assembled by the Commission have appeared in widely read sources such as *Social Trends*. Undoubtedly the reports themselves are authoritative and weighty, likely to appeal to an educated and relatively specialist readership rather than a popular mass audience, with the exception of one publication referred to at the end of this chapter.

It is difficult to provide an entirely cut and dried picture of the uses made of research by the Commission for three main reasons, though each emphasises the extent to which the RCDIW is strongly oriented to statistical research and intelligence activity. First, the Commission works closely with statistical divisions of government departments, who provide much of its data and who themselves have considerable expertise in the field, for example, in the Inland Revenue and the Central Statistical Office. Moreover, one role that the RCDIW plays is to improve the quality of official data, so that they feed back suggestions to those from whom they are receiving data. Examples of such changes brought about by the Commission include the revival of the Blue Book income distribution figures, which the CSO actually ceased to publish in the late 1960s. The revival of this series is an important contribution. Another case is that of sector balance sheets. When Atkinson and Harrison began work in the early 1970s, no one had continued the pioneering balance sheets of Revell. The Commission's role in getting these established was crucial.[24]

Secondly, given the nature of the Commission's work, the line between submitting evidence, acting as a consultant and doing research on the Commission's behalf is not a hard and fast one, particularly for academic experts. Some of those who have given written and oral evidence have subsequently been used as consultants. Some of the consultancy work appears to draw heavily on pre-existing research by the individual concerned. Those who have done research for RCDIW have then been examined orally.

Thirdly, and most important, the degree of expertise among the Commissioners themselves is unusual. First, three out of nine, and since 1978 two out of eight, members of the Commission have been academic experts in the field. This clearly has been very important, not only in the formal work of the Commission. Though Professor Greve's report on low incomes in Sweden is the only published report by a Commissioner,[25] commissioners have played a very active role behind the scenes. The Secretary commented that the Commission received a great deal of help from its academic commissioners, not only at meetings. 'We almost come to expect – quite outrageously – comments on papers on relatively detailed matters where we do get very considerable advantage from an independent and extremely authoritative view.' Informal discussion with the staff is a hidden means by which academic (and other) expertise plays an important role in the work of the Commission.

Unlike some Royal Commissions, members of the Commission do not appear to play a primary role in the actual drafting of the Commission's reports; their contribution is greater at the stage of shaping the strategy for the report and determining what shall be covered and how it shall be treated. As outlined earlier (p. 166), the first stage of a reference is for the Commission to receive, modify and approve a planning paper which forms the basis, after an interval, for the second stage, a review of the evidence collected by the Office. This in turn forms the basis for the third stage, producing a draft report for publication. In the Chairman's words, 'We consider a report as a whole, what is going into the report, the structure of the report, the order of events, and so on, and then the draft report is produced by the Office. We work on that, and then a further draft, and a further draft, and then the final thing.'

The Commission has recognised that its task is not limited to the production of one single, true, factual description of any particular aspect of income or wealth distribution. Though its objective throughout is to make available the facts, these facts are not always uncontested. 'What are seen as relevant facts', the First Report commented,

> will, in part, reflect the values of the people using them. In an area like the distribution of income and wealth there will never be one correct set of statistics. Thus we have followed a policy of offering alternative approaches and measurements based on different definitions, so that readers may make their own choice of the most appropriate statistics for the problems they wish to study.

Lord Diamond elaborated:

> The Commission made a very early decision that the truth is not one-sided; there are many aspects of the truth, and the sensible way was for the Commission to show these different aspects. And we have therefore, for the distribution of wealth, shown the details of wealth under Series A, B, C, D, E and F. These are all relevant answers, depending on what you are looking at and what point of view you are looking at the truth from. These are all true, and you may draw certain conclusions, depending on what you regard as important and what you regard as the relevant point of view. That's not for us, that's for the policy-maker.

One former Commissioner has described the process which went on in developing work on a reference as follows:

> On receipt of a reference, staff would prepare a paper summarising sources and issues in relation to the reference. At this point the Commissioners became involved in the crucial process of deciding what was a relevant 'fact' or question which we should attempt to answer and what particular areas should be selected for a programme of work. We would engage in a process of bargaining, which explains why the reports show varying degrees of willingness to engage in estimation on sensitive issues, and to pursue different topics in depth ... [For example] the Commission decided that it would not attempt to estimate the value of fringe benefits for higher incomes from employment because, it argued, insufficient data was available, even though it was clear that such benefits were of considerable and increasing value at the top income levels.[26]

This chapter is not intended as an evaluation of the work of the RCDIW so much as an analysis of its mode of operation. A proper evaluation of its work would clearly involve discussion of what is a 'social fact', and the extent to which 'social facts' can be defined and constructed independent of particular theoretical or value standpoints. (Some evaluations of the Commission that have appeared to date place primary emphasis on a different point, the failure of the RCDIW to make policy recommendations.)[27]

The Commission was also brought sharply up against the problem of interpretation by the reference on lower incomes, which asked it in part 'to examine the economic, social and other factors which give rise to low incomes'.[28] It received written and oral evidence on this aspect of the reference, and commissioned its own research. Indeed, the most important contribution which the Commission may have made to the elucidation of social and economic factors may have been to commission Layard, Piachaud and Stewart's re-analysis of GHS data, published as Background Paper No. 5, entitled *The Causes of Poverty*, a report which may turn out to be as significant a contribution in the 1970s as Abel-Smith and Townsend's re-analysis of FES data was in the 1960s.[29]

The Commission itself failed to reach any definite conclusion on the relative importance of different social and economic factors in accounting for low incomes. It commented that:

> questions of causation are notoriously difficult to answer, especially in the economic and social fields . . . moreover, the nature of the statistical evidence is such that it may identify factors associated with low incomes but cannot establish a causal link . . . The present state of knowledge does not point with certainty to any single explanation as to why some families and individuals have lower incomes than others. The complex interplay of heredity, family background, early environment and education – and the extent to which chance enters in – raise basic issues of human behaviour going far wider than incomes.[30]

Lord Diamond explained that the Commission had listened to different theories being propounded and

> having listened to them all, came to the conclusion that the truth had not been clearly established to our satisfaction, and said so. A cowardly way out, if you like, but that's what we felt was the objective way of looking at it. The view we formed was that this was a vast field requiring separate, lengthy, study with enormous resources all on its own. Far too important for us to pronounce upon, as a side issue to the distribution of income and wealth. Our job was to draw attention to the importance of it, and the

implications of it, and we drew the conclusion which would be a tenable conclusion, in our view the right conclusion.

All six reports of the Commission have been unanimous, reflecting the achievement of the Chairman's aim of providing an authoritative and objective statement of the facts. Two reports have, however, contained addenda. In Report No. 3 on *Higher Incomes from Employment,* three members signed an addendum which called attention to 'the rapid erosion in the real value of managerial salaries' and urged 'that it is essential that the problem of rewarding management adequately should be recognised and dealt with as soon as possible'. This went well beyond the terms of reference of the report to deal with an issue of policy.

The other addendum appears in Report No. 6 on *Lower Incomes*, by Mr George Doughty, Mr David Lea and Professor Dorothy Wedderburn,[31] in effect saying that the main report is too cautious in its approach to the weighing of economic, social and other factors. It notes, for example, that the Commission decided that the evidence for the view that personal characteristics associated with earnings' capacity are genetically determined, was inconclusive.

> We would go beyond this. In our view, the genetic argument contributes nothing to an understanding of the causes of lower incomes in contemporary society . . . The level and distribution of lower incomes are largely determined by interaction between economic and social arrangements, including market forces, which are capable of modification in the course of economic and social development, if society so decided.[32]

The addendum also argues that studies of trends over time should not be allowed to carry prescriptive overtones. Stability in the position of lower incomes between 1968 and 1976, in relation both to other income levels and as between lower income groups with different characteristics, should not be taken to mean inevitability. To demonstrate that lower level incomes, national insurance and SB benefits have all increased roughly in line with the increase in earnings in recent years is not enough. A study of living standards would call into question the adequacy of such benefits.

These addenda are indicative of understandable differences of outlook between members of the Commission drawn from different industrial or political settings. 'The statistics of income and wealth', a former Commissioner, Sir Henry Phelps-Brown, has written,[33]

> are far from straightforward, but raise many questions of definition, presentation and evaluation; and what any one person sees

as the appropriate and reasonable answers will depend in part on the extent of his concern with equality – take the question, for example, whether the capitalised value of pensions should be included in estimates of personal wealth. Generally there is no one right answer, and the figures can and should be cast up in alternative ways. The unanimity of the Commission on its presentation of its factual materials has been reached only after long discussion, and its *Reports* are the more valuable for that reason. But this experience makes me doubtful whether panels of persons of different social and political attitude and conviction can form an effective instrument of enquiry and report in questions not of fact but of social causality.

Such points suggest that there may be limits to the extent to which the distribution of income and wealth may be examined purely empirically without encountering problems of both theoretical interpretation and value-judgement. The Chairman's view is that such more theoretical inquiries are not properly a matter for the Commission, but for other bodies to finance and for others, such as academic researchers, to undertake. (The DHSS-SSRC research programme on transmitted deprivation would be one example.) The Commission's principal work lies in the field of gathering objective and authoritative facts and figures on the distribution of income and wealth.[34]

It is appropriate to conclude by stressing the extent to which the RCDIW is unique, and how it is also of interest as a possible future model for inquiry sponsored by central government. As a standing Royal Commission, of course, it is not alone. Three long-established standing Royal Commissions include the Royal Commission for the Exhibition of 1851, which was set up after the affairs of the Great Exhibition were settled to promote scientific and artistic education by means of funds derived from its Kensington estates. The Royal Commission on Historical Monuments (England) (there are similar bodies for Wales and Scotland) was set up in 1908 to survey and publish an account of every building, earthwork or stone construction up to 1714 (a date later extended to 1850). It is purely a recording body and, although it can recommend the preservation of certain structures, does not possess powers to implement those recommendations. The Royal Commission on Historical Manuscripts, set up in 1869, now has responsibility, as a central co-ordinating body, to promote, assist and advise on the preservation and storage of all historical records outside of the Public Records, though its original purpose was to inquire and report on collections of papers of value for the study of history in private hands.[35]

None of these three commissions is comparable to the RCDIW.

The first is a historical oddity. The second and third provide independent advice to government on matters of public interest of an antiquarian, scholarly or cultural character, preserving for posterity the fabric of British civilisation, but unlikely to be involved in current economic or social policy issues.

The only other standing Royal Commission with which the RCDIW may be compared is the Royal Commission on Environmental Pollution (RCEP), set up in 1970 'to advise on matters, both national and international, concerning the pollution of the environment; on the adequacy of research in this field; and the future possibilities of danger to the environment'. The work it does has been described as that of a watchdog, to keep a watchful eye on developments in the field of environmental pollution, to identify areas where it appears that insufficient attention is being given to pollution problems, and to advise the government on action that should be taken.

Like the RCDIW, its membership includes a number of academic scientific experts, and it has produced a number of reports, beginning with a general review of pollution in Britain.[36] However, the differences between the RCDIW and the RCEP are more striking than the similarities.[37] The reports of the latter are short and, so far from being factual, principally contain recommendations for action by government and industry, in fields such as nuclear power, air pollution and agriculture and the environment. The RCEP is scientifically authoritative – its three chairmen have all been leading academic scientists[38] – with the collective capability of weighing scientific evidence and making informed recommendations for further research. (By others; its own total staff of ten includes only one scientific assistant; another difference from RCDIW.) But its main task seems to be to keep a sharp and watchful eye on current developments and make policy recommendations where appropriate. Being a watchdog implies a readiness to bite, whereas the role of providing authoritative facts is more analogous to the steady drip of water on stone, gradually wearing the stone away.

Among the vast majority of Royal Commissions, those with a limited life, the closest parallel to the RCDIW is with the Royal Commission on Population, which reported in 1949. It was set up in 1944 'to examine the facts relating to the present population trends in Great Britain; to investigate the causes of these trends and to consider their probable consequences; to consider what measures, if any, should be taken in the national interest to influence the future trend of population; and to make recommendations'.[39] The parallel is limited, for this Commission was charged to make recommendations too. The parallel lies in the scale of the factual inquiries which it undertook. Three scientific committees – biological and medical, economic and statistical – were set up to advise the Commissioners, and the Statement which the Commission issued after one year of existence placed great emphasis on the role of inquiries into facts, causes, and motives. In particular, it sought the co-operation of the public in a voluntary family census of a representative sample of the population, in order to be clearer about the structure of the present population and likely trends. 'More facts and continuous study will be needed . . . The Royal Commission can only hope to make a beginning: but it is of the utmost importance that this beginning should be soundly based on facts.'[40] The Commission mounted a major programme of research, published in six volumes, several of which remain classic treatments of their subject.[41]

Some of the work initiated by the Royal Commission on Population is today undertaken by the Population Statistics Division of OPCS, using government census, registration and social survey data. In that it does not make recommendations, and pursuing the parallel with the study of population, there is a sense in which the RCDIW may less resemble a Royal Commission than either a small statistical department of government or a large statistical division of a mainstream government department. The Department of Employment is its sponsoring department. The Secretary of State for Employment appoints the Chairman and Commissioners, and in consultation with the Commission decides upon matters for special reference. The cost of the Commission is borne on the DE parliamentary vote, and their Establishments branch supply the Commission with certain common services which it cannot afford to provide for itself. Though it is not part of the DE Group (which includes the DE itself and the hived-off parts such as the Manpower Services Commission and the Training Services Agency), the RCDIW is dependent administratively upon that department for its resources.

If resources were made available, some of the statistical work which it undertakes could be carried out within government. The close links with government are indicated by the role which recommendations from RCDIW have to play in improving official statistics. And though many government statisticians are under heavy day-to-day or week-to-week pressure from policy-makers, other parts of the Government Statistical Service – for example, parts of OPCS – are more distanced from the *immediate* demands of policy-makers.

Nevertheless, the RCDIW is quite clearly *not* a department of government, despite the close ties of various kinds. It is an independent body, run by an independent Chairman and Commissioners, and resting for its authority both upon its Royal Warrant of appointment and upon the quality of the work which it has done. Its independence also ensures fuller co-operation from non-governmental bodies, since it is not linked to government departments such as the Inland Revenue. Indeed, its Royal Warrant expressly states: 'No report [of the RCDIW] shall disclose information which would enable persons whose income or wealth had been inquired into to be identified or would damage the legitimate business interests of any person.'[42] It can deploy academic and professional expertise, and can do so publicly, in a way not at present possible within government. It can take evidence, debate the merits of particular approaches, and publish its findings, and in doing so act as an influence (albeit a very light and discreet one) upon the development of policy in relation to the distribution of income and wealth.

In another, quite different, respect the RCDIW resembles *in form* (if not in either the content or purpose of its work) a number of independent bodies in the industrial relations field. This also reminds one of its origins. The appointment of the Chairman of the Commission, and of the ACAS, were announced in the same speech by the Secretary of State for Employment. The DE has given birth to a range of institutions, from the Prices and Incomes Board to the Comparability Commission, which are intended to provide a more objective and detached view of aspects of industrial relations, pay, and collective bargaining than the government itself is capable of. Though in each case the *functions* of these bodies are quite different from the RCDIW, the reason for setting up the body seems to be similar, to provide authoritative and independent advice to the Department of Employment from outside government.

None of these parallels is wholly convincing, and one concludes that the RCDIW is, for the present at least, *sui generis*. It may, however, provide a model for how government could in future promote more in-depth research and statistical inquiries into relatively controversial social and economic issues. Social research located within government is at the present time handicapped in various ways: by the constraints of official secrecy, by the low status of social science (other than economics and statistics) in Whitehall and the marginal status of social scientists; and by isolation from outside academic influences. Social research for policy outside government is often equally handicapped; by unfamiliarity and lack of contact with the civil service; by lack of resources which government can mobilise to support social investigation; and by isolation from the world of current policy.[43] The RCDIW provides one model for devoting more government resources to social investigation, doing so in an impressive and authoritative manner, while harnessing academic expertise and preserving the independence of social inquiry from political and bureaucratic control.

Sic transit

This chapter was completed in March 1979. In May 1979 a new Conservative government was elected at the general election. On 11 June 1979 the Secretary of State for Employment, Mr James Prior, announced in a written parliamentary answer that the Royal Commission on the Distribution of Income and Wealth had

> made a valuable contribution to improve understanding of the trends in the distribution of income and wealth. As a consequence of the Commission's recommendations the Government's own regular statistics on income and wealth are now providing more and better information. There is therefore no continuing need for a standing commission, and the Queen has approved that the Royal Commission be dissolved. This will take effect at the end of July when the appointments of the chairman and other members expire.[44]

The cost of the Commission's work from its foundation in 1974 to 31 March 1979 was £1·431 million.[45] In five years it produced eight reports and seven background papers. Its last two reports, numbers 4 and 5 on the Standing Reference, were published as the Commission closed down.[46] Its final step was to publish through HMSO a more popular short report, summarising in one place in a readable form findings from all its standing and specific references. *An A to Z of Income and Wealth: A Guide to the Reports of the Royal Commission* appeared after the Commission's demise in the autumn of 1979.

Starting life as a standing Royal Commission with an indefinite term ahead of it, the RCDIW existed for not very much longer than the average term of an *ad hoc* commission. The reasons for its dissolution will be for future historians to discover, though they are clearly related to the new government's attitude to its subject, to their desire to cut public expenditure, and possibly (as A. R. Prest suggests in the next chapter) Conservative scepticism about the value of Royal Commissions as instruments of government. Be that as it may, political change rendered the life of the RCDIW finite.

NOTES: CHAPTER 11

1 This chapter is based upon a reading of the *Reports, Evidence* and *Background Papers* of the Royal Commission on the Distribution of Income and Wealth, and upon an interview with its Chairman, Lord Diamond, and Secretary, Mr N. S. Forward, in December 1978. All quotations from Lord Diamond and Mr Forward in this chapter are from this interview or from a background note prepared for it, unless otherwise stated. The writer is greatly indebted to Lord Diamond and Mr Forward for their interest and assistance in his work. He is also pleased to acknowledge the helpful comments on an earlier draft which he

received from Professor A. B. Atkinson, Professor Sir Henry Phelps-Brown, Mr David Piachaud and Professor Dorothy Wedderburn, none of whom, however, is to be held to endorse the interpretation of the work of the Commission presented here, which is the writer's own.

2 *The Labour Party Manifesto 1974* (London: February 1974), p. 10.

3 *Hansard, HC*, Vol. 877 (July 1974), cols 700–1.

4 The Royal Warrant of the RCDIW is reprinted at the beginning of each of its reports.

5 Respectively: Sir Neville Butterworth; Mr Leslie Murphy; Mr David Lea; Mr George Doughty; Mr Roy Cox; and Professor Sir Henry Phelps-Brown, Professor Dorothy Wedderburn and Professor John Greve.

6 Mr Murphy retired and was replaced by Mr Deryk van der Weyer at the beginning of 1977. Mr Doughty, Professor Phelps-Brown, Professor Wedderburn and Mr Cox retired during 1978, and Mr Tony Christopher (General Secretary of the Inland Revenue Staff Federation) and Professor A. B. Atkinson (an academic economist) were appointed in their place.

7 One former Commissioner dissents. 'Royal Commissions are supposed to be chosen to represent the views of the "man on the Clapham omnibus" and this is usually seen to be achieved by a suitable balance in the representation of different interest groups . . . This . . . may help to explain the choice of a Royal Commission as the vehicle for the investigation of a subject which might be thought to be highly technical and yet is politically charged.' D. Wedderburn, 'Policy issues in the distribution of income and wealth: some lessons from the Diamond Commission', paper presented to the Conference on Canadian Incomes, sponsored by the Economic Council of Canada, Winnipeg, May 1979, p. 2.

8 RCDIW, *Report No. 1: Initial Report on the Standing Reference*, Cmnd 6171 (London: HMSO, July 1975), p. v.

9 RCDIW, *Report No. 4: Second Report on the Standing Reference*, Cmnd 6626 (London: HMSO, 1976).

10 RCDIW, *Report No. 5: Third Report on the Standing Reference*, Cmnd 6999 (London: HMSO, 1977).

11 RCDIW, *Report No. 2: Income from Companies and Its Distribution*, Cmnd 6172 (London: HMSO, 1975).

12 RCDIW, *Report No. 3: Higher Incomes from Employment*, Cmnd 6383 (London: HMSO, 1976).

13 RCDIW, *Report No. 6: Lower Incomes*, Cmnd 7175 (London: HMSO, 1978).

14 Sometimes on behalf of other government departments. The specific reference on income from companies was received from the Treasury, with the knowledge and agreement of DE.

15 *Selected Evidence Submitted to the Royal Commission for Report No. 1* (London: HMSO, 1976), p. 346.

16 ibid., p. 70.

17 For an example of the political sensitivity of the subjects of income and wealth, a prime case is provided by the failure of the House of Commons Select Committee on a Wealth Tax to agree upon a report. See their *Report(s)*, House of Commons Papers, Session 1974–5, HC 696–I and II. See also C. T. Sandford, 'The wealth tax debate', in F. Field (ed.), *The Wealth Report* (London: Routledge & Kegan Paul, 1979), pp. 109–28.

18 *Selected Evidence Submitted to the Royal Commission for Reports Nos 1, 2 and 3* (London: HMSO, 1976), 3 vols; *Selected Evidence Submitted for Report No. 6* (London: HMSO, 1978).

19 cf. T. Stark, *The Distribution of Income in Eight Countries: A Background Paper to Report No. 5*, RCDIW Background Paper No. 4 (London: HMSO, 1977); A. J. Harrison, *The Distribution of Wealth in Ten Countries*, RCDIW Background Paper No. 7 (London: HMSO, 1979).

20 R. Layard *et al.*, *The Causes of Poverty: A Background Paper to Report No. 6*, RCDIW Background Paper No. 5 (London: HMSO, 1978).

21 *Analysis of Managerial Remuneration in the UK and Overseas: A Report by Hay-MSL Ltd*, RCDIW Background Paper No. 2 (London: HMSO, 1976).

22 This expenditure can be compared with the *total* expenditure for *ad hoc* Royal Commissions of £434,000 on the Royal Commission on the Constitution (Kilbrandon), 1971; £286,000 on the Royal Commission on Local Government in England (Redcliffe-Maud), 1969; £85,000 on the Donovan Commission on Trade Unions and Employers' Associations, 1968; the Finer Committee on One-Parent Families (1974) cost £180,000; the Seebohm Committee on the Personal Social Services cost £18,000 (1969); the Robbins Committee on Higher Education £128,000 (1963); the Royal Commission on Population, 1944–9 cost £201,000, equivalent to well over £1 million at 1980 prices. There is clearly a quite strong correlation between the extent of the research and intelligence work of a commission and its cost. (Figures from T. J. Cartwright, *Royal Commissions and Departmental Committees in Britain* (London: Hodder & Stoughton, 1975).

23 See RCDIW, *Report No. 6: Lower Incomes*, Appendix D, p. 165.

24 I am indebted to Professor A. B. Atkinson for these examples.

25 J. Greve, *Low Incomes in Sweden: A Background Paper to Report No. 6*, RCDIW Background Paper No. 6 (London: HMSO, 1978).

26 D. Wedderburn, 'Policy issues in the distribution of income and wealth', p. 2 (see Note 7, above).

27 cf. C. Pond, 'The poor and the pundits', *New Society*, 29 March 1979, pp. 740–1; C. Pond, chapter in M. Brown and S. Baldwin (eds), *Yearbook of Social Policy 1979* (London: Routledge & Kegan Paul, forthcoming).

28 RCDIW, *Report No. 6: Lower Incomes*, p. viii.

29 B. Abel-Smith and P. Townsend, *The Poor and the Poorest* (London: Bell, 1965).

30 RCDIW, *Report No. 6: Lower Incomes*, pp. 135, 153.

31 ibid., pp. 155–7.

32 ibid., p. 157.

33 In a personal communication to the author.

34 For a picture of the overall situation in regard to sources of data on income and wealth, see A. B. Atkinson, A. J. Harrison and T. Stark, *Wealth and Personal Income* (Oxford: Pergamon, 1978). For an example of academic research in the field ranging considerably more widely than the Commission, see A. B. Atkinson and A. J. Harrison, *The Distribution of Personal Wealth in Britain* (Cambridge: Cambridge University Press, 1977).

35 cf. *Whitaker's Almanac 1979*, (London: Whitaker's Almanac, 1979), pp. 430, 397.

36 cf. Royal Commission on Environmental Pollution, *First Report: Priorities for Action and Enquiry*, Cmnd 4585 (London: HMSO, 1971), and reports on *Industrial Pollution*, Cmnd 4894 (London: HMSO, 1972); *Pollution in Estuaries and Coastal Waters*, Cmnd 5054 (London: HMSO, 1972); *Pollution Control*, Cmnd 5780 (London: HMSO, 1974); *Air Pollution Control*, Cmnd 6371 (London: HMSO, 1976); and *Nuclear Power and the Environment*, Cmnd 6618 (London: HMSO, 1976).

37 Much of the data in this and the previous paragraph are drawn from a factual memorandum about the RCEP and its work, kindly made available by the Commission's Secretary, Mr L. F. Rutterford.

38 Currently Sir Hans Kornberg, Professor of Biochemistry of Cambridge University. Previously Sir Brian Flowers, and Sir Eric (now Lord) Ashby.

39 Royal Commission on Population, *Statement by the Commission* (London: HMSO, 1945), p. 2.

40 ibid., p. 7.
41 cf. E. Lewis Fanning, *Report of an Inquiry into Family Limitation* (1949); *Report and Selected Papers to the Statistics Committee* (1950); D. V. Glass and E. Grebenik, *The Trend and Pattern of Fertility in Great Britain: A Report of the Family Census of 1946* (1954) (all *Papers* of the Royal Commission on Population 1944–9, London, HMSO).
42 RCDIW, *Report No. 1, Initial Report on the Standing Reference*, p. iv.
43 cf. M. Bulmer (ed.), *Social Policy Research* (London: Macmillan, 1978), ch. 1 by the editor and chs 3 and 15 by L. J. Sharpe.
44 *Hansard, HC,* Vol. 968 (11 June 1979), Written Answers, Col. 75.
45 See Note 22 above.
46 RCDIW, *Report No. 7: Fourth Report on the Standing Reference,* Cmnd 7595 (London: HMSO, 1979); and RCDIW, *Report No. 8: Fifth Report on the Standing Reference*, Cmnd 7679 (London: HMSO, 1979). The latter, rather than merely updating previous standing reference reports, focuses in more detail on income from employment and self-employment.

Chapter 12

Royal Commission Reporting

A. R. PREST

I INTRODUCTION

As someone who has recently experienced five years' hard labour as a member of a Royal Commission, I hope an account of my reflections, even if not exactly comparable with 'The Ballad of Reading Gaol', may not be without interest, most especially to past and potential future victims of the system. It might be said that it is highly presumptuous for someone who has served on but one Royal Commission to expatiate on the subject, if only because of the obvious risk of arguing from the particular to the general. Nevertheless, five years is more than most people, especially those responsible for setting up such commissions in the first place, have spent on such activities.[1] Moreover, if one spent more time on such activities one might become so immersed in the system as to find it impossible to take a detached view about it.

The Royal Commission in question was the Royal Commission on Civil Liability and Compensation for Personal Injury (Chairman: Lord Pearson). The establishment of the Commission was announced in Parliament in December 1972 and the *Report* (Cmnd 7054–I) appeared in March 1978. The sixteen members of the Royal Commission, which first met in March 1973, were mandated to consider compensation for personal injury on a wide basis. The terms of reference, briefly if loosely described, were to consider compensation (and its financing) for death or personal injury suffered in the course of employment; as a result of transport accident; arising from production, distribution or use of goods and services; due to accidents on other people's premises; or 'otherwise through the act or omission of another' in cases where damages can be obtained on proof of fault or strict liability. The remit of the Commission, the conclusions which were arrived at and the initial response to its recommendations were described in detail in *Three Banks Review*, no. 119 (September 1978), pp. 4–19.

In this chapter I shall discuss first of all some problems which academic economists may encounter when serving on bodies of this kind, and secondly, and perhaps most controversially, offer some thoughts to those responsible for setting up such bodies. These comments are of a general nature and inevitably somewhat speculative and subjective in character. Although there are some formal differences between Royal Commissions and Departmental Committees of Inquiry, it seems to be generally agreed that the practical differences between them are small nowadays. So I shall have both types of body in mind.

II HARD TRUTHS FOR ACADEMIC ECONOMISTS

What may an academic economist have to expect when serving on official committees, meeting witnesses from many walks of life and reading evidence of enormously varying character?

The first thing he has to recognise is that his role as a member of an official body is different in a number of ways from that to which he is accustomed in his normal milieu. Such bodies are expected to produce specific recommendations on specific problems and so he cannot sit on the fence crying 'on the one hand . . . but on the other hand'. Then he has to be aware of the suspicions which many 'practical' men in the world at large have of many academics. There is a strong feeling that those who dabble in theoretical issues are likely to have both feet firmly planted in the air and be totally incapable of coming to grips with the things which really matter. If the academics concerned are social scientists the degree of suspicion is likely to be even stronger than would apply to those from such 'practical' subjects as, say, chemistry or engineering. Matters are made even worse if an academic happens to be on the staff of the London School of Economics; the belief that all such people have private telephone lines to Peking dies very hard indeed!

The next point is that there is likely to be an ingrained feeling on some people's part that a committee should produce a package of recommendations likely to appeal to the government of the day and to its supporters whether in Parliament or outside. Time and again one is likely to hear the argument that although certain suggestions might be desirable in principle they would cause such mortal offence to a certain powerful section of opinion that no government would pick up that ball; and so on that account it must be put out of court. In other words, there is a wide gap between the academic view of searching in an entirely disinterested way for an intellectually satisfactory solution – and then operating on the principle of 'publish and be damned' – and the object of making sure that one produces a set of recommendations which is not likely to give great offence in any quarter that really counts. Then an academic may or may not be interested in the finer details of recommendations; but an official committee is by its very nature obliged to pay great attention to the pernickety aspects of its work.

Another feature facing any academic worker is a very variable level of numeracy, some people being highly skilled, but others much less so. The attitude of some people to statistical inquiries is likely to be of a rather naive character in that it may well be thought that there is a set of ultimate truths which can be elicited by such investigations; the notion that the way the questions are phrased will to some extent determine the answers is something which those unused to statistical methods and techniques find extremely hard to grasp. Another illustration is the way in which the application of algebra is likely to produce looks of incredulous horror. It is also a plain fact that compound interest is beyond the comprehension of quite a lot of people. The notion that a given capital sum and an annual level of income for a given period are connected by a particular discount rate is a mystery which some people seem to find impossible to penetrate. (One possible explanation is that compound interest is a subject which has traditionally been taught fairly late in the O-level syllabus. Given that most people in this country do not pursue mathematics beyond that stage the chances of retaining a lifetime's understanding of the processes involved are relatively small.) As the author does not make any pretence to mathematical expertise himself, it must follow that the mathematical weaknesses described above would be even more striking to people with such expertise.

So much for the general nature of the background against which economists are likely to have to work when undertaking tasks of this sort. Let us now look at some of the consequences which are likely to follow. The first is that consideration of abstract principles and literature setting out such principles is unlikely to commend itself. There is likely to be a strong tendency to take the existing situation as it stands and to try to think of the ways in which it can be improved rather than to think about wider issues. In other words, there is likely to be an overwhelming predisposition to discuss what the law is rather than what the law is for.

It follows from this general aversion to abstract principles that there is a strong presupposition that any major change in the existing system is likely to be unacceptable and that the most one should do is a little tinkering rather than ever dream of branching out into new directions.

As an illustration, one might argue that the Australian medical care system (that is, people can either pay Federal Health Insurance Levy along with their income tax or alternatively contribute to private health insurance schemes) is something which would be a possible model for some accident insurance in the United Kingdom. In other words, people could either have government benefits and pay for them or alternatively take out insurance policies and get a corresponding remission in government levies. Likewise, if one is thinking of an occupier's liability in respect of injuries happening to people on his premises (for example, a woman slipping on a highly polished floor in a department store) it would not seem impossible to organise a system of guaranteed benefits. If the benefit is payable from the public purse then an additional contribution should be payable by the store along with the rates; if the benefit is covered by a private insurance policy and evidence can be produced to that effect no contribution would then be payable with the rates. But it may be a somewhat daunting task to pursue such ideas.

There is also likely to be a strong feeling that the present economic atmosphere (for example, whether the Treasury is or is not conducting a cut-back of public expenditure) is of overwhelming importance. It is very hard for people to think several years ahead and ask themselves whether policy options which seem inappropriate in the present circumstances of the economy will remain so in several years' time, when there are likely to be substantial productivity increases if past experience is any guide at all.

Given these general consequences arising from the nature and methods of inquiry of official committees, one must now ask what role economic concepts are likely to play in their councils. The answer is extremely little, at least in those cases where economists do not dominate the proceedings. One is likely to find extreme difficulty in communicating the fundamental propositions of economic thought. For instance, the difficulty of distinguishing between a 'cost' which is purely a transfer of purchasing power from one person to another, and one which absorbs real resources, is not something which goes down easily with those without any exposure to the elements of economic theory. Nor is the proposition likely to be self-evident to many, that from an economist's viewpoint there is no fundamental distinction between goods and services. Another example is to be found in the concept of externalities. This is a staple diet to all economists and the basic notion that any one economic transaction may result in uncompensated costs (or benefits) to a third party in a transaction would seem to be simple enough. Nevertheless, the idea that the subject of road injuries can be handled fruitfully in this way may come hard to many people. Similarly, the notion that public regulations governing smallpox inoculations and the like tie in with economists' theories relating to public goods (that is, those characterised by benefit-jointness) and externalities is again likely to be far too much for many people.

Another example is to be found in systems of charging for state benefits. It is often loosely stated that the charges should fall on those who create the risks which give rise to the need for state benefits. But the meaning of 'risk creation' is by no means straightforward.

It is true that a man would not be injured in, say, a foundry unless the foundry had been established by someone; but it is also true that accidents would not occur to particular individuals unless they chose to work there. So the meaning of allocating charges according to the degree of responsibility for risk creation is by no means straightforward.

The lesson from these illustrations is that an academic economist will be lost if he does not recognise that the extent to which he can hope to impart economic principles must be very limited indeed. Even to secure a minimal adherence to elementary economic propositions and the consequences of disregarding them, what is really needed is a persuasive tongue and a willingness both to repeat the same points *ad nauseam* and to rebut insubstantive objections with patience and tolerance rather than detailed knowledge of the most recent theoretical developments as set out in the most highly abstract economic journals. In other words, one is likely to reap greater dividends by being tiresome than by being highly skilled in modern economic techniques, even if this tiresomeness can give rise to feelings akin to 'who will free me from this turbulent Prest'!

III HOME TRUTHS FOR GOVERNMENTS

If anything, this section is even more speculative than the preceding one and I certainly do create a risk – that of pontificating on subjects of which I have no knowledge. Justification for such an invasion of foreign, and perhaps even hostile, territory is that unless people who have earned long-service medals on these exercises speak out those responsible for setting up commissions or committees may fail to understand or be aware of some basic problems.[2] However, I hope to protect myself against charges of complete amateurism by confining myself to a small number of the possible topics on which one could embark.

The first point, by no means new[3] but worth repeating, is that governments should show responsibility in setting up Royal Commissions and similar bodies. It is all too easy for a politician to pacify an importunate questioner in the House of Commons by saying that he proposes to set up a Royal Commission to study the subject. It is all too easy for a permanent secretary of a government department to persuade his minister that he ought to set up a Committee of Inquiry and thereby delay matters before engaging in some practice of which the permanent secretary disapproves. Obviously, a commission or committee may also be set up as a panic reaction. It is quite clear that one major reason for setting up the Royal Commission on Civil Liability was the thalidomide controversy in the autumn of 1973. The Conservative government of

1970–4 did not set up any other Royal Commission during its tenure of office; but on the other hand the succeeding Labour governments went to town with Royal Commissions on the administration of justice, the press, gambling, the distribution of income and wealth, the health service and the legal profession. There is no doubt that the tendency to dodge importunate questions by referring matters to a commission which can be trusted not to report for some time and to fend off all inquiries in the meanwhile is a well-tried and well-known one. Perhaps all that one can hope is that those in power will behave in a rather more responsible fashion than has sometimes been the case in the past and confine bodies of this sort to questions which both justify and admit of sustained inquiry, as distinct from those which are a nuisance at a particular time.[4]

Having taken a decision to set up a commission or committee the next issue is the formulation of exact terms of reference. There are two major points here: first, the terms must steer a middle course between being over-wide and over-narrow; and, secondly, they must be carefully thought out and well drafted.[5] Governments always like to have it both ways; but it does make life difficult if they insist on the one hand that a commission must stick more or less to its terms of reference, but on the other hand the terms of reference themselves are badly formulated. Quite apart from specifying terms of reference in a careful and precise manner, there are some other important matters to be dealt with at the outset. The first is whether a time-limit should not be fixed for the length of an official body's deliberations.[6] It simply is not the case that the more discussion continues the better the report is likely to be – any more than that the larger the number of times a new building is re-designed the better the final outcome is likely to be. And the longer matters drag on the more necessary it may be for a government to take short-term or remedial stop-gap action on some pressing problems which may in turn make a commission's task more difficult when formulating long-term solutions. One would have thought that something of the order of a two to three years' absolute time-limit depending on the precise nature of a commission's work is really all that should be tolerated. If in fact it could be shown in advance that any particular terms of reference would take longer to inquire into then that is a condemnation of the terms of reference. Another point is that it would be more sensible if commissions were encouraged to take a longer view rather than to have a fixation on purely short-term ephemeral matters. Explicit instructions at the beginning would not guarantee the observance of such a guideline but nevertheless would be an encouragement in that direction.

Another consideration is the relationship between the sponsoring government department and a committee or commission. The first problem here is that the subject-matter for any official body may fall between two or more government departments. It should always be made clear from the beginning that one particular department must have the prime responsibility and if that department has this responsibility it has the duty to facilitate the work of the commission at all possible times and at all possible levels. Naturally, it may be necessary, depending on the subject, for one department to have primary responsibility and another to have secondary responsibility but any such division of functions should be specified at the outset. Another clear responsibility of the sponsoring department should be the provision of a full secretariat. There is one particular point here which is not always fully recognised but is nevertheless vital. There is no presumption that all civil servants will necessarily have the talents for writing long committee reports as distinct from organising the flow of evidence, making arrangements for meetings and matters of that kind. The writing of what may be a long book or series of books will, after all, call for skills in which civil servants have no particular training and for which they may or may not have a particular aptitude. What one needs to recognise is that it is necessary to have somebody with experience of writing, journalistic talents essentially, which can be put to work at the relevant stage of a committee's work. No one would argue that the report of an official body should be thought of as light bedside reading; on the other hand, there is no reason why it need be written in such a way as to be a cure for sleeplessness.

Now we come to the membership of a commission or committee. The traditional principle is what I shall call the Noah's Ark one, with the animals going in two by two (two of one profession, two of another, two Scotsmen, two women, and so on). This idea of combining a number of different ingredients in fixed proportions in the cooking pot and hoping (praying?) that the end-result will be palatable is extremely debatable. The first principle should be that one wants a certain degree of expertise, but not too much. If one has too little expertise and no people who are acknowledged experts on the subjects under review, obviously there is a very high risk that the report will be a disaster. There are also dangers of having too much expertise. The first is that some experts may be so used to their own habits, their own modes of thought and methods of working that they are incapable of seeing or accepting any different ideas. Another danger is that if one particular group of experts has a substantial representation on a commission it may dominate the proceedings and slant the whole weight of the report in one particular direction. Another danger is that experts in technical fields may be over-concerned with keeping the status quo intact.

Experts may also be so inclined to sympathise with the interests of those with whom they feel emotional bonds that the wider interests of other groups of society are neglected. In other words, the extent to which a committee should be peopled with experts reminds one of the old remark about Los Angeles – that one cannot get around it without a car and that one cannot get around with one either. In the same way one clearly cannot conduct a committee's business satisfactorily without any experts, but one may also not be able to do with nothing but experts.

Those deciding on the composition of an official body should not just look at the ages of the members when they start their work but also think ahead and ask what their ages may be by the time their work finishes. Given the usual ages of members of such bodies there are always dangers of inflexibility of attitudes. If governments wish to avoid such risks they must face the fact that it may be an expensive proposition[7] to persuade younger people who are in the prime of their careers to give up some of their activities for purposes of this sort.[8] Finally, in thinking of the membership of a committee one does need to have a number of people who recognise the elementary economic proposition that time does have a cost. It is all too easy to think that one can go on indefinitely asking questions, examining witnesses, proceeding at a leisurely pace, and so on. Nevertheless, it can be a source of immense difficulty. Obviously this temptation would be taken care of directly by imposing a time-limit on a commission's discussions but it nevertheless needs to be thought about in the choice of membership.

Finally, one must ask whether a Royal Commission is an outmoded method of inquiry,[9] and under what conditions it is reasonable to expect that a commission consisting of a large number of different interests will come out with anything as clear-cut as did, say, Beveridge in his report on social security. Even if results of this latter kind are unlikely to be repeated,[10] it would be premature to consign such a historic mode of investigation, stretching back to mediaeval times, to the dustbin without further thought.

What is surely needed is some sort of cost-benefit analysis of such methods of inquiry. One must not think that this would be a very formal exercise in that the costs and benefits are not easy to formulate in such a way that one can give them quantitative precision. And one may be crying for the moon in that the very people who would have to make such an assessment may well be unlikely or unwilling to think in such 'scientific' terms. Nevertheless, it would be a highly desirable exercise to undertake.

NOTES: CHAPTER 12

1 According to T. J. Cartwright, *Royal Commissions and Departmental*

Committees in Britain (London: Hodder & Stoughton, 1975), p. 190, no Royal Commission lasted for more than five years during the period 1945–69. More generally, in numbers of meetings, the volume of evidence submitted and numbers of recommendations, the Royal Commission on Civil Liability scored far in excess of the average. The end-product was three volumes totalling over 1,000 pages in all.

2 Lord Rothschild, Chairman of the Royal Commission on Gambling, was reported as having raised questions about the Royal Commission method of inquiry (*The Times*, 30 June 1978).

3 cf. Sir K. C. Wheare, *Government by Committee* (Oxford: Clarendon Press, 1955), pp. 89 ff., for an analysis of the motives for setting up official committees. Gladstone is quoted as writing in 1869, 'A Committee keeps a cabinet quiet'. And for an anthropological view of the functions of Royal Commissions in terms of the functions of performing tribal dances (to distract public attention) and retirement to the medicine hut (to give the impression of prolonged meditation), see remarks by Lord Kennet in M. Greenwood, 'On the value of Royal Commissions in sociological research with special reference to the birth rate', *JRSS*, 100 (1937), p. 400.

4 Greenwood (op. cit., p. 399) distinguished three desiderata – a comparatively narrow range of subject-matter, the requirement that those most closely affected would read and understand the report and the absence of political difficulties in giving legislative effect to any findings.

5 The terms of reference of the Royal Commission on Civil Liability were not in fact well drafted with obvious and demonstrable lacunae.

6 There are precedents for this. See Cartwright, op. cit., p. 171.

7 cf Sir K. C. Wheare, op. cit., p. 252, for a reference to the House of Commons debates in 1911 on the payment of members and the remark of Lloyd George that 'gratuitous work necessarily means bureaucracy'.

8 The Treasury might be so concerned at the expense involved that it would insist on cutting down the number of such bodies; this might improve the quality of those remaining.

9 Once again not a new question. Thus John Bright wrote in 1879: 'Some people still have faith in Parliamentary Committees and Royal Commissions on matters of this kind. I confess I have none . . . If an enquiry such as you refer to is granted I hope it may do some good if it only shows once more how useless such enquiries are.' See H. J. Hanham, *The Nineteenth Century Constitution 1815–1914, Documents and Commentary* (Cambridge: Cambridge University Press, 1969), pp. 313–14.

10 *Committee on Social Insurance and Allied Services*, Cmd 6404 (HMSO, 1942). As the recent biography of Beveridge has made clear, the report was in reality a one-man band. See José Harris, *William Beveridge* (Oxford: Clarendon Press, 1977), ch. 16.

Select Bibliography

LISTS OF INDIVIDUAL COMMISSIONS

Several sources contain comprehensive lists of Royal Commissions and/or Departmental Committees of Inquiry. They include, chronologically:

Clokie, H. M. and Robinson, J. W., *Royal Commissions of Inquiry* (Stanford: Stanford University Press, 1937), pp. 58–9, 76–8, 143–7 (covers the period 1800–1935, but not complete or exhaustive).

Cole, A. H., *A Finding-List of British Royal Commission Reports 1860–1935* (Cambridge, Mass.: Harvard University Press, 1935).

Vernon, R. V. and Mansergh, N. (eds), *Advisory Bodies* (London: Allen & Unwin, 1940). Lists (pp. 443–500) advisory bodies, including Departmental Committees appointed between 1919 and 1939, grouped by the department which appointed them.

Pemberton, J. E., *British Official Publications* (Oxford: Pergamon, 1971). Chapter 6 lists Royal Commissions from 1900 to 1969 in alphabetical order, chapter 11 does the same for Departmental Committees from 1900 to 1969.

Cartwright, T. J., *Royal Commissions and Departmental Committees in Britain* (London: Hodder & Stoughton, 1975). Appendix A, pp. 227–38, discusses historical sources and gives numbers appointed and in existence for each year from 1800 to 1969. Appendix B, pp. 239–61 lists the 356 major commissions and committees appointed between 1945 and 1969, and gives data on purpose, size, membership, number of meetings, cost, and so on.

Hanser, C. J., *Guide to Decision: The Royal Commission* (Totowa, New Jersey: The Bedminster Press, 1965). Appendix 2, pp. 239–54, lists all commissions appointed between 1900 and 1965, classified by type (impartial/expert/representative) and by kind of problem handled. Appendix 4, pp. 262–4 lists all commissions 1900–64 having divided reports.

Rhodes, G., *Committees of Inquiry* (London: Allen & Unwin, 1975). The appendix, pp. 213–25, lists all Departmental Committees appointed between 1959 and 1968, classified under broad subject headings.

Whitaker's Almanac (London: Whitaker's Almanac, annual), lists new Royal Commissions giving title, date of appointment, terms of reference and names of members. Also lists the few Standing Royal Commissions (see above, Chapter 11).

MAJOR SOURCES

Cartwright, T. J., *Royal Commissions and Departmental Committees in Britain* (London: Hodder & Stoughton, 1975). Contains useful bibliography, pp. 266–74.

Chapman, R. A. (ed.), *The Role of Commissions in Policy-Making* (London: Allen & Unwin, 1973).

Clokie, H. M. and Robinson, J. W., *Royal Commissions of Inquiry: The*

Significance of Investigations in British Politics (Stanford, Calif.: Stanford University Press, 1937).

Gosnell, H. F., 'British Royal Commissions of Inquiry', *Political Science Quarterly*, 49 (1934), pp. 84–118.

Hanser, C. J., *Guide to Decision: The Royal Commission* (Totowa, New Jersey: Bedminster Press, 1965).

Herbert, A. P., 'Anything but action', in R. Harris (ed.), *Radical Reaction* (London: Hutchinson, 1961), pp. 249–302.

Mansfield, H. C., 'Commissions, government', in *International Encyclopaedia of the Social Sciences*, Vol. III (New York: Macmillan/Free Press, 1968), pp. 13–18.

Merton, R. K., 'Social knowledge and public policy', in M. Komarovsky (ed.), *Sociology and Public Policy* (New York: Elsevier, 1975), pp. 153–77.

Rhodes, G., *Committees of Inquiry* (London: Allen & Unwin, 1975).

Webb, S. and B., 'Royal Commissions and Committees of Inquiry as sources for the investigator', in *Methods of Social Study* (London: Longman, 1932), pp. 142–57.

OTHER GENERAL DISCUSSIONS OF BRITISH COMMISSIONS

Beattie, A., 'Commissions, committees and competence', *New Society*, 29 July 1965, pp. 10–12.

Checkland, S. G. and E. O. A., *The Poor Law Report of 1834* (Harmondsworth: Penguin, 1974), esp. Introduction pp. 9–59.

Jackson, R. M., 'Royal Commissions and Committees of Inquiry', *Listener*, 1411, 12 April 1956, pp. 388–90.

Kogan, M. and Packwood, T., *Advisory Councils and Committees in Education* (London: Routledge & Kegan Paul, 1974).

Pinker, R. A., *Social Theory and Social Policy* (London: Heinemann, 1971, chapter 2.

Plowden, W., 'An anatomy of commissions', *New Society*, 15 July 1971, pp. 104–7.

Political and Economic Planning, *Advisory Committees in British Government* (London: Allen & Unwin, 1960).

Prest, A. R., 'Royal Commission reporting', *Three Banks Review*, 119 (September 1978), pp. 3–30.

Report of the Departmental Committee on the Procedure of Royal Commissions (Balfour Report), Cd 5235 (1910).

Smith, B. C., *Advising Ministers* (London: Routledge & Kegan Paul, 1969).

Smith, G. and Stockman, N., 'A sociological approach to the study of government reports', *Sociological Review*, 20 (1972), pp. 59–77.

SSRC, 'Seminar on research for government Committees of Inquiry', *SSRC Newsletter*, 18 (March 1973), pp. 20–2.

Toulmin-Smith, J., *Government by Commissions Illegal and Pernicious*, (London: Sweet, 1849).

Vernon, R. V. and Mansergh, N. (eds), *Advisory Bodies: A Study of Their Uses in Relation to Central Government* (London: Allen & Unwin, 1940).

Wheare, K. C., *Government by Committee* (London: Oxford University Press, 1955), esp. chs 3 and 4.

SOME DISCUSSIONS OF SPECIFIC BRITISH COMMISSIONS

See Chapters 3 to 11 above and references therein. R. Chapman (ed.), *The Role of Commissions in Policy-Making*, contains chapters which discuss the Fulton Committee on the Civil Service, 1966–8; the Donovan Royal Commission on the Trade Unions, 1965–8; the Plowden Committee on Primary Education, 1964–7; the Redcliffe-Maud Royal Commission on Local Government, 1966–9; and the Seebohm Committee on Personal Social Services, 1965–8. In addition, see:

Greenwood, M., Kennett, Lord *et al.*, 'On the value of Royal Commissions in sociological research, with special reference to the birth rate', *Journal of the Royal Statistical Society*, 100 (1937), pp. 396–414.

Hamilton, Lord George, *Parliamentary Reminiscences and Reflections 1886–1906* (London: Murray, 1922), ch. 35. (RC on the Poor Law, 1905–9).

Herbert, A. P., 'Sad fate of a Royal Commission', in *Mild and Bitter* (London: Methuen, 1936). (RC on Kissing, 1874 —— .)

Hood, R., 'Criminology and penal change', in R. Hood (ed.), *Crime, Criminology and Public Policy* (London: Heinemann, 1974), pp. 375–90. (RC on Penal System 1964–6 and its dissolution.)

McGregor, O. R., 'The Morton Commission: a social and historical commentary', *British Journal of Sociology*, 7 (1956), pp. 171–93. (RCs on Marriage and Divorce including Gorell, 1909–12, and Morton, 1951–5).

Pahl, R. E., 'Playing the rationality game: the sociologist as hired expert', in C. Bell and H. Newby (eds), *Doing Sociological Research* (London: Allen & Unwin, 1977), pp. 130–48. (Greater London Development Plan Inquiry, 1970.)

Webb, B., *Our Partnership* (London: Longman, 1948), ch. 7. (RC on Poor Law, 1905–9.)

COMPARATIVE PERSPECTIVES

A *Canadian Royal Commissions*

Brady, A., 'Royal Commissions in the dominions: a note on current political practice', *University of Toronto Quarterly*, 8 (1939), pp. 284–92.

Cole, A. H., *A Finding-List of Royal Commission Reports in the British Dominions* (Cambridge, Mass.: Harvard University Press, 1939).

Courtney, J. C., 'In defence of Royal Commissions', *Canadian Public Administration*, 12 (1969), pp. 198–212.

Hanson, H. R., 'Inside Royal Commissions', *Canadian Public Administration*, 12 (1969), pp. 356–64.

Hodgetts, J. E., 'Royal Commissions of Inquiry in Canada', *Public Administration Review*, 9 (1949), pp. 22–9.

Sellar, W., 'A century of Commissions of Inquiry', *Canadian Bar Review*, 25, (1947), pp. 1–28.

Walls, C. E. S., 'Royal Commissions: their influence on public policy', *Canadian Public Administration*, 12 (1969), pp. 365–71.

B *United States Presidential Commissions*

Tollefson, A. M. and Chang, A. C., *Bibliography of Presidential Commissions, Committees, Councils, Panels and Task Forces, 1961–72* (Minneapolis: University of Minnesota Library, Government Publications Division, 1973).

Bell, D., 'Government by commission', *The Public Interest*, 3 (1966), pp. 3–9.

Derthick, M., 'On Commisionship – Presidential variety', *Public Policy*, 19 (1971), pp. 623–38.

Drew, E., 'On giving oneself a hotfoot: government by commission', *Atlantic*, vol. 221, no. 5 (May 1968), pp. 45–9.

Komarovsky, M., *Sociology and Public Policy: The Case of the Presidential Commissions* (New York: Elsevier, 1975). Contains chapters on the role of sociology in the Presidential Commissions on Population Growth, Obscenity and Pornography, the Causes and Prevention of Violence, and Law Enforcement and the Administration of Justice.

Lipsky, M. and Olson, D. J., *Commission Politics: The Processing of Social Crisis in America* (New Brunswick, NJ: Transaction Books, 1977). Discusses particularly the work of the National Advisory Commission on Civil Disorders (the Kerner Commission), 1968.

Platt, A. M. (ed.), *The Politics of Riot Commissions* (New York: Macmillan, 1971). Considers commissions on American riots and disturbances from 1917 to 1970.

Skolnick, J. H., 'Violence commission violence', *Transaction*, 7 (October 1970), pp. 32–8.

Wilson, J. Q., 'Violence, pornography and social science', *The Public Interest*, Winter 1971, pp. 53–7.

Wolanin, T. R., 'Presidential Advisory Commissions, 1945–68', unpublished Ph.D. dissertation, Department of Government, Harvard University, 1971.

Index